The Gospel according to
The Simpsons™

The Gospel according to *The Simpsons*™

The Spiritual Life of the World's Most Animated Family

MARK I. PINSKY

Foreword by Tony Campolo

Westminster John Knox Press
LOUISVILLE
LONDON • LEIDEN

Scripture quotations from the Revised Standard Version of the Bible are copyright
© 1946, 1952, 1971, and 1973 by the Division of Christian Education of the
National Council of the Churches of Christ in the U.S.A. and are used by permission.

Scripture quotations from *The Holy Bible, New International Version*
are copyright © 1973, 1978, 1984 International Bible Society.
Used by permission of Zondervan Bible Publishers.

Cover image of Bart Simpson printed with permission.
Reprinted from *Bart Simpson's Guide to Life,*
published by HarperCollins © 1993, Matt Groening Productions, Inc.
All Rights Reserved.
The Simpsons © and ™ Twentieth Century Fox Film Corporation.
All Rights Reserved.

Book design by Sharon Adams
Cover design by Mark Abrams

First edition
Published by Westminster John Knox Press
Louisville, Kentucky

This book is printed on acid-free paper that meets the
American National Standards Institute Z39.48 standard. ∞

PRINTED IN THE UNITED STATES OF AMERICA
01 02 03 04 05 06 07 08 09 10 — 10 9 8 7 6 5 4

Library of Congress Cataloging-in-Publication Data is on file
at the Library of Congress, Washington, D.C.

ISBN 0-664-22419-9

For
Sallie, Liza, and Asher
and
In memory of my parents,
Charlotte and Oscar Pinsky

Contents

Foreword

If you have never watched *The Simpsons*, you will want to after reading this book, especially if you are religious. Mark Pinsky gives us a thoughtful probing into the beliefs and practices of this now famous American family.

At first glance, what you see and hear while watching *The Simpsons* might be a "turn off" because it can easily be mistaken for an assault that ridicules middle-class Christianity. It is not! What the show is really depicting through the antics of the Simpsons is the character of some of the people who are in our churches, and the ways in which they choose to live out their faith. People in Middle America understand what it means to be religious in a variety of ways, and they express Christianity in diverse modes of behavior. That is what the author lifts out of his viewing of *The Simpsons*, and after you read Mark Pinsky's book, you may well make the same observations.

As an evangelical Christian, I find that *The Simpsons* provides me with a mirror that reflects my own religious life. When I make judgments about the inadequacies of their religiosity, I am sorry to say that they are often judgments of the ways in which I live out my own faith. Contrary to what some critics say, the Simpsons are basically a decent American family with good values. They go to church on Sunday. Homer and company triumphantly conquer the serious temptations of life, like adultery, and they even conquer some of the lesser sins, such as taking advantage of an illegal cable television hookup.

I easily identify with much about the Simpsons. First of all, the names of my two children are Bart and Lisa (really!), and if you know me you would have to admit that I look a lot like Homer. My wife's name is Margaret (no kidding!). But there are more serious comparisons that cause me to identify with the Simpsons, even though it took me awhile to recognize them. Like King David, when the prophet Nathan told him a story in which harsh judgment was meted out to the story's main character, I sense a finger being pointed at me, and hear an inner voice saying, "Thou art the man!"

Fred Craddock, the famous homiletics professor, once said in a comment that was a takeoff on something from Søren Kierkegaard, that sermons are not so much heard as overheard. He made the point that you can hear a story that is supposed to be about other people, revealing *their* character, exposing *their* foibles, critiquing *their* lifestyles, and examining *their* beliefs, and then suddenly realize that the story is about you. Without ever pointing a finger in a Nathan-like manner, you sense that the storyteller has you in mind, and that you are being judged.

That is certainly the case for me when I watch *The Simpsons*. This cartoon sitcom is supposed to be about an outrageous dysfunctional family in Middle America, but all too often I realize that it's about me—and about my religious convictions and lifestyle. In one way or another, I find in the beliefs and behaviors of the Simpson characters, those same beliefs and behaviors that at one time or another have been evident in my own life. Both the hypocrisies and the virtues of the Simpson family and the other characters on the show are too often my own.

When I'm feeling good about myself, I would think of myself as being like Homer Simpson's next-door neighbor, Ned Flanders. Ned is an evangelical Christian who would feel at home at a Promise Keepers gathering. He is on a mission, such as you would expect of an evangelical, to lead Homer and others around him into a living faith relationship with Jesus. Ned is sometimes so aggressive in his evangelistic efforts that he appears both ludicrous and obnoxious. But, in spite of his single-mindedness about bringing his neighbors into God's Kingdom, he is, overall, a nice guy.

Ned is sincere and good-hearted. He tries to live out a consistent commitment to his faith. Because the writers of *The Simpsons* are probably afraid of offending people of other religions, they never let Ned say anything about what is at the heart of evangelical Christianity—that salvation comes by faith in a Christ who saves us by His grace and is in the evangelical tradition, a gift of God, "not of works, lest any man should boast." No, instead of making faith and grace the basis of salvation, Ned Flanders, like other characters in the show, believes that salvation is the result of doing good deeds. In this sitcom, you get the popular media impression that, on Judgment Day, there will be a weighing of our good deeds against our evil deeds, and if a person's good deeds outweigh the evil, then heaven is his or her reward. Obviously, to those of us who are evangelicals, this is diametrically opposed to what we believe.

In pointing out this misrepresentation of evangelicalism (as represented by Ned), we must remember that *The Simpsons* is a comedy show meant to entertain, and not a religious TV show promoted by the Billy Graham Association. In the popular mind, salvation *is* earned, in spite of all our preaching to the contrary. If the writers did the grace thing, as we evangelicals believe it, I am not sure most of the audience would get it, and if they did, they would probably question it. One of my friends criticized the show, complaining that Ned, the evangelical, gets lampooned and made to look silly. But, I had to remind her that everything is lampooned on *The Simpsons* and everybody is made to look silly. What else would you expect of a sitcom?

In many respects, I am quite comfortable with the way in which Ned is presented. He is committed to his church. He really loves his neighbor (Homer) and he does his very best to live out what he believes. Ned is not a superficial Christian who pretends there are no doubts or struggles with his faith commitments. He goes through times of confusion and questioning—especially when his wife dies. But, he never gives up on God, and Ned always comes out as a true believer. I hope that I come across to my friends as being as sincere and having as much integrity as Ned does in the hands of the writers of this show.

One thing I would add to the image of Ned Flanders' Christianity is a more pronounced commitment to the social justice requirements of biblical Christianity. And this I find strongly exemplified in the beliefs and the practices of the character of Lisa Simpson. Lisa is everything that I find good in mainline denominational churches and their commitment to the "social gospel." Hers is a rationalistic approach to religion that leaves little room for the mystical or miraculous, but is strong on humanistic moralism. She is cynical about those flimflam artists who present themselves as television evangelists. She is certainly skeptical about faith healers with their ministries of miracles.

Lisa is committed to seeing to it that all forms of social behavior and all social institutions treat people with equality. True religion for her is in the prophetic tradition that declares: "What does the Lord require of you? To act justly and to love mercy and to walk humbly with your God" (Micah 6:8). Deeply sensitive to the oppressed and needy, she is dedicated to the justice issues that seem to preoccupy those denominations that are part of the National Council of Churches. You can count on Lisa to stand up for the underdog. Hers is a religiosity that undergirds such causes as racial equality, feminism, and the peace movement.

Many of us long for a holistic Christianity that would bring personal evangelism and concerns for social justice together. We wish that the caring for others expressed by Lisa, and the zeal for saving souls, so evident in Ned Flanders, could be synthesized.

In Homer, we find still another form of Protestant Christianity. He is one of the best examples of what sociologists call *folk* religion. He is the kind of religious person who goes to church regularly, but is in reality more into a religio-magic belief system than into anything that resembles biblical Christianity. For Homer, God is like a parachute he hopes he never has to use, but he wants God to be there, just in case. When Homer is in deep trouble he turns to God and begs for miracles, but when miracles do happen, they do not make him into a man of faith or deep moral convictions. Once a crisis is passed, Homer's thinking about God is over. God, for him, is somebody you bargain with in times of trouble, making all kinds of promises to change (which are never lived out), if God will just deliver on a needed miracle.

The anthropologist, Bronislaw Malinowski, in his book *Magic, Religion and Science*, explains some key differences between religion and magic. Magic, he says, is an attempt to *manipulate* spiritual forces so that the supplicant gets what he or she wants, whereas in pure religion the individual *surrenders* to spiritual forces so that those forces (i.e., God) can do through him or her what those forces desire. Given these definitions, Homer is certainly into magic rather than religion.

Do not go too hard on Homer Simpson because more people in our churches are where he is than any of us in the mainline denominations want to acknowledge. If you ask probing questions, you quickly will learn that most church members are into some form of religio-magic Christianity. For instance, I remember my Sunday School teacher telling me when I was a boy that, if I wanted my prayers to be answered, I had to make sure that I ended them with the right words—"In Jesus' name, Amen." Without that "magic" formula I was told I would be unlikely to get the desired results. My teacher led me to believe in a petty God who could look down on people who were begging for help and say, "I really would love to meet your needs, but you didn't give your prayers the proper ending." God, for Homer, is a great big Santa Claus in the sky who gives people what they want if they just remember to state things with the right incantation.

Prayer, for Homer, is not a time of intimate communion with God. Instead, it is something you do when you can't get what you want on your own. There is an infantile quality in Homer, which reminds me of when my son, as a very little boy, came into our living room and said, "I'm going to bed! I'm going to be praying! Does anybody want anything?"

Church, for Homer, has nothing to do with the worship. Its value lies in the fact that it teaches moral lessons to his children. Homer wants his children in church every Sunday, not so much to express gratitude to God for the blessings of life, but to receive lectures about what is right and wrong. He believes, as do most people who are into the folk religion of our society, that those who learn from these moral lectures and do what is right will go to heaven, and that those others who on Judgment Day discover that the bad they have done outweighs the good, will go to hell. This TV series leaves little doubt that Homer has a psychologically repressed conviction that he, himself, falls into the latter category of those bound for hell. His subconscious fears about Judgment Day surface when he dreams. In his dreams, Homer generally sees himself as not quite measuring up to the standards of goodness required for passage through the pearly gates, and ending up in hell. This is a fear that most people have.

In the book you are about to read, you will see how the Simpson family lives out the Christian religion in a pluralistic society. Other religions, such as Judaism and Hinduism, are viewed through the eyes of the popular culture. There is a desire on the part of the Simpsons for tolerance of other religions, though their ignorance of what others believe leads to mistakes. But all in all, you will find in the Simpsons positive models in handling diversity.

I don't want to make you think that what Pinsky has written here is a sociological tome on the worst and the best in American religious life. But, on the other hand, his book does provide a pretty good picture of our religious thinking and behavior without the sometimes heavy jargon of social scientists. And beyond that, this book is just fun to read!

Tony Campolo
Emeritus Professor of Sociology
Eastern College
St. Davids, PA

Introduction: Epiphany on the Sofa

George Bush the Elder once denounced it; his wife, Barbara, called it dumb. Former Education Secretary William Bennett questioned its values. So the dilemma loomed: Should my wife, Sallie, and I allow our young kids to watch *The Simpsons*? Many considered the show to be abrasive, abusive—even abominable. We were concerned, as most parents are, that our children would grow up too quickly because of what they saw on the screen. When our son Asher (then 11) and our daughter Liza (then 8) took an interest in *The Simpsons*, I began to watch it with them—and was I ever surprised! At first, the popular program featuring a spikey-haired kid seemed to be the antithesis of *Leave It to Beaver*, a program my brother Paul and I watched with our parents in our suburban home. But the modern cartoon sitcom turned out to be family-friendly and full of faith. Even Barbara Bush and Bill Bennett eventually back-pedaled. George Bush *pere*, who was able to embrace *Saturday Night Live* impersonator Dana Carvey, has not yet recanted his criticism of the series.

How did it happen? What made *The Simpsons* so popular and its popularity so durable? Would regular viewers be catching some glimpses of faith that the spiritually faithful have been trying to communicate for years? What lessons might the program have for viewers of varying spiritual, moral, political, and social stripes?

On Sunday nights, when America's best-known dysfunctional family is a fixture in millions of households, many Christians are in church. At home, the less devout are probably tuned to the competition, *Touched by an Angel*, which usually wins the ratings time period when the two shows go head to head. But a lot of people *are* watching *The Simpsons*, and have been watching faithfully and, yes, religiously for more than a decade. "*Simpsons* fans treat Sunday as a day of worship," wrote Jon Horowitz of Rutgers University in an unpublished paper. "Not early mornings at church; 8 P.M. in front of the holiest of holies, the TV tuned into the FOX network."[1]

In addition to the estimated 14.7 million who watch the series each week (ratings during the 2000–2001 season, according to *Entertainment Weekly* and Nielsen Media Research), another four million people tune in each week to watch reruns of the show in syndication (it was rated first among all rerun shows in the 1994–1995 season). More than 180 Fox affiliates carry the new episodes on Sunday nights. Over 250 stations in the U.S. and Canada aired the highly rated reruns, some twice a day or more. Around the world, it is more popular than *Baywatch*, reaching sixty million people a week in more than seventy countries (though not in Costa Rica or the Dominican Republic, where it is banned as an affront to family values), dubbed in dozens of languages. A syndicated Sunday comic strip in 250 newspapers reaches an audience of fourteen million, and hundreds of thousands of copies of more than two dozen authorized books about the show have been sold—part of a billion-dollar *Simpsons* merchandise industry. In the early 1990s there were more than a thousand *Simpsons* web sites in cyberspace, and there are plans for a full-length feature film when the series ends.

During more than a decade in prime time, the series has ranged from the fringes of the top 15 in the Nielsen ratings to the 30s, doing best among males ages 18–49. In the 2000–2001 season, eleven years after it began, the show actually *gained* in the ratings, and its 2000–2001 premiere pulled sixteen million viewers. The series ended the 2000–2001 season ranked 21 of 150 network shows, but was still the third most watched show on Fox. As important to Fox as the show's enduring ratings success was *The Simpsons'* continued critical acclaim, superlatives that rained on Rupert Murdoch's fledgling network like manna from heaven. In its first dozen years, the show was nominated for thirty-four Emmys and has won sixteen. It has also won a Peabody award, which recognizes distinguished achievement in radio and television. *Time* magazine called *The Simpsons* the twentieth century's best television show, and the entertainment industry took note of the series' tenth anniversary with a star on Hollywood Boulevard. The show has made the cover of *TV Guide* a dozen times. During the same two-week period in early 2001, the Simpsons appeared on the covers of both *Christianity Today* and *The Christian Century*, two magazines at opposite ends of the Christian theological spectrum. *Life* magazine, in a cover story titled "The Shows That Changed America: 60 Years of Network Television," called *The Simpsons* the "millennium family unit: struggling, skeptical, disrespectful, ironic, hopeful. . . . The Simpsons verify our country's strength: If they can make it in today's America, who can't?"[2] In the words of cultural guru Kurt Andersen, it is "smarter, sharper and more allusive than any other show on television."[3] Robert Thompson, founding director of the Center for the Study of Popular Television at Syracuse University, said in a newspaper interview that the series "doesn't compare just with other television programs, but with the best of American humor. Will Rogers, Mark Twain and *The Simpsons* can happily occupy the same stratosphere of respect in the annals of American humor."[4]

The Simpsons has exerted an ongoing influence on American culture, high and low. "D'oh!" Homer's expression of consternation, has been added to the *Oxford English Dictionary*. Bad boy Bart became a giant, sixty-foot balloon in the Macy's Thanksgiving Day parade. The *New York Times* predicted in its millennium edition, perhaps with tongue in cheek, that *The Simpsons* would still be a top-rated show in 2025, and suggested that one of the show's characters, the avaricious nuclear plant owner Montgomery Burns, was a better-known exemplar of capitalism than Ayn Rand. A 1999 survey conducted by Roper Starch Worldwide found that 91 percent of American children between the ages of 10 and 17, and 84 percent of adults, could identify members of the Simpson family. In each case, this was a greater percentage than knew that the vice president of the United States was Al Gore—a man who later identified himself as a fan of the show to a high school crowd in Concord, New Hampshire.

This influence may be nearly as great outside America. In Britain, where the show is now more highly rated than in the United States, Prime Minister Tony Blair revealed himself to be a fan of the series. Campaigning for reelection in May of 2001 in the city of Norfolk, he confessed that he "is a bit of a Simpson's addict." His wife, Cherie, rolled her eyes in embarrassment and confirmed that the English leader is devoted to the show.

All this began in 1987 with 30 two-minute, animated vignettes that ran between segments of *The Tracey Ullman Show* on the Fox Television Network. The family was created by cartoonist Matt Groening, then best known for a comic strip called *Life in Hell*, which appeared in alternative weekly newspapers.

The Simpsons are a lower middle class family living in the town of Springfield, in an unidentified state. They consist of:

> Father—Homer, bald and overweight, with a weakness for beer, pork chops, television, and donuts. Employed as a safety inspector at the local nuclear power plant. Named for character of the same name in Nathaniel West's Hollywood classic, *Day of the Locust*. Also shares first name with Groening's father.
>
> Mother—Marge, a long-suffering, stay-at-home mom with a towering beehive of blue hair. Same first name as Groening's mother.
>
> Son—Bart (an anagram for "brat"), a ten-year-old with a world-class attitude. Stand-in for young Matt.

Daughter—Lisa, a good-hearted and gifted eight-year-old, usually dressed in a strapless red frock and a strand of Barbara Bush pearls. Name of one of the Groening sisters.

Baby Maggie, who does not speak and is rarely seen without her pacifier. Name of another Groening sister.

So popular were *The Simpsons* snippets on *The Tracey Ullman Show* that in 1990 the family got its own half-hour series on Fox. In the ultimate counterprogramming move, Fox first put their edgy new series into what was considered a suicide slot on Thursday nights, opposite the wholesome and high-flying *Cosby Show*, then number one in the ratings. The contrast between the two family comedies could not have been more stark, and *The Simpsons* caused a sensation, sparking denunciations throughout the nation over the next few years as the animated show moved to Sunday nights and became even more popular. Across the country, merchandise featuring Bart Simpson and his disrespectful catch phrases such as "Don't have a cow, man," and "Eat my shorts" caused outrage. In April 1990, the principal of Cambridge Elementary School in Orange County, California, banned students from wearing the Bart shirts to school. In June, Mayor Sharpe James of Newark, New Jersey, asked retail stores and street vendors in his city to stop selling the shirts, according to the Associated Press. "Just at a time when we are trying to get our young people to develop their abilities to the fullest, we get a tee-shirt with a popular cartoon character saying he is proud to be an underachiever," James told the Associated Press.[5] J.C. Penney halted sales of the offending shirt.

Nowhere was the initial uproar more vigorous than in America's pulpits. Upset by his child imitating Bart at the dinner table, an outraged member of Willow Creek Community Church near Chicago complained to one of the ministers, Lee Strobel, who in turn preached a widely reprinted sermon titled "What Jesus Would Say to Bart Simpson." A Baptist pastor, Dan Burrell, recorded an educational audiotape entitled "Raising Beaver Cleaver Kids in a Bart Simpson World," instructing parents how to rear their children with "value and character."

America's moral leaders thundered that this nuclear but troubled family was the latest evidence of the fall of Western civilization. When drug czar and former education secretary William Bennett visited a rehabilitation center in Pittsburgh in 1990, he spotted a Bart Simpson poster on the wall with the caption, "Underachiever and Proud of It." Bennett then asked, "You guys aren't watching *The Simpsons*, are you? That's not going to help you any." Bennett later retreated from his criticism, acknowledging that he didn't watch the show. Making the best of the backlash, he retorted several days later, "I'll have to sit down and have a talk with the little spike head."[6]

From his own bully pulpit, President George H. W. Bush told the National Religious Broadcasters in 1992, "We need a nation closer to the Waltons than the Simpsons." Not to be outdone, Bart responded in an episode that followed three days later. The segment featured the family watching the president's attack on them on TV, puzzled. Noting the sharp economic downturn attributed to the Bush administration, Bart cracked, "We're just like the Waltons. We're praying for an end to the depression too." Barbara Bush shot back, "*The Simpsons* is the dumbest thing I've ever seen." Then, and in much the same fashion as Bennett, she back-pedaled. In a letter to "Marge Simpson," the First Lady called the animated family "charming" and complimented them for "setting an example for the rest of the country."[7] The series returned this conciliatory gesture with the back of its hand, portraying the First Lady in the White House bathtub. Several years later, *The Simpsons* took an episode-length shot at the former president in retirement, in which the otherwise genial Bush was driven to spank Bart, infuriating Homer, whose preferred form of corporal punishment is strangulation.

These early controversies branded the series in the minds of many—especially some Christians—as negative and juvenile. In the years that followed, this impression obscured a fundamental shift in *The Simpsons*, as the narrative focus of the episodes moved from rebellious son Bart to his hapless dad, Homer. The show was delving deeper in the issues it tackled and was friendlier to faith, but many viewers who might have appreciated this dimension had tuned out or had never tuned in.

You can find God in the funniest places. "Humor is a prelude to faith, and laughter is the beginning of prayer," Reinhold Niebuhr observed.[8] Or as Conrad Hyers wrote in *The Comic Vision and the Christian Faith*, "If humor without faith is in danger of dissolving into cynicism and despair, faith without humor is in danger of turning into arrogance and intolerance."[9] Tuning in nearly a decade after the series premiered, I found God, faith, and spirituality in abundance on *The Simpsons*. Like most of the show's episodes, my involvement with the series began on the family couch. I had been vaguely aware of the series since its debut, but I was not a fan or even a regular viewer; the hype and the controversy put me off. If I happened to see an episode every now and then, I enjoyed it, but I would never rearrange my schedule to watch. It was only during the summer of 1999, when my young son and daughter became interested in the program, that I started to tune in regularly. In light of the show's reputation for rude behavior, bad language, and sexual innuendo, I insisted on sitting with them. Watching the weekly episodes—supplemented by a double dose of nightly reruns through the summer—led to valuable discussions with the kids about moral issues, and I was relieved to see that most of the naughty stuff sailed over their heads (I hope).

The real epiphany for me, as a longtime religion writer for daily newspapers, was the surprisingly favorable way religion, in its broadest sense, was presented in the series, and what a central role faith played in the lives of the characters. In many ways, Simpson family members were both defined and circumscribed by religion. The family attended church every Sunday and said grace before meals. Their next-door neighbors were committed evangelical Christians. When faced with crises, the Simpsons turned to God and prayed aloud. God often answered their prayers and intervened in their world. Here was a complete (if inconsistent) cosmology—God, the devil, angels—and a fully realized universe of faith. Characters believed in a literal heaven and hell, and, like most Americans, they ridiculed cults. Clearly, Christians and Christianity were more a part of *The Simpsons* than of any other prime-time network sitcom or drama, excluding shows specifically devoted to religion such as *Touched by an Angel* and *7th Heaven*.

The Simpsons, wrote Jim Trammell in a 2000 master's thesis for the University of Georgia's Grady School of Journalism and Mass Communication, "proves it is possible to produce a profitable, respected program that credits religion as a part of the American lived experience. In an industry where spirituality is either absent or merely glossed over for a cheap, dispensable laugh, this cartoon proves religion can be featured as a theme without isolating the audience."

Still, no one would mistake Homer Simpson and his family for saints. In many ways, in fact, they are quintessentially weak, well-meaning sinners who rely on their faith—although only when absolutely necessary. *The Simpsons* is consistently irreverent toward organized religion's failings and excesses, as it is with most other institutions and aspects of modern life. And Bart is still Bart. He is not the youngster of which the prophet Isaiah said "a little child shall lead them"; with Bart, it is literally a case of "suffer the little children" (Mark 10:14). Homer's grasp of theological complexity is, at best, fuzzy. Asked by Bart what the family's religious beliefs are, his father answers, "You know, the one with all the well-meaning rules that don't work in real life. Uh, Christianity." Inexplicably, along with Catholics, Unitarians have been the butt of most denomination-specific jokes ("If that's the one true faith, I'll eat my hat," Homer cracks), although Lutherans, Mormons, and Jehovah's Witnesses come in for stray shots.

The gift of *The Simpsons* is that the characters' fundamental beliefs are animated but not caricatured. God is not mocked, nor is God's existence questioned. Springfield, where the family lives, possesses a rich spiritual life, according to Gerry Bowler, professor of philosophy at Canadian Nazarene College in Calgary and chairman of the Centre for the Study of Christianity and Contemporary Culture. (Like me and many others, he had been drawn to the show by the requests of his children to watch.) "The satiric *Simpsons* program takes religion's place in society seriously enough to do it the honor of making fun of it," he later wrote. "As satires go, these criticisms are not overly harsh and indeed most Christians would find much truth in them. . . . If this is a show with attractive Christian characters, where good usually triumphs, where the family virtues are always affirmed in the end, why are Christians put off by it? It's a case of where if you're a mature Christian and you get all the jokes, you could watch it."[10]

William Romanowski, author of *Pop Culture Wars: Religion and the Role of Entertainment in American Life*, found that "*The Simpsons* is not dismissive of faith, but treats religion as an integral part of American life." At the same time, the Calvin College professor said, "Episodes generally leave the matter of God and religion open to multiple interpretations, perhaps so as not to potentially alienate audience members, but also as a reflection of American attitudes."[11] The Reverend David Bruce, webmaster of hollywoodjesus.com, which uses popular culture to spread the gospel, put it more simply. He called the Simpsons "the best Christian family on television."

This aspect of the series was spotted very early on, in a 1992 master's thesis written by Beth Keller at Pat Robertson's Regent University. While "it is safe to say that the Simpson clan does not represent an ideally religious family," she wrote, and "it may not completely resonate with the evangelical Judeo-Christian belief system, *The Simpsons* does portray a family searching for moral and theological ideals. . . . I believe religion is viewed positively, overall."[12]

In retrospect, the opening seconds of *The Simpsons* should have tipped me off: Harp strings accompany a heavenly choir as the clouds part and the show's title appears on the screen and the camera swoops down over Springfield. As my summer viewing wore on, I found myself watching the show with my reporter's notepad, scribbling feverishly. Then I bought a copy of *The Simpsons: A Complete Guide to Our Favorite Family* and read through a decade of episode summaries, which confirmed my initial impression. Interviews with media experts, academics, and the show's executive producer led me to write a lengthy essay that appeared in the "Sunday Insight" section of the *Orlando Sentinel*, a piece reprinted widely in newspapers around the country. Fans of the show sent me e-mails referring me to other newspaper articles and academic papers on the show's spiritual side. The more I saw in the show, the more I wanted to understand its spiritual dimension. Since very little of what appears on television and in the movies is there by accident, I wanted to know why religion was treated the way it was.

Mike Scully, at the time the series' executive producer and "showrunner," explained to me that the series wanted to reflect through its characters the fact that faith plays a substantial part in many families' lives, although it is seldom portrayed on television. "We try to represent people's honest attitudes about religion," he said in another interview. "You see the Simpsons and all the townspeople in church together, just like real life. You're in church giving the sign of peace to somebody and then in the parking lot afterward, you're giving them the finger because he's blocking your way. It's just human nature," he told another interviewer.[13] As creator Matt Groening put it in a 1999 interview with the Associated Press, "You're inviting yourself into someone's home when you do a TV show. . . . For all of *The Simpsons'* darker strains of satire, ultimately it's a celebration of America and the American family in its exuberance and absurdity."[14]

And its faith. Some in the religious world have recognized this phenomenon, making *The Simpsons'* beliefs the subject of at least half a dozen favorable academic journal articles and Web sites. According to one study by a theologian (and fan), fully a third of all the episodes include at least one religious reference. Another random study of 30 percent of the episodes, by John Heeren of California State University at San Bernardino, found that there was some religious content in 70 percent of these episodes and that 10 percent of the episodes surveyed were constructed around religious themes. Religion was more prominent in the show in the jaded, decadent decade of the 1990s than in other programs in the more religious 1950s, he said. *Simpsons'* writers and producers, Heeren said, "think religion is important in people's lives, and that's why they put it in the center of the work they do."[15]

The accolades have continued to pour in: Christian humor magazine *The Door* said, "There is more spiritual wisdom in one episode of *The Simpsons* than there is in an entire season of *Touched by an Angel*."[16] David Dark, writing in the Christian monthly *PRISM*, published by Evangelicals for Social Action, called the series "the most pro-family, God-preoccupied, home-based program on television. Statistically speaking, there is more prayer on *The Simpsons* than on any sitcom in broadcast history."[17] David Landry, a theologian and New Testament scholar at the University of St. Thomas, a Catholic college in St. Paul, Minnesota, agreed. "This is not the be-all and end-all of theology on TV, but the most consistent and intelligent treatment of religion on TV is on *The Simpsons*," he told a newspaper interviewer.[18]

Paul Cantor, professor of political science at the University of Virginia, was not willing to go that far. "*The Simpsons* is not pro-religion—it is too hip, cynical and iconoclastic for that," he wrote in the journal *Political Theory*. Yet, "even when it seems to be ridiculing religion, it recognizes, as few other television shows do, the genuine role that religion plays in American life. . . . [I]n Homer Simpson it also suggests that one can go to church and not be either a religious fanatic or a saint."[19]

As a journalist, I have covered religion in the American Sunbelt, from Orange County, California, to Orlando, Florida, for the better part of fifteen years. The current cultural disconnect in the United States over faith and values, which began in the 1980s and was manifest in the 2000 presidential election, is such that I can think of few groups with as little in common as committed evangelical Christians and hard-core fans of *The Simpsons*. Many of the former are no more likely to watch the show than they would be to turn on a boombox and dance naked in front of the church—which Homer actually did when he thought he was the lone survivor after Springfield was wiped out by a neutron bomb launched by France.

Dedicated fans of *The Simpsons*, I have learned in researching this book, miss very little of what goes on in the series, and they analyze the show's minutiae with the intensity of committed Talmudists. There are Web sites devoted to religion in the series and to Springfield's pastor, Reverend Lovejoy, yet I suspect that even most of these fans have not noticed the consistent fabric of belief that the show's writers and producers have been weaving over the years.

If this little book can in some way create a common ground for these two groups—and the many between them—I will be happy. And there is evidence that this has already begun.

"*The Simpsons* is one of the most important common experiences in the American home," said Stewart Hoover, a religion and media scholar at the University of Colorado. In a study funded by the Lilly Foundation, Hoover found that "*The Simpsons* consistently comes up in our interviews as a subject for family discussion and family interaction around issues of values and morality and religion. It's kind of a meeting place for families. The show has quite a cross-generational appeal and effect," he told me.

This has been true in the Tilley household in Orlando. Mike Tilley works for Campus Crusade for Christ as the worldwide evangelical organization's national director for U.S. expansion. His son, Jonathan, began watching *The Simpsons* when he was 11 or 12, he recalled, probably behind his parents' backs. But he became convinced the show was not something to hide after watching an episode called "Homer vs. Lisa and the Eighth Commandment." In that show there was an extended discussion involving Simpson family members and their pastor about whether an illegal cable television hookup was theft, as defined by the Bible. Jonathan approached his dad and, as a result, watching the show together on Sunday evenings became a ritual for father and son.

"I saw it as a time to get into my son's world," Mike said. "It was a chance for us to connect. It was a great bridge, a relationship-building thing. Sometimes I think Christians are a little too uptight to share a good laugh. I wanted to do something together with him that was fun; I didn't want him to see his Christian upbringing as overly serious." Jonathan, now a college student, agreed. "It was humor I would relate to then and can relate to now," he said, acknowledging that in the early years of their viewing his father probably understood some of the humor that he did not. Still, "it was a special time. My dad and I like to do things [together]. It's cool when we find something that is truly enjoyable for both of us."

One episode in particular, in which Homer resists the temptation to commit adultery, rang a bell with father and son, and provoked a conversation both recall vividly years later. "That show won me over," Mike said. "These guys—the show's writers—despite the fact they were exposing the apparent idiosyncrasies of religious people, they obviously had a moral message they wanted to reinforce." Said Jonathan: "He liked the fact that Homer was able to turn it down. The value of a long-lasting loving relationship was there. Marge said she would always love him. My dad said he liked that."

These days, Mike and Jonathan still talk about *The Simpsons*, usually via e-mail or by phone. Jonathan, who wants to be a missionary, found the show valuable in his relationships with his classmates at Florida State University, even in those episodes when the foibles of organized religion and religious people are the targets of humor. "Pretty much everyone watches *The Simpsons* at college, and it's important for me in my faith to have common ground with everyone."

This book is a distillation, an interpretation and analysis of material about God, faith, and religion contained in approximately 275 episodes of *The Simpsons*. In that sense it is a magnification, but I hope it is not a distortion. As Neil Postman wrote in 1985 in *Amusing Ourselves to Death: Public Discourse in the Age of Show Business*, religion on television, "like everything else, is presented, quite simply and without apology, as . . .

entertainment." I'll be discussing concepts like prayer, the Bible, sin and grace, and examining the ways in which Catholics, Jews, and Hindus are portrayed in *The Simpsons*. The evidence I present here notwithstanding, the series is not a television show *about* religion, and I would not want uninitiated viewers tuning in thinking it is. *The Simpsons* is a situation comedy about modern life that includes a significant spiritual dimension; because of that, it more accurately reflects the faith lives of Americans than any other show in the medium. For that, I am grateful.

One

Divine Imagery: "Perfect Teeth. Nice Smell. A Class Act All the Way."

God answers all prayers. The problem, ministers say, is that some-times the answer is "no"—not a thundering denial but often a silence that implies that a request will not be fulfilled, for reasons best known to the Almighty. For Homer Simpson, this conundrum represents an opportunity rather than a reason to question the validity of prayer. In a flashback episode we see him at home, ostensibly thanking God for his life—his marriage, his two children, his job—a constellation in balance that is "absolutely perfect the way it is." Homer asks that everything be frozen in place. This is impossible, of course, sort of the equivalent of praying for a protective "hedge around him and his household and every-thing he has," as the book of Job (1:10) puts it. It is at this point that Homer, at best an imperfect believer, attempts to toy with God. He prays that if the Almighty agrees to keep everything exactly as it is, Homer won't ask for anything more. Confirmation of the deal, he prays, will come in the form of "absolutely no sign." There is no sign. In gratitude, Homer presents an offering to God of cookies and milk. Should God want Homer to eat the cookies himself, he asks again for "no sign." After a pause, Homer utters the benediction, "Thy will be done."

Homer's theological sophistry caught the attention of more than one Christian thinker. The incident appears in the opening lines of William A. Dembski's *Intelligent Design: The Bridge between Science and Theology*, a book designated one of the ten best of 1999 by *Christianity Today* maga-zine in the category of "Christianity and Culture." In a chapter titled "Recognizing the Divine Finger," Dembski argues that something very serious is going on in the dialogue. "What's the matter with Homer's prayer? Assuming God is the sovereign ruler of the universe, what is to prevent God from answering Homer's prayer by providing no sign? Granted, usually when we want God to confirm something, we look for something extraordinary, some sign that leaves no doubt of God's will. But presumably God could have made it thunder when Homer asked God to

13

freeze everything and God could have made the earth to quake when Homer asked to eat those cookies and milk. Presumably, it is just as easy for God to confirm Homer's prayer with no sign as to disconfirm it with a sign."[1]

Dembski's answer is that the flaw in Homer's reasoning is that the prayer is self-serving. There is asymmetry in "tying a course of action to a sign and tying it to no sign" and of "seeking confirmation through the absence of a sign." Actually, the series writers may be providing a simpler answer, in the form of an underlying cosmic joke. Homer begins his prayer by brushing off his wife, Marge, who we later learn has been trying to tell him that she is pregnant with their third child, an event guaranteed to turn his life upside down. Even before Homer asks, God has already given him both a sign *and* an answer (no), if he will only listen.

"Right-wingers complain there's no God on TV," *The Simpsons'* creator Matt Groening said in a 1999 interview in *Mother Jones* magazine. "Not only do the Simpsons go to church every Sunday and pray; they actually speak to God from time to time. We show Him, and God has five fingers—unlike the Simpsons, who have only four."[2] *The Simpsons* is consistently irreverent toward organized religion's failings and excesses, as it is with most other institutions of modern life. However, God is not mocked. When *The Simpsons* characters are faced with crises, they turn to God. He answers their prayers, often instantaneously, and he intervenes in their lives. Mike Scully, the series' executive producer, insists that God is not off-limits as a target, although there are considerable challenges. "It's more difficult to satirize something than to mock it," he says, and "it's hard to satirize something you don't see."

Characters in the series are admittedly a little hazy on the essence of the Almighty and His plan for humanity. Homer mistakes a waffle stuck to his ceiling for God, and then compounds the error by eating the waffle and mocking Communion by describing the taste as "sacrelicious." "I don't know who or what God is exactly," says Lisa to her brother Bart. "All I know is, he's a force more powerful than Mom and Dad put together." In an attempt to con the neighbor boys, evangelical Christians Rod and Todd Flanders, Bart impersonates the voice of God. Mother Marge, the most faithful member of the family, believes that when she sings "You Light Up My Life," she is singing about God. And the sign outside Springfield Community Church offers multiple views, from "God, the Original Love Connection" to "God Welcomes His Victims."

Predestination makes an appearance from time to time, where God's plan is used sometimes as an excuse, sometimes as an explanation. "Until this moment," says Bart, poised to buy a rare issue of *Radioactive Man*, "I never knew why God put me on this earth. But now I know . . . to buy that comic book." Informed that his house is teetering on its foundation, Homer says the situation is simply "all part of God's plan," and when he causes a traffic accident, he shouts, "Act of God, not my fault!" After a giant sturgeon falls to Earth from a Russian spacecraft and crashes onto his car hood, Homer complains, "God conned me out of sixty-five hundred dollars in car repairs." Criticized for using bad language, he says, "Maybe I curse a little, but that's the way God made me and I'm too old to stop now." Homer does a dance on top of a baseball dugout during a game, to the delight of the crowd. "We all have a calling, a reason the Almighty put us on earth, and yours might be to dance on dugouts," says Marge. Lisa equates her family's weekly menu with predestination: "Friday night. Pork chops. From cradle to grave, etched in stone in God's library somewhere in heaven."

It is Homer, however, who has the most personal relationship with God. Denounced by some as a simple-minded pagan, he is much more than that. According to the book *God in the Details: American Religion in Popular Culture*,

> Homer fulfills the role of the American spiritual wanderer. Though linked culturally (if unsteadily and unenthusiastically) to biblical tradition, he regularly engages a mosaic of other traditions, mythologies, and moral codes. In the face of these ever-shifting layers of meaning, he stumbles along, making the most of his limited understanding of their complexities. His comic antics remind us that the making of meaning (religious or otherwise) is even an unfinished business, and that humor and irony go a long way toward sweetening and sustaining the endeavor.[3]

In his spiritual searching, Homer is not shy about going directly to the source and asking God for help in his daily life. Uncertain how to help his gifted daughter Lisa, Homer asks for a sign from God. Suddenly he sees a storekeeper putting a sign in his window, "Musical Instruments: The Way to Encourage a Gifted Child," that answers his question exactly, beginning her saxophone career. Over the years that the series has run, Homer has gone back and forth about God's fundamental nature: "He's always happy. No wait, He's always mad." Homer is not alone in this confusion. The Jewish philosopher and theologian Abraham J. Heschel, in his study of the prophet Amos, noted this stark duality of God. On one hand, he is "the Deity of stern, mechanical justice." On the other, he is the God who overlooks and forgives a faithless Israel.[4] So maybe *The Simpsons*' writers are after more than a cheap laugh.

Without question, this is also a jealous God that does not like to be challenged. Montgomery Burns, the richest man in Springfield and Homer's boss at the nuclear power plant, fancies himself divine when a cult sweeps the town. Likening himself to "The New God," he tells workers at the nuclear plant, "You may now praise me as the almighty"—whereupon his robe catches on fire and he is left standing naked before the people. Homer falls into a similar trap when he finds a six-foot Tiki statue in the trash, sets it up in his backyard, and runs a gas line to the idol so it can spew flames. "Can your god do that?" he asks Ned Flanders. Actually, his neighbor replies, "we worship the same God." Not so, says Homer, yelling "I am your god now!" as the Tiki drops from his hands and sets the yard afire. In another episode, Homer and a friend engage in a vicious competition for snowplow customers, one so intense that Homer uses an opportunity to read the Bible from the pulpit during Sunday service to plug his plowing service. After reconciling with his competitor, Homer proclaims, "When two best friends work together, not even God can stop them." The words "Oh, no?" then appear large in the sky, and the rays of sunshine instantly melt the accumulated snow. Sometimes fire and sometimes ice, but the result is the same.

Homer is never entirely certain of God's love, which he tests repeatedly. Driving the family car during a Halloween fantasy sequence, he flees a zombie—the undead Ned Flanders. "Dear God," he cries, "it's Homer. If you really love me, you'll save me now," after which, he runs out of gas. In a Christmas episode, Homer is horrified to discover the family's gifts and tree missing on Christmas morning, and he reaches an inescapable conclusion: "Kids, God hates us!"

In another episode, he struggles to express God's universality: "You're everywhere. You're omnivorous." He's also somewhat confused about God's sense of self and what he does when not conversing with Homer. "I feel this incredible surge of power," Homer says in one episode, "like God must feel when he's holding a gun." In another, after shaking up Springfield with revelations on his personal Web site, he believes he has changed the world: "Now I know how God feels."

On a Pacific island, where he finds himself an accidental missionary, Homer is asked why an all-powerful Lord cares how or even whether he is worshiped. The question, profound and serious, is answered on this occasion with a disappointingly superficial quip. "It's because God is powerful, but insecure," Homer replies, "like Barbra Streisand before James Brolin." Homer is on even shakier ground when he tries to explain God and heaven to the islanders. After overseeing construction of a primitive church, he says, "I may not know much about God, but I have to say we built a pretty nice cage for him." Explaining why church bells have to be rung, he says, "God's palace is way up on the moon. So if you want him to hear us, you have to crank up the volume."

Embroiled in an escalating feud with George H. W. Bush when the former president moves into the neighborhood, Homer asks himself, "What would God do in this situation?" The next scene shows Bart carrying a box of locusts. In another episode, after watching a biblical epic about Noah on television, Bart gets carried away, telling Homer that God is cool because he is so "in-your-face!" Homer agrees, sort of, saying that God is his favorite "fictional character." After being accidentally hit in the face with an ice cream cone while on a hunger strike in another episode, he snaps, "Nice try, God, but Homer Simpson doesn't give in to temptation that easily." For his part, the Almighty is not without a sense of humor, at least where Homer is concerned. He leaves Homer a note reading, "IOU one brain, God."

Like many biblical figures and religious mystics through the ages, Homer has his most intense encounters with the Divine while dreaming. A vivid and extended example of this takes place in the 1992 episode "Homer the Heretic," written by George Meyer, long a guiding force in the series. The episode is used in college and seminary classes on religion and popular culture around the country. On a cold Sunday morning, Homer splits his pants as he dresses for church, so he decides not to go. Again, he offers what he takes as a clever, if familiar, theological justification: What's the big deal about going to some building on Sunday, he asks his wife. "Isn't God everywhere?" What he is asking is, How does God want to be worshiped? It is a question people of most cultures have been asking for thousands of years. Homer believes that if God wanted people to worship him for an hour a week, he should have made the week an hour longer.

At Springfield Community Church, where the furnace has broken, the other members of the Simpson family shiver, warmed only by Reverend Lovejoy's sermon promising hell's fire and brimstone. Meanwhile, Homer luxuriates in a hot shower and a warm house, with loud music and fattening food. Thus, the dichotomy is established: The faithful suffer for their belief, while the prodigal father enjoys the sybaritic life. As if the point is not made well enough, the contrast deepens. Together with the rest of the congregation, Marge and the children are stuck in church *after* the service, since the doors have frozen shut, and are forced to listen to the minister fill time by reading from the bulletin. At home, Homer wins a radio trivia contest, then watches an exciting football game on television and even finds a penny on the floor. After the congregation is finally able to leave the building, Marge's car won't start, leaving the family cold and stranded. When his family finally trudges in with their tales of woe, Homer proclaims that he has been having a wonderful day, perhaps the best of his life. Based on his analysis of divine favor, he decides never to go to church again. Marge can't believe that her husband intends to give up his faith. At first, he denies that is his intention, but then he admits it.

Homer's decision to abandon church provokes a full-blown theological debate in the Simpson household, with Bart supporting his father's choice with call-and-response evangelical fervor. In his defense, Homer offers a corollary to the "one true faith" argument: "What if we picked the wrong religion?" he asks. "Every week we're just making God madder and madder." That question, undermining as it is to more than one denomination, cannot remain unanswered. Before going to sleep that night, Marge kneels by her bed and prays for Homer to see the error of his ways, as he drifts off to sleep.

As so often in *The Simpsons*, God hears and answers. God comes to Homer in his dream, and provides as dramatic and direct an answer as can be imagined. Sitting on his couch, watching television, Homer feels the house begin to shake. A beam of light shines through the clouds and a large hand—with five realistic fingers—removes the roof. God is standing in the Simpsons' living room. In deference to several faiths, God's countenance is not shown. He is seen from the flowing beard down, wearing a robe and, it appears, Birkenstock sandals. At first, God is in no mood for pleasantries: "Thou hast forsaken my church!" he thunders.

Homer is frightened, but is nothing if not quick on his feet: "I'm not a bad guy! I work hard and I love my kids. So why should I spend half my Sunday hearing about how I'm going to hell? . . . I figure I should try to live right and worship you in my own way." God seems won over, acknowledging that Homer has a point as God pets the family cat. God agrees with Homer's complaints about Reverend Lovejoy's sermons. Because the minister displeases him, the Almighty will give him a canker sore. Here, truly, is God alive in the world. God agrees to let Homer worship him in his own way and departs, explaining that he has to appear in a tortilla in Mexico. Is this a dig at believers who report seeing religious visions in unlikely places? Clearly not, because God says he will actually *be present* in the tortilla.

After waking, Homer dives wholeheartedly into his new religion, donning a monk's robe and a mien of inner peace. In the manner of Saint Francis of Assisi, he attracts backyard birds and squirrels. Naturally, he decides his new religion needs holidays—what would a religion be without holidays? From the neighborhood bar, Moe's Tavern, Homer calls the nuclear power plant where he works to inform his employer that he will be out for a religious holiday. Asked the name of the holiday, he spies a sign on the wall of the bar and replies, "the Feast of Maximum Occupancy." Homer invites Moe to join his new religion, pointing out that it has the advantages of no hell and no kneeling. The bartender, a self-professed lifelong "snake handler," declines.

Lisa cautions against her father's apparent blasphemy, but Homer explains that he is covered. In his own variation of Pascal's wager, he says that if he is wrong he can always recant on his deathbed. Lisa does not remind him that this strategy may contain a fatal flaw, in light of the biblical warning that "no man knows when his hour will come" (Eccl. 9:12). Marge takes a more assertive approach to saving her husband from perdition by inviting Reverend Lovejoy to dinner. At the table, Homer describes to Bart how God appeared to him in the dream: "Perfect teeth. Nice smell. A class act, all the way." Under divine instructions, Homer tells the minister, he is seeking a new religious path. Lovejoy quotes Matthew 7:26 about the foolish man who built his house on sand. Homer replies with a bogus verse from Matthew, plucked out of the air, which is completely irrelevant.

How silly is Marge's concern with her husband's apparent loss of faith? Not silly at all, to judge from the numerous books, television, and radio shows that discuss the dilemma of spouses with different religions or different levels of religious commitment—what Christians call "unequally yoked." Homer's decision to abandon the church, and his persistence in this course, continue to have serious repercussions within his family. His wife makes an argument familiar to many households with divided beliefs: She has an obligation to raise the children with moral values, and church is a part of that obligation. Exasperated, Marge tells the children that Homer is wicked, and warns her husband not to force her to choose between him and God, because he will lose. At church the next Sunday, the sign out front reads "When Homer Met Satan." Inside, Reverend Lovejoy—who understands the struggle he is engaged in—preaches that the devil is at work among them, in a seductive incarnation. As he speaks, Homer is again at home enjoying himself, drooling over a pornographic magazine. Lovejoy continues from Exodus 20:8, "Remember the Sabbath day to keep it holy," as Homer is seen buying beer and cigars at the convenience store. "Pride goeth before destruction," the minister intones, and once more Homer takes the opposite message, smoking his cigar and reading his magazine while concluding that "everyone is stupid except me." He's right; he has abandoned organized religion with no discernible consequence. What is the lesson? What does God say?

This time—with or without God's canker sore—Reverend Lovejoy is onto something with his warning about haughtiness going before a fall. Homer dozes off, and his lighted cigar starts a fire in the couch, setting the house ablaze. The volunteer fire department comes to his aid. Homer is saved—twice—by his next-door neighbor, Ned Flanders, an evangelical Christian. The fire is put out by Lovejoy and the other members of the ecumenical crew, including Krusty, the Jewish clown, and Apu, the Hindu convenience store operator. Homer, always quick to learn the wrong lesson, takes the fire as a sign of divine retribution for abandoning his traditional Christian faith for a self-indulgent, personal religion. Converted by what he takes to be God's vengeance, Homer falls to his knees and prays for new marching orders: "O Spiteful One, show me who to smite, and he shall be smoten!"

Here the Christians come through, validating the essence of their faith rather than pressing their advantage on a weak mind. Ned assures Homer that the fire was not God's vengeance. Lovejoy explains that God was "working in the hearts of your friends and neighbors when they came to your aid." The minister asks if Homer would like to give church another try, and next Sunday he is back in church, snoring in the front pew. He dreams that he resumes his dialogue with God, albeit God with only four fingers. God takes him under his arm and tells him not to worry about his unsuccessful foray into religion, since nine out of ten new faiths fail in their first year. Homer then asks God about the meaning of life, and God replies with an old joke. He can't reveal the meaning of life until Homer dies. When Homer says he can't wait that long, God asks, "You can't wait six months?" as the two are bathed in a heavenly glow.

This episode, said author and Calvin College professor William Romanowski, is instructive because "it tries to get at the role of God and religion in people's everyday lives." Like Romanowski, David Landry uses "Homer the Heretic" in his religion and mass media classes at the University of St. Thomas. Michael Glodo, professor of Old Testament and preaching at Reformed Theological Seminary in Orlando, said the series writers "have captured a very common understanding of who God is." The lesson of the episode, wrote David Owen in *TV Guide*, is disarmingly simple: "Going to church may not be a terrible idea."[5]

In *The Simpsons*, God is a cross between Mel Brooks's Two-thousand-year-old Man and Charlton Heston's aged Moses, "a familiar stereotype with a humorous and not-too-blasphemous sting," according to one book on religion and popular culture.[6] Having fun with the image of God the Father is one thing in *The Simpsons*; Jesus is another matter entirely. When characters are in peril or crisis, they pray to "God" or "Lord" but rarely to Jesus. In one exception, Homer cries out, "Jesus, Allah, Buddha—I love you all!" Here the writers tread lightly. Why? Is the series that is not afraid to satirize anything afraid of offending Christians? Or are they afraid that any reference to Jesus might offend people of other, non-Christian religions? Perhaps. Jokes about God can refer to any of the major monotheistic faiths, and so are less likely to offend any particular denomination. (Compare this caution with the scatological animated cable show *South Park*, which in one episode featured a fight between Jesus and Satan—that the devil throws to win a side bet—and that features Jesus in a recurring role as host of a public access television program.)

Neil Postman, in *Amusing Ourselves to Death*, was as prescient on this point as he was on many others. "Christianity is a demanding and serious form of religion," he wrote. "When it is delivered as easy and amusing, it is another kind of religion altogether."

Each episode of *The Simpsons* begins with a fleeting sequence featuring Bart in the classroom after school, writing and rewriting an admonition on the blackboard, presumably punishment for some misbehavior that day. Sometimes the sentence refers to a theme of the story to follow, and sometimes it is a stand-alone gag, as in an episode in 2000 when Bart writes, "I was not touched by an angel"—a dig at *The Simpsons*' Sunday night competition. In the case of the Easter Sunday 1999 show, Bart writes "I cannot absolve sins." Yet in the episode that follows, the context for which is an Easter Sunday service, there is no mention of crucifixion or resurrection, something that would never happen in any Christian church. Reverend Lovejoy drones on about other things, including a chocolate bunny. All of the biblical dream sequences that follow are from the Old Testament, except for a short, closing sequence about the rapture. This is no accident.

One of the few physical images of Jesus in the history of *The Simpsons* is in the same episode, a quick *People's Court* parody, "Jesus Christ vs. Checker Chariot," depicting a silent, bearded Jesus in a business suit and neck brace. In another episode, when Homer gets his first computer, he calls up a real Web site, "Dancing Jesus." There are offhand and throwaway references to Jesus in a dozen or more episodes, some just this side of sacrilege. As a winter storm approaches Springfield, neighbor Ned Flanders takes down his manger scene because "if Baby Jesus gets loose, he could really do some damage." A Sunday school teacher assures one of the children that Jesus "did not have wheels." Barney, the town drunk, suggests at one point that Jesus "must be spinning in his grave." Jesus is also used as a way to take a shot at an easy target—commercialism and Christmas. A store sign proclaims, "In honor of the birth of Our Savior, Try-N-Save is Open All Day Christmas." Bart believes that "Christmas is the time when people of all religions come together to worship Jesus Christ."

More specific references are oblique or problematic. Upon reading his Bible, Homer says, "Everybody's a sinner, except this guy," without naming "this guy." Bart asks why he has to wear shoes to church since Jesus wore sandals. Homer replies that "maybe if he had better arch support they wouldn't have caught him." In Sunday school, Bart says he learned that lepers were cured by "a bearded dude." When the boy, reacting to drugs he takes for attention deficit disorder, steals a tank and aims the cannon at the church, Reverend Lovejoy shouts, "Not the church! Jesus lives there!" Outside the sanctuary building in the same 1999 Easter show, the sign reads, "Christ Dyed Eggs for Your Sins." At times, even Lovejoy is a little unclear on the concept of Jesus. "I remember another gentle visitor from the heavens," he says. "He came in peace and then died, only to come back to life. And his name was E.T., the extraterrestrial. I loved that little guy."

If anything, Homer is even hazier on the nature of Jesus and Christianity than he is about God. Asked by Bart what religion his father is, Homer answers, "You know, the one with all the well-meaning rules that don't work in real life. Uh, Christianity." While walking through the Springfield Airport, he and Bart cross paths with a Christian evangelist holding a Bible and quoting the Golden Rule: "Do unto others as you would have them do unto you" (Matt. 7:12). Homer replies sarcastically, "That'll work."

Homer has the unsettling habit of comparing himself to Jesus, often under trivial circumstances. "Kids, let me tell you about another so-called wicked guy," he says in his defense in "Homer the Heretic." "He had long hair and some wild ideas. He didn't always do what other people thought was right. And that man's name was . . . I forget. But the point is . . . I forget that too." After bowling a perfect game, Homer is briefly the center of Springfield's attention, only to have the spotlight inevitably fade. "They did it to Jesus and now they're doing it to me," he tells his wife, who is shocked. "Are you comparing yourself to Our Lord?" Marge asks. "In bowling ability, yes," Homer replies blithely. In a Halloween fantasy, Homer dies and can only get into heaven if he returns to earth to do a good deed. Marge offers his hovering spirit a simple list of choices, which her husband rejects, saying, "I'm not running for Jesus!" Driven to delirium during a hunger strike to protest the move of Springfield's minor league baseball team to another city, Homer tells the crowd that he is, himself, "kind of like Jesus, but not in a sacrilegious way."

In the extreme, Homer even gets Jesus' name wrong. In one episode, he becomes involved in a madcap comedy of errors involving an unpaid pledge to a PBS telethon that leaves Homer trapped on a Christian relief flight heading for a remote Pacific island. He runs to the cockpit and begs the pilots to stop the plane and let him off, sounding a lot like Peter before the cock crowed. "I don't even believe in Jebus," he pleads, using the ancient name for Jerusalem before it was conquered by King David. Yet when the plane takes off, the desperate Homer knows where to go for help. "Save me, Jebus!" he cries. Sacrilege has its costs: Homer attributes part of the fall of his popular barbershop quartet, the Be Sharps, to the group's decision to name their second album "Bigger Than Jesus," a play on John Lennon's celebrated boast.

Homer thinks Ned Flanders is "holier than Jesus" and so turns to him in the mistaken belief that he and Bart have been afflicted with leprosy. Bart wonders aloud why God would punish a kid with such a disease, most particularly "an American kid." Homer correctly identifies the divine figure in question as Jesus but tells his son not to hope for a similar miracle because "I think we're on the outs with him." Even this may be changing. Twice in a single episode in May 2001, Homer says, "Christ be with you," once as a way of expressing gratitude and once expressing irony.

There have been surprises, especially in recent years. In the same 2001 episode where Homer starves himself to keep the baseball team in Springfield, Duff Man—the superhero mascot of the team's owners, the Duff Beer Company—is torn between helping Homer do the right thing and the orders of his boss. Uncertain, Duff Man asks himself, "What would Jesus do?" In what is arguably a loose interpretation of the biblical Jesus, Duff Man tosses his employer out of the stadium.

Salvation by grace is never mentioned in *The Simpsons*. Crucifixion and resurrection, essential elements of Christianity, are also not often referred to in the series because neither is "a big laugh getter," according to executive producer Mike Scully. The writers would use such imagery only if there were some point in doing so, he said, although in a May 2001 episode Reverend Lovejoy is seen serving "Cruci-fixins" ice cream toppings at a church social. More particular Christian concepts like the Trinity or the Holy Spirit can be difficult enough for believers to grasp, so it is not surprising that *The Simpsons* make little effort to bring them into the series. Yet there is something more at work in this reluctance of *The Simpsons* to deal with Jesus as divine, as well as the refusal to deal with the other specific details of Christianity in the series.

In her 1992 master's thesis at Regent University, "The Gospel according to Bart: Examining the Religious Elements of *The Simpsons*," Beth Keller provided an in-depth context for the presentation of religion in popular culture. She analyzed five episodes from the first few seasons, not including "Homer the Heretic," which had not aired at the time of her research. She concluded, perceptively, that the theological construct that informs the series and the churchgoing Simpsons is actually the Old Testament.

> The show seems to promote the idea that following the law, or being ethically good, is all that is required to gain entrance to heaven. While this is theoretically true, the evangelical believes that "keeping the law" is impossible. That is why grace by faith in Jesus Christ is understood to be the way to stand before God in the afterlife. . . . However, the viewer is given the strong impression that the Simpsons represent a Protestant Christian family, so there is a dichotomy between the full truth from an evangelical perspective and the "truth" that is represented in *The Simpsons*.[7]

In the years of episodes that have followed, this dichotomy has been reinforced time and again, much like the one between a vengeful God and a loving God. Homer and Bart watch a television movie about Noah's ark, which ends with God telling Noah, "Remember, the key to salvation is. . . ." Just then, a news story interrupts the show. But this poses no problem for most monotheists. "After the key to salvation remains ambiguous," writes Trammell, "the Simpsons still pray to God."

Gerry Bowler, of Canadian Nazarene College, has a simpler explanation: "Though he claims to be a Christian, Homer is essentially a pagan. Religion for him consists of placating or bribing an angry god or gods."[8] Support for Bowler's position—or that Homer is satanic—came in an episode in the show's 2000–2001 season, when Homer shapes a snow angel with his body. Getting up, all that remains is a dark outline of a devil with pitchfork, something Homer says happens whenever he tries to be an angel.

Another reason Jesus may be largely off-limits for *The Simpsons* is the problem many Christians have associating their Savior—or any aspect of the New Testament—with humor. (The Hebrew Bible offers more opportunities, as the book of Psalms (2:4) notes: "Who sits in the heavens laughs.") This subject has drawn the attention of numerous authors over the years, who have produced works such as *Laughing Out Loud and Other Religious Experiences* by Tom Mullen, *Humor: God's Gift* by Tal Bonham, *Serve Him with Mirth* by Leslie Flynn, and *The Ontology of Humor* by Robert Parrott.

A book on this subject preferred by many evangelicals is *Humor of Christ*, by the late Elton Trueblood, a slim volume first published in 1964 and now out of print.[9] At the outset, Trueblood acknowledges that many Christians, perhaps a majority, believe that finding humor in the person of Jesus is at least inappropriate and may be sacrilegious. "Religion, we think, is serious business, and serious business is incompatible with banter." He agrees that some elements of the gospel, such as the crucifixion, are so tragic as to be "intrinsically unhumorous." Still, he argues, humor is a fundamental part of Jesus' message and method. He wrote his book to "help overcome an almost universal failure to appreciate an element in Christ's life which is so important that, without it, any understanding of Him is inevitably distorted." Trueblood is determined "to do something to challenge the conventionalized picture of a Christ who never laughed. . . . If Christ laughed a great deal, as the evidence shows, and if He is what He claimed to be, we cannot avoid the logical conclusion that there is laughter and gaiety in the heart of God."

The humor of Jesus is ironic, sardonic and, occasionally, sarcastic, according to Trueblood. Thus, Jesus dubs the inconstant Peter his rock, or "Rocky," as Trueblood puts it. His wit is sly and wry, the absurdist imagery most evident in the parables and paradoxes: the beam and the mote, the gnat and the camel, the camel and the eye of the needle. Trueblood believes that even more of Jesus' humor was probably lost in the transcription, if not in the translation. Examples from the Gospels, when properly analyzed, "are luminous once we become liberated from the gratuitous assumption that Christ never joked." In Matthew 24:20, for example, Jesus explains his ability to draw a crowd by observing, in apparent self-deprecation, that, "Wherever the corpse is, there the vultures will gather."

But a joking Jesus is not the same as a Jesus joke, which may be why, in the end, *The Simpsons* writers treat Jesus so gingerly. There is a great tradition of gentle Christian humor, much of which centers around the clergy, the inconsistencies of church life, and getting into heaven. Portraying Jesus as a humorous character in an animated comedy may simply be too much to ask of a sitcom audience. Here, Trueblood offers some useful—if unsolicited—advice to the show's writers: "The only kind of laughter which can be redemptive is that which goes beyond scorn to recognition of a common predicament."

Two

Personal Prayer: "Dear God, Give the Bald Guy a Break!"

In the Simpson household, prayer most frequently takes the form of blessings at mealtimes, including grace over take-out fast food and, on at least one occasion, in a restaurant. Often, the prayers are perfunctory, as in Bart's "Rub a dub, dub, thanks for the grub" or Homer's equally succinct but barely more reverent, "Good drink, good meat, good God, let's eat." On one occasion, Bart seems to speak the unspeakable: "Dear God, we paid for all this stuff ourselves, so thanks for nothing." In the early 1990s, the young child of a member of Willow Creek Community Church, the megachurch in South Barrington, Illinois, offered a version of this grace at the family table, shocking his father. The man complained to a minister, Lee Strobel, saying that the child was prohibited from watching *The Simpsons* but had picked up the prayer from a commercial advertising an upcoming episode.

Strobel, a former journalist at the *Chicago Tribune* who became a teaching pastor at Willow Creek, used the incident to introduce a sermon titled, "What Jesus Would Say to Bart Simpson." Strobel explained that the episode's grace was "an exaggerated look at life from a kid's perspective, with a kernel of truth at its core." Because Bart is so uninhibited, he

> says things that other people only think. When he prays, "Why should we thank you, God—we bought this ourselves," people recoil in horror. Yet isn't he just expressing a sentiment that a lot of people secretly harbor? They'd never *say* it, but don't many people live their lives with the attitude they they've earned what they've received and that God really had nothing to do with it? So, in ways, Bart is merely more honest than most.[1]

Grace at mealtime is far more common than prime-time television would suggest. A 1999 Gallup survey found that 51 percent of Americans says a blessing over food always or frequently. In *The Simpsons*, such prayers can express a larger gratitude, beyond simple sustenance. Next door to the Simpsons, at the home of the evangelical Flanders family, father Ned prays, "Dear God, thanks for *Ziggy* comics, little baby ducks, and 'Sweatin' to the Oldies' volumes one, two, and three."

The Simpsons are "a family where God has a place at the table," said Robert Thompson of Syracuse University in a newspaper interview.[2] Homer gives thanks for his job. One evening he takes the opportunity to thank God "most of all for nuclear power, which has yet to cause a single, proven fatality, at least in this country." And at Thanksgiving he prays, "We especially thank you for nuclear power, the cleanest, safest energy source there is, except solar, which is just a pipe dream." Yet the family sometimes acknowledges during grace that its blessings are mixed and, this being *The Simpsons*, things simply spin out of control. After one particular Thanksgiving turns into a disaster, Homer loses it, offering thanks "for the occasional moments of peace and love our family's experienced . . . well, not today. You saw what happened. O Lord, be honest! Are we the most pathetic family in the world, or what?" (His sister-in-law Selma comments, "Worst prayer yet.") By the conclusion of the episode, the conflicts are resolved and, as the soundtrack plays "We Gather Together," the family eats turkey sandwiches. "O Lord," Homer says, "on this blessed day, we thank thee for giving our family one more crack at togetherness."

On another occasion, Homer gives way to exasperation. "Dear Lord, thank you for this microwave bounty, even though we don't deserve it," he says. "I mean . . . our kids are uncontrollable hellions. Pardon my French, but they act like savages! Did you see them at the picnic? Of course you did; you're everywhere, you're omnivorous, O Lord! Why did you spite me with this family?"

As in many homes, prayer at the Simpsons' is fervent in the face of disaster, like a hurricane or a comet bearing down on their cartoon town. It often comes in the form of a bargain: "Dear God, this is Marge Simpson. If you stop this hurricane and save our family, we will be forever grateful and recommend you to all of our friends"; likewise, during a nuclear meltdown begun at Homer's workplace, Marge prays, "Dear Lord, if you spare this town from becoming a smoking hole in the ground, I'll try to be a better Christian. I don't know what I can do. Ummm . . . oh, the next time there's a canned food drive, I'll give the poor something they actually like, instead of old lima beans and pumpkin mix." In desperation, Homer can even forget the exact nature of the divine: "I'm not much of a praying man, but if you're up there, please save me, Superman." And the Simpsons are not unique in this respect. In the face of these and other imminent disasters, all of Springfield is seen praying, in church, at the nuclear power plant, and even on a hillside where a divine apparition seems to have appeared. Even lesser primates pray. When Mojo, Homer's abused pet monkey, is dropped off at the Animal Assistants Program, he frantically taps out on a keyboard the message: "Pray for Mojo."

Intercessory prayer is rare in the series. Characters pray directly to God for what they want. Between the extremes of grace for meals and appeals for physical survival come appeals for some of the simple—sometimes trivial and absurd—things for which most people pray. Bart promises to build a church if God will stop Homer from embarrassing him. When the Simpsons' television reception goes out, Homer prays, "Dear God, just give me one channel!"

When God responds favorably to pleas like these, there is often a twist. Larry Dossey explores this issue in *Be Careful What You Pray For . . . You Just Might Get It*. He discusses the notion of "toxic prayer," which can do damage to the petitioner or others. For example, Homer wants a hair-restoring formula to work: "Dear God, give the bald guy a break!" It does work, but only for a time, and it turns Homer's life upside down. Desperate to attend the big football game, Homer prays, "God, if you really are a God, you'll give me tickets to that game." As soon as the words are out of his mouth, the doorbell rings and it is his next-door neighbor, Ned Flanders, whose company he does his best to avoid. Ned has tickets to the game and asks Homer to join him. Homer slams the door and cries out, "Why do you mock me, O Lord?"

This illustrates a fundamental and very thorny theological issue presented by *The Simpsons*. For hundreds of years, Jewish sages have debated whether a God who is truly kind and compassionate would grant prayer requests that are not in the best interests of the petitioners. "What limitations or controls does God put in place to prevent us from experiencing our destruction?" asks Rabbi Sholom Dubov of Maitland, Florida. "Faith drives an inner mechanism." But in the Judeo-Christian tradition that has free will at its core, there is no guarantee that faith will not drive human beings in the wrong direction. The Roman philosopher Juvenal, a pagan, wrote of "enormous prayers which heaven in vengeance grants." Thus, Bart gives spontaneous thanks to God "for all the bad things adults do, which distracts attention from the stuff I am doing." (His protective mother, overhearing, adds a postscript: "He's also thankful for your bounty, Lord.") When the boy discovers a cache of lethal police equipment in a closet while playing at the home of the chief's son, Bart voices gratitude "for this bounty I am about to receive." Why thank God? Would a merciful God put murderous paraphernalia in the hands of children?

On several occasions, characters ask for things so clearly beyond the pale that they are called on it. Bart prays for God to kill his nemesis and tormenter, Sideshow Bob, only to have Marge separate his praying hands and explain that such a prayer is wrong. When it comes to tasks like that, his father tells him, "you do your own dirty work." In another episode, Homer and Bart hatch a typically hare-brained, money-making scheme to steal a load of kitchen grease from the elementary school kitchen. As the two are preparing to pump out the grease, Homer pauses to recognize the power of the Almighty. "All right, son," he says, "we're about to embark on a most serious mission. Let's bow our heads in prayer. Dear Lord, if you help us steal this grease tonight, I promise we'll donate half the profits to charity." To which Bart responds, "Dad, he's not that stupid." Homer agrees but is undissuaded from his course. "Screw it," he says. "Let's roll!"

"Bart Gets an F" offers the most detailed portrayal of the dynamic of prayer on *The Simpsons*. After the boy blows an oral book report of *Treasure Island* (which he neglected to read) and fails a test in colonial American history, Marge and Homer are called in and told by the teacher and the district psychologist that Bart is in danger of failing fourth grade. The boy pledges to do better, yet he fails to prepare for the next, crucial test and engineers a reprieve only when he fakes an illness. A makeup test, using cribbed answers, is a disaster. Time runs out the night before the test that will determine whether Bart has to be held back. He squanders his study time and faces a dire future.

At this point, Bart, kneeling by his bed, turns to God. "Well, Old Timer, I guess this is the end of the road," he says. "I know I haven't always been a good kid, but if I have to go to school tomorrow, I'll fail the test and be held back. I just need one more day to study, Lord. I need your help!" (His sister Lisa overhears and scoffs, "Prayer, the last refuge of the scoundrel," echoing the sentiments of many in recent years who have seen criminal defendants enter the courtroom with their Bibles and newfound faith.) Bart continues, listing God's alternatives: "A teachers' strike, a power failure, a blizzard. . . . Anything that'll cancel school tomorrow. I know it's asking a lot, but if anyone can do it, you can! Thanking you in advance, Bart Simpson." And God delivers. After Bart turns out the light, the first flakes of snow begin to fall as the strains of the "Hallelujah" chorus from Handel's *Messiah* are heard—the series' standard signal of divine intervention. A deep snow covers Springfield the next morning, prompting the closing of school. Bart, forgetting everything and reverting to type, prepares to head out for a day of carefree fun—until he encounters Lisa. "I heard you last night, Bart," she says. "You prayed for this and your prayers have been answered." Bart acknowledges his obligation: "I asked for a miracle, and I got it. I gotta study, man!" Bart passes the test by a single extra-credit point, and he tells his father, "Part of this D minus belongs to God."

"I like to think that Bart Simpson is in line with Abraham and Moses in that he talks to God directly," says Robert Thompson.[3] In his previously discussed Willow Creek sermon, Lee Strobel deconstructs this exercise and finds that this example is also theologically consistent with the New Testament concept of prayer. In Matthew 6:6, believers are advised, "When you pray, go into your room, close the door and pray to your Father, who is unseen. Then your Father, who sees what is done in secret, will reward you." In Philippians 4:6, they are told, "In everything, by prayer and petition, with thanksgiving, present your requests to God." And Proverbs 28:13 instructs, "He who conceals his sins does not prosper, but whoever confesses and renounces them finds mercy."

Bart does most things a praying Christian should do, Strobel says. He speaks directly and personally to God from the heart. He confesses his powerlessness. He admits his sinfulness. He voices faith in God's ability and power to grant his petition, and he expresses gratitude before *and* after it is granted. "Maybe—as outrageous as it sounds—we can come away with a few good ideas about how to notch up our own interaction with God," says Strobel, taking a lesson from *The Simpsons'* bad boy.[4]

While, as Trammell notes, prayer serves the narrative purpose of exposing character's feelings and furthering the plot, "prayers are also used as quick, cheap, dispensable jokes." Thus Bart also prays to Santa on Christmas Eve: "If you bring me lots of good stuff, I promise not to do anything bad between now and when I wake up." The boy is a fervent believer in holiday miracles, despite his father's skepticism. In the original Christmas episode, when the family's presents are destroyed, Bart says, "Aw, come on, Dad. This could be the miracle that saves the Simpsons' holiday. If TV has taught me anything, it's that miracles always happen to poor kids at Christmas. It happened to Tiny Tim, it happened to Charlie Brown, it happened to the Smurfs, and it's going to happen to us!"

The mutual hostility between the secular culture and religion—in the context of the national conflict over moral values—pops up frequently on

The Simpsons. An inmate performing in a prison rodeo is booed after being identified as having been convicted of erecting a nativity scene on city property. In another episode, Bart's elementary school teacher excuses two students, obviously Christian, when a sex education film is shown in class. "Ezekiel and Ishmael," she says, "in accordance with your parents' wishes you may go out into the hall and pray for our souls." The authors of a chapter on the show in *God in the Details: American Religion in Popular Culture* ask, "Does *The Simpsons* reflect our attitudes—particularly toward religion—or does it shape them? Does television act as a mirror to show us ourselves as we really are, or as we ought to be? As the reactions to *The Simpsons* suggest, it is an important debate."[5] How different, for example, is the personal prayer life of characters in *The Simpsons* from that of most Americans? John W. Heeren, professor of sociology at California State University at San Bernardino, writes that the series is "not a reflection of religious reality, but a pop culture version of religion. As the postmodernists say, it is a 'copy of a copy.'"[6]

I am not so sure that when it comes to religion, faith, and prayer that *The Simpsons* shapes, reflects, or copies our attitudes; it may simply portray our practice. The 1999 Gallup survey alluded to earlier found that 90 percent of Americans pray, and 75 percent pray on a daily basis. Ninety percent said that religion was very important or fairly important in their lives, although that reality is rarely evident in other series on prime-time television. By contrast, a 1994 study that surveyed the portrayal of religion on prime-time television found that it was "a rather invisible institution." Religion was infrequently the focus of the narrative in the one hundred episodes studied over a five-week period, and fewer than 6 percent of 1,462 characters had a recognizable religious affiliation. Through this fiction, the study's authors found, religion is "delegitimized" by television.

As with all things demographic in the United States, the trend toward prayer was strongly influenced and accelerated by the baby boom generation. By the end of the twentieth and the beginning of the twenty-first century, increasing numbers of the generation that believed it would be, in Bob Dylan's words, "forever young" were coming face-to-face with mortality, if not their own then that of their parents. And—some would say at long last—they began to shift their attention from themselves to their children, the generation that will succeed them. This happened to me in much the same way as it has to others of my peers. During one Jewish High Holiday service, around the time my son was three and my daughter was an infant, our rabbi at Temple Israel in Long Beach, California, Howard Laibson, suggested in his sermon one small way to get in touch with the divine: reciting the *Sh'ma* ("Hear, O Israel, the Lord is my God, the Lord is one") each night with the children before bed. When I heard those words they took me back to my own childhood when I would say the prayer with my parents and my younger brother. From that day to this, evening prayers became a part of our home life. In religion, one thing has a tendency to lead to another. Some years later, at the suggestion of my wife, Sallie, we began to observe the arrival of the Sabbath on Friday evening, lighting the candles and blessing the braided challah bread, which she learned to bake herself. More recently, we have added grace before dinner, holding hands while we recite the Hebrew blessing for breaking bread and sing a simple Girl Scout grace my wife sang with her own family at dinner ("For health and strength . . .").

Something seismic was at work in this look to the heavens by Americans, and I believe, at a deeper level, that "something" is reflected in the way the supernatural is portrayed in *The Simpsons*. Season after season, the Simpsons have continued to pray, especially Marge. Despite a "No Praying" sign in her husband's hospital room, she asks for divine intervention. Faced with the latest in a never-ending series of sanity hearings endured by family members, she calls on God (in a soft but audible voice) to help her as she pleads her case to three psychiatrists. They ask her if she is praying, and she acknowledges that she is. Concerned by what they consider obvious evidence of mental instability, they inquire whether she thinks God is in the room. She replies that, yes, He's pretty much everywhere. Case closed: Marge is certifiably nuts.

Of course, there is a downside to this new spiritual consciousness and openness to the supernatural that is also reflected in the series. New Age beliefs are consistently mocked and disparaged. But two green, slimy beings from another universe (the planet Rigel-4), Kang and Kodos, visit Springfield from time to time for typical alien undertakings: either to abduct, breed with, or probe Simpson family members, or to conquer or destroy the earth. The aliens' presence in *The Simpsons* universe is as "real" —which is to say as unquestioned—as that of God. Characters on the show have no difficulty accepting both unconditionally.

Recent books such as Joel Achenbach's *Captured by Aliens: The Search for Life and Truth in a Very Large Universe* and Wendy Kaminer's *Sleeping with Extra-Terrestrials: The Rise of Irrationalism and Perils of Piety* explore this puzzling coexistence of belief in God and UFOs by many Americans. "No religion can simply be trusted to balance faith with reason," Kaminer writes, "but regular social rituals, like attending church or New Age lectures, and private rituals, like prayer, or maybe watching *Touched by an*

Angel once a week, can provide people with the opportunity to compart-mentalize their beliefs, so as not to be consumed by them."[7]

Unlike the regular characters on *Touched by an Angel,* the extraterres-trials on *The Simpsons* are in no way divine. To a degree, the difference between the irrationality of faith and the irrationality of extraterrestrials in Springfield is quantitative. Prayer and appeals to God are a much more routine and regular part of the Simpson family's life and the lives of their friends than are the appearances of Kang and Kodos on the show. In one episode, the two extraterrestrial siblings reveal that they too are creatures of faith (sort of): They identify themselves as "Quantum-Presbyterians."

Three

Does Lisa Speak for Jesus?
"There's Something Wrong
with That Kid. She's So Moral."

O ne of the more enduring images of Lisa Simpson is of the precocious eight-year-old fluttering above the earth in angel's wings and a sparkling halo. The wings might come in handy, since Lisa seems to carry the weight of the world on her shoulders. When she gets into one of her funks, her father tries to cheer her up, but she replies by asking what the point of existence is: "How can we sleep at night when there's so much suffering in the world?" When her brother and her father put their souls in jeopardy through sin, it is Lisa who takes the initiative to save them. Her essential goodness is manifest and acknowledged in a brief sequence imagining the rapture. Alone among her family, she begins to drift from the earth with the other elect, only to be yanked back by her sinful and earthbound (and, presumably, hell-bound) father.

In an essay in *Simpsons Comics Royale*, Matt Groening writes that Lisa is his favorite character. "I like her idealism, her stubbornness . . . [her] politics, convictions, and ability to learn from her mistakes. If I had to be suddenly transmorphed into the Simpsons cartoon universe (a horrifying thought), I'd like to be Lisa Simpson." The girl is as conscientious a student as her brother Bart is a slacker, and is so reliable that Reverend Lovejoy advertises her baby-sitting availability from the pulpit. Even as she plays her saxophone, she marches to the beat of a dramatically different drummer. During a tortured group rendition of "My Country 'Tis of Thee" in the school's music room, Lisa takes off on a bebop riff, drawing a reproof from the band teacher. She explains that her solo is "what my country is all about," that she is wailing out for the homeless family living out of a car, the farmer whose land has been taken away by heartless bureaucrats, and West Virginia coal miners. That may well be, the music teacher replies, "but none of those unpleasant people are going to be at the recital next week."

Lisa tries—and fails—to preserve Springfield's fragile civility when a food fight breaks out in a city park. Writing a letter to the newspaper, she asserts her purpose is "not to nag or whine, but to prod." In the super-market, she castigates her mother for eating two grapes, shaming her into paying for them at the checkout counter. When the family is caught up in a cult, it is Lisa who resists the group's mind control, noting that while they toil in the group's fields, the cult's leader tools around in a Rolls Royce. Unlike much that goes on around him, this does not escape Homer's attention. "There's something wrong with that kid," he says. "She's so moral." Pressed for income tax deductions, he lists Lisa's occupation as "clergy."

In contrast to some other series characters, Lisa retains her essential nature even in fantasy episodes. In one Halloween special, she accidentally creates a microworld in a school science experiment and is venerated by that world's tiny people as a god, complete with a statue of herself. Seeing one of the tiny people nailing something to a cathedral door, she assumes she has created Lutherans. Later, shrunk down to the little world's size, she is asked a familiar metaphysical question: As the Creator, why does she allow bad things to happen? Stuck for an answer, she falls back on blind faith, asking, "Shouldn't you people be groveling?" In another Halloween segment, Springfield reprises the Salem witch trials. Although the Flanders family is condemned to the stake, Lisa refuses to participate in the burning, quoting the Bible verse, "Judge not, lest ye be judged."

If the Simpsons' next-door neighbor Ned Flanders is an exemplar of evangelical Christianity (see chapter 4), Lisa represents the essence of mainline denominations, with their commitment to a socially conscious gospel and rational, religious humanism. She rejects the faith healing of a Pentecostal preacher at a tent revival as "mumbo-jumbo." In her own way, she speaks for a Christianity as envisioned by many modern believers. James Lawler, in a collection of essays entitled *The Simpsons and Philosophy: The D'oh! of Homer*, contrasts Lisa's acute sense of moral duty to

> the self-assured, institutionally based morality of Flanders, confident in the authority of his Bible and Church. Lisa's morality arises out of a precocious personal reflection on the great themes of moral life: truthfulness, helping others in need, a commitment to human equality, and justice. . . . Lisa focuses attention on inescapable moral principles and makes people uneasy with the conventional compromises. Hence she is typically isolated and suffers intensely from her isolation.[1]

Lawler argues that Lisa is motivated not by religion but by the moral theory of the eighteenth-century German philosopher Immanuel Kant and his Categorical Imperative: "Act only on that maxim through which you can at the same time will that it should become a universal law." Some suggest that, on occasion, her political views echo another German philosopher—Karl Marx. Yet consider the ways in which Lisa's words and actions parallel those of Jesus:

1. Lisa supports the poor, the powerless, and the downtrodden and is critical of the rich. Her goal is to do good in the world, to alleviate suffering and, when necessary, through guilt to persuade others into doing the same. She backs the rights of striking workers in Springfield and, in the years when South Africa had a white-ruled government, she had anti-apartheid posters hanging in her bedroom. When Bart asks how the comic character Richie Rich died, she explains, "Perhaps he realized how shallow the pursuit of money was and took his own life." In another episode, her grandfather, Abe Simpson, unexpectedly inherits one hundred thousand dollars and wonders what to do with it. Lisa urges him to give it to the needy. "The people who deserve it are on the street and they're in the slums. They're little children who need more library books, and they're families who can't make ends meet."

2. Lisa questions the conventional wisdom, regardless of how unpopular such questioning might be. Like the ancient prophets, she is a compulsive truth teller, seeming to take a perverse joy in whom and how she offends. Athletics are a particular sore point with her. Children's leagues, she says, are places "where parents push their kids into vicious competition to compensate for their own failed dreams of glory," and professional football is little more than "a savage ballet." It seems that the more inopportune the occasion, the more likely she is to speak out, to speak truth to power. As Little Miss Springfield, Lisa is asked to sing "The Star Spangled Banner" before a football game. She uses the occasion to announce, "Before I sing the national anthem, I'd like to say that college football drains funds that are badly needed for education and the arts." Her subsequent denunciation of the tobacco company that sponsors the Little Miss Springfield contest costs her the tiara.

In Washington, D.C., to participate in a patriotic essay competition, Lisa discovers that her congressman is involved in a plot to cut down Springfield National Forest for timber. Naturally, she incorporates this information into her oratory: "The City of Washington was built on a stagnant swamp some two hundred years ago, and very little has changed. It stank then and it stinks now. Only today it is the fetid stench of corruption that hangs in the air." (A subsequent headline in the Springfield paper reads, "Imprisoned Congressman Becomes Born-Again Christian.") Lisa loses the contest to a Vietnamese immigrant whose essay celebrates his family's triumph over adversity in the United States.

3. Lisa believes in the concept of stewardship of the earth and its resources, and defends the rights of God's lesser beings. A committed environmentalist and vegetarian, she opposes the needless killing of creatures—including snakes at Springfield's annual "Whacking Day"—and condemns her mother for ordering veal in a restaurant. She agrees to help her father's boss, Mr. Burns, recover his lost fortune only "by doing good, responsible things. Nothing evil." As one might predict, things go awry when she discovers that the "Li'l Lisa Recycling Plant," while environmentally sound, is using plastic six-pack holders to construct a giant fishnet to sweep the sea clean of marine life. Lisa rejects Mr. Burns's royalty check of $12 million, but she also rejects her father's suggestion that the lesson of the experience is "Never help anyone."

4. Lisa takes pity on scorned individuals, offering solace and affection for the unloved. Her concern is not only for the collective good. She tries to transform a playground bully and all-around bad boy named Nelson Muntz, whose parents are in prison, with her puppy love. She takes pity on dim-witted Ralph Wiggum, whom she notices has not received a single valentine, by changing the name on one of her cards to his. The effort backfires, naturally, as Ralph becomes obsessed with the girl and is hurt even more when she rejects him as well.

There are ways in which Lisa clearly stands apart from a fundamentalist view of Christianity. She opposes religious hysteria, denounces blind faith, and tries to reconcile science with belief. In "Lisa the Skeptic," she confronts all of these issues in a trial that is a reprise of the Scopes Monkey Trial in Dayton, Tennessee, in the 1920s.

Concerned that a new shopping center being built in Sabertooth Meadow might endanger fossils, she organizes a dig by elementary students and community residents. She uncovers what appears to be a fossilized skeleton with wings, which Flanders suggests is the remains of an angel. Lisa replies that the configuration could be that of a Neanderthal man attacked by two angry fish. A sensation ensues over what it is and what to do with it. In the confusion and growing hysteria, Homer ties the object to the roof of his car, takes it home, and stashes it in his garage.

The Flanders family comes to the door, asking to pray with the angel, the first of a stream who want to venerate what they believe to be a relic. Homer decides to decorate the image with Christmas lights and charge admission. Lisa objects to her father's plan and tells him she plans to take a sample of the remains to the local museum for testing. Harvard's Stephen J. Gould, an expert on evolution, is in residence there. Homer accuses his daughter of being sacrilegious, signaling an unfolding confrontation between science and faith. Lisa asks the scientist to determine the age of the "so-called angel," which Gould suggests is quite preposterous. Of course, no one makes the obvious and elementary theological observation—that angels are spiritual entities and thus unlikely to leave skeletal remains.

The garage attraction shrine is an instant success, although there is a nasty argument about whether the object on display is the angel of peace or the angel of mercy. When Gould arrives to say that his tests have been inconclusive, Reverend Lovejoy crows that "science has faltered once again in the face of overwhelming religious evidence." Lisa storms into the kitchen, telling her mother that "those morons" in the garage infuriate her. Marge tells her daughter that, while she may be right about the angel, she would appreciate it if Lisa would not refer to those people in the garage as morons. The girl asks what grown person could believe in angels. "Your mother, for one," Marge replies. Lisa protests that her mother is an intelligent person. Her mother sees no contradiction between the two: "There has to be more to life than just what we see, Lisa. Everyone needs something to believe in." Lisa backs down, acknowledging that she has a spiritual side. She just finds it difficult to believe that "there's a dead angel hanging in our garage." Marge offers sympathy to her daughter. "If you can't make a leap of faith now and then, well, I feel sorry for you."

Still convinced that the remains are bogus, Lisa takes her case to television and has to respond to a newsman's argument that the remains must be of an angel because they look like an angel. She asserts that those who believe the remains are heavenly probably believe in sea monsters, unicorns, and leprechauns. "You can either accept science and face reality, or you can believe in angels and live in a childish dream world," she says. Her remarks inflame believers watching the show at the church, where the television set is perched atop a piano. Flanders compares science to "a blabbermouth who ruins a movie by telling you how it ends. Well, I say there are some things we don't want to know—important things!" His words set off a riot against all things associated with science: the museum, a robotics laboratory, and a Christian Science reading room. The mob comes to the Simpsons' home for their angel, believing it is not safe in the presence of Lisa, "the unbeliever."

They find that the angel is missing from the garage, and suspicion naturally falls on Lisa. Reverend Lovejoy suggests that the girl "found something science couldn't explain, so she had to destroy it." Lisa is arrested and tried on charges of destruction of property. After hearing testimony, the judge acquits the girl and issues his order: Science and religion are to remain five hundred yards apart. Miraculously, through the courtroom window, the angel reappears on a hillside near where it was found. The crowd stampedes to the site, where they find something has been added: words carved at the base that read, "The End Will Come at Sundown." With this, Reverend Lovejoy says that even Lisa must admit that they have witnessed a miracle. The girl is steadfast, insisting that someone could have moved the image to the site, prompting Homer to denounce his daughter to the angel as a "child of Satan."

Springfield assumes that Judgment Day is coming, and so its residents anxiously prepare, with the Simpsons donning their Sunday best. When Lisa resists, her mother tells her that, while she is not certain what will happen, she wishes the two could make peace before sunset. The towns-people gather on the hillside as the sun approaches the horizon. Even Lisa is frightened, squeezing her mother's hand at the climactic moment. When the chips are down, there are no atheists in foxholes or on Spring-field's hillside. Suddenly a deep, disembodied voice intones that "the end" is the end of high prices at the new Heavenly Hills Mall; the angel is des-tined to perch atop the shopping center's entrance. With shades of scien-tific hoaxes like the Cardiff Giant and the Piltdown Man, the remains had been buried as a publicity stunt by the mall's developers. Rather than gloating at her apparent vindication, Lisa is outraged: "You exploited peo-ple's deepest beliefs just to hawk your cheesy wares." The rest of the crowd is more interested in racing down the hill to take advantage of opening-day bargains at the new shopping center. Left on the hillside, Lisa thanks her mother for squeezing back when the girl clutched her hand. "Any-time, my angel," Marge says.

Lisa is "the avatar of logic and wisdom" in the series, according to Aeon J. Skoble, writing in *The Simpsons and Philosophy*. "Although her wisdom is sometimes presented as valuable, other times it is presented as a case of being sanctimonious or condescending." In a way, he writes, "her treat-ment in the show captures the love-hate relationship American society has with intellectuals."[2] For all her exemplary characteristics, Lisa is not with-out sin, including some of the major ones. In one episode, she clearly does not honor her father, calling him a baboon. The show's writers have said that there came a time when Lisa's character—even her sardonic sense of humor—began to grate on them. Even in the absurdist context of the series, the girl wasn't convincing as an adult in an eight-year-old's body.

Her still, small voice had become a *shrill*, small voice. So they began to lighten up, building up the little-girl side of her without eliminating the self-righteous side. For example, after suggesting that her grandfather give his unexpected windfall to the poor, she adds, "Of course, if you really wanted to, you could buy me a pony."

Oddly, Lisa's relationship with the Divine is less direct than that of other characters, such as Marge, Flanders, and even Homer. But when Lisa does resort to prayer, she is not above taking advantage of her record of rectitude, as if it were some form of entitlement. Needing help for a test she is not prepared for, Lisa says, "I need a miracle. C'mon, you owe me."

It may seem strange, after three decades in which evangelical Christianity has been so identified with political and social conservatism, for a character like Lisa Simpson to emerge—someone with a strong (but not evangelical) faith in God coupled with an equally strong commitment to issues identified with contemporary liberal activism. If so, it should not. From the second half of the nineteenth century through the early twentieth, Christian activists were at the forefront of movements for political and social reform, including the abolition of slavery, women's suffrage, prohibition, and worker's rights. And in the second half of the twentieth century, when white religious conservatives largely and disgracefully fell silent on the preeminent moral struggle of the generation—racism and civil rights—it was the mainline denominations that picked up the banner of Christian activism, agitating for civil rights, peace, gender equality, economic justice, gun control, environmental protection, and nuclear arms control. Lisa is not an anomaly; she is part of a proud and consistent tradition.

Four

The Evangelical Next Door: "If Everyone Were Like Ned Flanders, There'd Be No Need for Heaven."

On American college and high school campuses today, the name most associated with the word "Christian"—other than Jesus—is not the pope or Mother Teresa or even Billy Graham. Instead, it's a goofy-looking guy named Ned Flanders. Homer Simpson's next-door neighbor is the evangelical known most intimately to nonevangelicals. Flanders's mustache, thick glasses, sweater, and irrepressibly cheerful demeanor have made him an indelible figure. There are an estimated 50 million evangelical and fundamentalist Christians in the United States—one in every five Americans. Although heterogeneous in their beliefs, politics, and lifestyles, they are easily recognizable to one another, and they would have no difficulty in recognizing Ned and his family as their own. Gerry Bowler, professor of philosophy at Canadian Nazarene College in Calgary and chairman of the Centre for the Study of Christianity and Contemporary Values, calls Flanders "television's most effective exponent of a Christian life well-lived," while conceding that may be a mixed blessing. "We may have to make do with Ned Flanders as our televised spiritual mentor," says Bowler, who characterizes himself as a "mainstream evangelical."[1]

In society at large, however, evangelicals are subject to other, unflattering stereotypes, the most infamous of which was Michael Weisskopf's designation in the *Washington Post* as a group of people that is "largely poor, uneducated and easy to command."[2] Flanders is the antithesis of Weisskopf's cliché, and he has eclipsed it, offering the fairest and most sympathetic portrayal of an evangelical Christian in American popular culture. *The Simpsons'* popularity and longevity account for much of this, but there is more. Throughout American history, the chief undermining sin of Christian character, in fiction and fact, has been hypocrisy. This strain runs from Reverend Dimmesdale in *The Scarlet Letter* to the title character in *Elmer Gantry* to televangelists Jimmy Swaggart and Jim Bakker. On this count, Ned Flanders is exemplary; his Christianity is unassailable. He may be a good-natured doofus, but he struggles mightily not to be a hypocrite. "American evangelicalism needs a good dose of demythologizing," says Christian Smith, professor of sociology at the University of North Carolina at Chapel Hill and author of *Christian America? What Evangelicals Really Want.* "In the American media, in the popular imagination and often in academic scholarship, American evangelicals are routinely cast as either angels or demons."

Not Ned Flanders. Like many of the series' characters, he is the object of satire and sustained ridicule. An Oral Roberts University graduate who is never without a Bible and a large piece of the "True Cross" of Jesus (which saved his life in one episode when he was shot), Ned believes that one of the essential elements of a good life is "a daily dose of Vitamin Church." Harry Shearer, the actor who provides the voice for Flanders, said in a *Texas* magazine interview, "His spirituality is probably slightly deeper than the plaques that are on sale in the Dallas/Fort Worth Airport that have various spiritual slogans printed on them."[3] But Steve Tompkins, who wrote for the series in the mid-1990s, including several episodes that focused on Ned, has a somewhat different view. "He's a great character. He appeals to a lot of people in the audience. But he also appeals to a lot of the writers. They have a great affection for Ned Flanders, and that's probably why he gets so many great jokes. He's so funny." Ned, named for Flanders Street in Matt Groening's hometown of Portland, Oregon, represents most of the television viewing audience—white, Christian, and middle class. Al Jean, a longtime writer for the series who took over as executive producer and "show-runner" for the 2001–2002 season, agrees. "We don't mock Ned's faith," says Jean, who, like Tompkins, is a Christian. "We actually think he's a guy with a lot of wonderful qualities. . . . We can never get enough Flanders. If people accuse us of being anti-Christian, we just ask whether they'd rather have Flanders as their neighbor or Homer." Jean's longtime writing partner, Mike Reiss, a self-described "atheist Jew," says he is gratified that "some religious, good-hearted people could see the humor in this character and not be offended by it."

Despite (or perhaps because of) the comic exaggerations, Ned's portrayal as a character is complex and nuanced, enabling him to raise serious issues on a regular basis. Consider his journey of faith. The root of Flanders's turn toward a structured religious framework—probably a conservative, mainstream form of Presbyterianism—is a traumatic childhood. When Ned suffers a breakdown and is institutionalized, he experiences flashbacks of his child psychiatrist, who employed eight months of sustained, "therapeutic" spanking to control the obstreperous little boy. Before the "Spankological Program," his parents were "freaky beatniks" who raised their son with no rules at all. Ned's reaction to this chaotic and unstructured environment mirrors many studies of those who came of age in the 1960s and 1970s and, finding the freewheeling lifestyle unsatisfying or repugnant, gravitated to religion.

Religion and morality inform nearly every aspect of Flanders's life, from the doorbell that alternates chimes of "A Mighty Fortress Is Our God" and "Bringing in the Sheaves," to his air horn that blares the "Hallelujah" chorus at football games. Together with his family, he prays at meals and before bed. He attends his church three times a week and tithes, contributing to seven other congregations just to be on the safe side. He belongs to a Bible study group and keeps notes stuck on his refrigerator with a fish magnet, and he turns his basement into a Christian youth hostel from time to time. Like many believers, he thanks God often for his blessings, for things as small as a beautiful day. He calls on the Almighty for everything from a better performance of *Guys and Dolls* at the local dinner theater to the backstage players—those who work behind the scenes to make the production work. At the dinner table, he gives thanks for the middleman responsible for inflating the price of the food on his table and for the "humane but determined guys at the slaughterhouse." The family carves Bible dioramas out of pumpkins at Halloween and gives out hugs instead of candy to trick-or-treaters. Vacation destinations include Verbal Johnson's "Praying Hands" ("America's Most Judgmental Religious Theme Park!") and Sunday Bob Picker's "America, U.S.A." ("Nuclear Warhead Museum and Religious Arts Center").

Sometimes the series writers have turned more playful than usual with Ned's character and have used him as a transgressive figure. Dream and fantasy sequences, as you might expect, have featured Ned as God, the pope, a cardinal, and a Puritan witch burner; in others, as the devil, a werewolf, and a zombie. When Homer is shocked to see that Flanders is Satan, he replies that it's always the one you least expect. Ned unconsciously runs a riff of naughty double entendres. His sons Rod and Todd wear jerseys 66 and 6 on their football team, so when they stand together the shirts read 666, the mark of the beast in the book of Revelation.

Ned believes in the second coming, certain that Jesus will return to earth at any moment. He mistakes Lisa's backyard saxophone practicing for the sound of Gabriel's trumpet and the arrival of Judgment Day, and an escaped elephant from the Springfield Zoo for one of the four horses of the Apocalypse. An episode set thirty years in the future has a dissolute Bart Simpson ringing Ned's doorbell, intending to ask for money. Flanders, who has lost his sight (but not his vision), hears the bell, taps his cane to the door, and asks matter-of-factly, "Is that you, Jesus?"

Yet Ned is also deeply immersed in the good works of the social gospel, beginning with the random (and typically improbable) donation of one of his kidneys and a lung for anyone who might need them. For a time, his elderly grandmother lived with the family, and Ned volunteers at a foster home, hospitals, soup kitchens, and a homeless shelter. He is a scoutmaster and Pee Wee football coach, recycles, is active in the PTA and the neighborhood association (but not, for some unexplained reason, Neighborhood Watch), and volunteers for the marital stress hotline. Wednesday is tithe day at the Flanders house, when the family tries to join together to do good deeds. A homeless man arrives at their front door on tithe day, the family bathes him and treats his sores, gives him a new suit and sends him on his way, singing "Onward, Christian Soldiers." This is a family Jesus would have no trouble recognizing as one of his own.

Nominally a member of the religious right, Ned is politically active, at least at the local level. He explains to Lisa that he is so well informed, presumably by scripture, that it is unnecessary for him to read the newspaper's editorial page: "I don't need to be told what to think—by anyone living." Yet his is not an angry activism. To be sure, he belongs to the Citizens Committee for Moral Hygiene, and he has picketed against cartoon violence. His most overt political act is one many Christians would consider inadvertent, and so ends in disaster. Homer objects to Ned's tenure as interim principal of Springfield Elementary School. Instinctively, Flanders says "Let's thank the Lord" over the intercom and, for this offense, is fired on the spot by the superintendent. "God has no place within these walls, just like the facts have no place within organized religion! Simpson, you get your wish. Flanders is history."

Ned's Christianity plays a major part in the way he raises his sons Rod and Todd, and, predictably, he often goes to extremes. A typical bedtime story has the father reading that Harry Potter and all his friends "went straight to hell for practicing witchcraft." Ned doesn't allow the kids to use dice when playing board games because dice are wicked. However, while attending the Springfield Animation Festival, he permits the boys to watch "The New Adventures of Gravy and Jobliath," a claymation show produced by the "Presbylutherans" in which a boy builds a pipe bomb to blow up a Planned Parenthood center. He is hesitant to buy the children Red Hots candy because there is a lascivious caricature of the devil on the package. The kids' favorite games are Good Samaritan,

Clothe the Leper, and Build the Mission ("Finally the villagers have a place to pray"). Their game is "Billy Graham's Bible Blaster," in which the goal is to zap nonbelievers into converts (those hit only by glancing shots become Unitarians). Cursing poses another problem, when Homer's foul language is picked up by one of the Flanders boys. Todd uses the word "damn" at the table and is punished by Ned, whose decree, "No Bible stories for you tonight!" sends the boy crying from the room. Later, Todd is seen wearing a tee-shirt with the name of the punk band "Butthole Surfers," which he finds in the church's donation bin after a disaster destroys their clothes.

The young Flanders boys are total innocents: They believe they are getting closer to God when they jump on the Simpsons' trampoline. The brothers believe Bart when he imitates the voice of God and tells them to walk into a wall, promising to remove it if they do. Of course, they crash, and—their faith thus tested—they balk when the voice of God/Bart tells them to take cookies to the Simpson household. "Look," the voice intones sternly, "do you want a happy God or a vengeful God?" The boys complain to their parents that they *only* get to go to church three times a week, and they decide to stop watching reruns of the original *Davey and Goliath* animated series because they think that the idea of a talking dog is blasphemous. In an apparent foray into Pentecostalism, Todd seems briefly to speak in tongues, a sequence that has been cut in reruns, without explanation. In a *Simpsons* comic book, Bart convinces the boys to dress up as a Druid priest and a sacrificial lamb when the Simpsons' basement is turned into a medieval dungeon. When Ned walks in on them he is outraged, saying the game smacks of "multiculturalism."

Ned is not immune to the familiar conflict between parental instruction on morality and the exigencies of modern life, especially when it comes to lying. Rod and Todd overhear Ned tell Homer that he can't come over to their house because the Flanderses are visiting relatives. The boys know it's untrue, though told to spare Homer's feelings. "Lies make Baby Jesus cry," Rod reminds his father. Ned gets away with a borderline fib when he tells the boys that the blood of a mangled cartoon character is really jam. Ned acknowledges that he has a temper, and his own language approaches the mildly blasphemous, including "crap," "hell," and "heckaroonie." Once, he gets halfway to taking the Lord's name in vain before catching himself. What really sets his temper off, he tells a counselor, is his wife's habit of underlining passages in *his* Bible.

Even Ned's various sideline businesses, some part of Flancrest Enterprises, reflect his faith. He sells religious hooked rugs on the Internet and

Bible trading cards at the swap meet. Flanders is honorable in his business, sometimes to his detriment. His major plunge into the entrepreneurial world occurs when he gives up his job in pharmaceutical sales to open the Leftorium, a boutique in the mall for all things left-handed, including tee-shirts reading "The Lord Loves a Lefty." His morality and good nature nearly do him in. He spends the day ignoring shoplifters and chasing down a customer he inadvertently shortchanged, and becomes known for validating parking for nonpatrons. Unbeknownst to Ned, Homer has wished failure on him and steers business away from his neighbor. Lisa accuses her father of *schadenfreude*, of taking joy from the misfortune of another. The Leftorium nearly goes broke, and Flanders has to sell everything he owns to pay off his debts. "At times like these, I used to turn to the Bible for solace," he tells Homer, "but the Good Book can't help me now." He hasn't lost his faith; it's simply that his neighbor picked up his Bible for seven cents at Flanders's desperation yard sale. In the end, Homer helps save the business and Ned forgives him for sabotaging the effort, preferring to thank him for warning him about the dangers of niche retailing. The warning is prescient; no sooner does the Leftorium recover than a competitor called Leftopolis moves next door. When economic times are tough at the Flanders home in December, they still celebrate, but with an "imagination Christmas."

Ned admits that most of the time he is "about as exciting as a baked potato." Yet for all his sweetness, he does have an unpredictable side. A part of him yearns to fit in with his worldly friends, even when his efforts are outlandish. Given his muscular physique, Flanders is selected to play the role of Stanley Kowalski in the community production of *A Streetcar Named Desire*, a musical version called "*Oh Streetcar!*" The director instructs him to play it as if he were "pulsating with animal lust." When his middle-aged friends decide to form an outlaw motorcycle gang, Ned goes along. He reluctantly accepts the name "Hell's Satans"—such blasphemy might send him to hell—only after hearing the alternative, "Christ Punchers." Still, he frets when the gang begins to pitch pennies on the sidewalk. In another episode, after asking Homer the "secret of your intoxicating lust for life," he sins on a grand scale, going with his neighbor to Las Vegas for a wild weekend, during which he goes on an all-night bender and (apparently) marries a cocktail waitress. In the casino, he tells Homer that gambling is forbidden by Deuteronomy 7, so naturally Homer bets the number on roulette and wins. Ned looks up and asks God if he should gamble, and is assured that he should by the voice of a security guard speaking from a camera in the ceiling, which Ned assumes is God.

Ned grapples with other temptations of popular culture in various incarnations and, on those rare occasions when he succumbs to temptation, is quick to see divine retribution. He angrily runs off a shady cable installer who offers an illegal hookup. Instead, he turns to satellite television, which enables him to view more than two hundred channels—almost all of which he then locks out for offensive content. Straying from his usual screen fare, such as reruns of the *Jim Nabors Show*, he once watched *Married . . . With Children* (on the same network that produces *The Simpsons*). He insists he is afflicted with the flu for this lapse: "Oh, the network slogan is true! Watch Fox and be damned for all eternity!"

Ned's relationship with the church and his pastor is ambivalent, although he tries to stand by the congregation, come what may. When Bart becomes a faith healer and holds weeknight services in a backyard tent, drawing away most of the congregation, only the Flanders family remains faithful to Springfield Community Church. (However, vigilant keepers of *The Simpsons* Archive Web site note Ned's absence in at least four panning shots of the church's pews. Family vacation, perhaps?) Ned is so quick to consult Reverend Lovejoy with his theological concerns, large and small, that he puts the minister's church and home telephone numbers on his speed dialer. As a younger man, Ned worried about coveting his own wife, and he admits to the minister that, while he's pretty meek, he could be meeker. Like many clergy in these situations, Lovejoy doesn't always appreciate this devotion. Interrupted during dessert or in the middle of the night over a seemingly trivial issue, the minister curses Flanders out of earshot. At a church picnic, Ned's questions about whether it's proper to engage in sports on Sunday prompts the exasperated minister to curse him to his face. When Ned suggests that a barbershop quartet might not be appropriate for a worship service, the pastor gets rid of him by sending him off to see an oil stain in the parking lot that looks "just like Saint Barnabas." Lovejoy's revenge is the perverse pleasure he takes in urging his dog do his "dirty sinful business" on Flanders's front lawn. The minister even suggests Ned try another denomination, since "they're all pretty much the same." Yet when Ned is in real trouble—held captive by angry, carnivorous baboons at the Springfield Zoo—it is the pastor who risks his life to save him.

For all his admirable qualities, Flanders occasionally exhibits the zealousness and narrow-mindedness that for many represent the darker side of evangelical Christianity. Homer has brain surgery that lifts his IQ fifty points and turns him into a genius. One of his accomplishments is writing a proof that there is no God, which he presents to Ned one Sunday when his neighbor is on his way to church. At first Ned scoffs at such proof, written on a single page, but he reads it through and agrees that it is airtight. "Can't let this get out," he says, burning the paper. Proselytizing is another touchy issue. Some true believers interpret the imperative of evangelism's Great Commission to mean never taking "no" for an answer. Homer's decision to stop going to church prompts Ned to show up at Moe's Tavern, complete with his guitar and his family, to bring his neighbor back to the fold. For their trouble, the door is slammed in their faces. Later, the Flanderses pursue Homer by car, as Todd calls out, "Dad, the heathen's getting away!"

After another typical misadventure costs Homer and Marge custody of their children, Bart, Lisa, and Maggie are placed in the Flanders's temporary care. Lisa observes to Bart that the house has a "creepy, Pat Boone-ish quality about it." A family parlor game, "Bible Bombardment," first reveals that Bart and Lisa have no grasp of the scriptural arcana that is common knowledge to the Flanderses. The Simpson offspring then let slip that, through their parents' neglect, they have never been baptized. So, rather than consulting Homer and Marge, who are taking court-ordered parenting classes, Ned dresses the Simpson children—who voice neither interest nor acquiescence—in white robes for baptism. At the Springfield River he prepares to immerse them and asks if they reject Satan.

This situation is not as far-fetched as it may appear. As often happens in *The Simpsons*, the scenario illustrates a serious and historic theological issue, in this case involving religious commitment and free will. Conversion at the point of the sword and the threat of the stake were staples of medieval Europe, by both Christians and Muslims. In a case that became a world controversy, a six-year-old Jewish boy named Edgardo Mortara was taken from his parents in Rome in 1858 and raised as a Catholic after a servant girl claimed to have secretly baptized the boy when he was an infant. Closer to home and the present, parents in Central Florida in the late 1990s sued a Christian day care center for baptizing their children without their consent.

In Springfield, the involuntary rite is interrupted just at the moment of immersion by Homer, who saves Bart from being saved by being baptized himself. "Wow, Dad, you took a baptismal for me," says a startled Bart. "How do you feel?" Put another way, the curious boy is asking, "What is the spiritual impact of this practice?" At first, the effect seems to be transcendent.

Homer, visibly aglow, replies, "Oh, Bartholomew. I feel like Saint Augustine of Hippo after his conversion by Ambrose of Milan." Ned, a world-class believer, is flabbergasted. It's not clear whether or not Flanders is familiar with this reference to one of Christendom's most famous turn-arounds, by a self-proclaimed reprobate of epic proportions. In any event, Ned is dumbstruck by the transformation of his neighbor: "Homer, what did you say?" As any modern theologian can explain, this is not what Christian conversion is about, and it cannot stand. "You don't force your faith on anybody," says Reverend Matthew Gibbs, a young Southern Baptist preacher from Orlando who watched the episode, even though his wife doesn't normally let him. Bill Merrell, vice president of the Southern Baptist Convention, agrees. "We believe that coercion cannot support faith. It completely erodes the value of any such profession."

James A. Smith, editor of the *Florida Baptist Witness*, the official weekly journal of the state's Southern Baptists, points out that even with the best intentions, manipulative evangelism "is really not evangelism at all. True evangelism is telling the Good News that God saves sinners and how human beings can be reconciled to Him. True evangelism does not happen when people are tricked." Sure enough, Homer's glow subsides and he returns to his natural state, snapping, "I said, shut your ugly face, Flanders!" For his part, Ned makes no apology or explanation for this breach, as he has in the past for lesser faux pas.

At times, Ned seems to have a direct pipeline to God. While making a movie based on the story of baby Moses for the first Springfield Film Festival, his son is swept away in a basket in a rushing river. "Flanders to God, Flanders to God, get off your cloud and save my Todd!" he shouts. Immediately, a bolt of lightning drops a tree across the river, catching the basket and saving the boy. Ned thanks God, who responds with a huge hand (with five fingers) making the OK sign through the clouds and, in a deep version of "Flanders-speak," says "Okily dokily."

Like some pious Christians, Ned is guilty of praying for trivial things. He and his wife, Maude, and Reverend Lovejoy and his wife comprise a bowling team called the "Holy Rollers." They arrive at the alley decked out in monks' robes and bathed in heavenly light, suggesting that there is more at stake in this league play than purely secular concerns. This is confirmed at one tournament when the Holy Rollers play Homer's team which is sponsored by Mr. Burns, the owner of the nuclear plant where Homer works. Burns asks, "Who's ready to kick some Christian keister?" As Ned leaves one pin standing after a frame, Homer mocks him and his religious faith, asking him where his God is. Flanders ignores the jibe and, again, turns his eyes above. "It's me, Ned," he says simply, and the lone pin drops. As a divine exclamation point, an electric charge from the machine that returns the bowling balls strikes Homer. His unfair appeal to the Almighty is troubling to Homer, and he says so when he sees Flanders praying, presumably to win a bet the two men have made on another occasion. Homer tells Ned it's no use praying, since he already did, and "we both can't win." Flanders replies that he is praying only that no one gets hurt in the contest.

Above all, Ned is the good neighbor, his basic role in the series. "Affordable tract housing made us neighbors," he tells Homer, "but you made us friends." In fact, the opposite is true. Homer does everything short of mayhem to abuse Flanders, and at one point Marge admonishes her husband: "You shouldn't be so hard on Ned. He's been a good neighbor ever since we moved here." Homer is unmoved and asks, "What has he ever done for us beside lend us things, do us favors, and save our children from the occasional house fire?" It is only by repeatedly turning to Matthew 19:19, Jesus' admonition to "love your neighbor as yourself," that Ned is able to survive the largely one-sided relationship, returning unconditional love for sustained abuse. Well, maybe not unconditional love. Because Ned is human, his acceptance has limits, a trait that reinforces his believability. Homer steps over the line when he rips out the Flanders's air conditioner during a heat wave. Discovered between their houses, Homer knows Ned well enough to try a biblical defense: "Haven't you ever heard, 'Let he who is without sin cast the first stone?'" Whereupon one of the Flanders boys lets fly with a rock that boinks Homer on the head.

Ned's faith is constant, and in the end it is always affirmed. Yet like most Christians, his faith is not perfect: God's will sometimes baffles him. Encouraged by the artist Jasper Johns, Homer floods Springfield one night as a conceptual art project. Ned wakes up the next morning and looks out of his second-story bedroom window. "It's a miracle!" he says to his wife, Maude. "The Lord has drowned the wicked and spared the righteous." Then he spies Homer in a rowboat and extends his leap to the wrong conclusion. "Looks like heaven is easier to get into than Arizona State." Maude grapples with the same conundrum but reaches her own conclusion: "I don't judge Homer and Marge. That's for a vengeful God to do."

Most frequently and most fervently, Ned prays for the strength to remain a good neighbor, which is his burden. Where Homer is concerned, Matthew 19:19 is never far from his mind. While Ned never suffers martyrdom for his faith, he comes in for more than his share of scorn, and it begins the day the Simpsons move into the neighborhood. Ned welcomes them and says cheerily that his friends call him by his first name; Homer immediately addresses him as "Flanders." Homer considers Ned "a big, four-eyed lame-o" who wears the same sweater every day, except to attend church. Homer tells Ned to shut up on innumerable occasions, calls him a liar and a square, nearly runs him over, and dumps garbage on his head. Even Marge, a believer, takes advantage of her neighbor, tossing a stray snake from their overgrown backyard into Ned's yard, where it bites him.

Homer refers to Ned by a variety of derisive terms such as "Saint Flanders," "Charlie Church," and "Churchy La Femme." Flanders is actually the physical embodiment of muscular, masculine Christianity, a man who would be right at home at a Promise Keepers rally, except, as Harry Shearer points out, Promise Keepers is for backsliders. Ned roots for the "Punishing Pilgrim" in professional wrestling. He is a former fraternity man and a football fan. Ned works out to a buff build that belies his age, which he insists is sixty. The secret of his youthful appearance, he explains to Homer, is that he "resists all major urges." He identifies himself as a recovering alcoholic, yet early in the series, he would have a beer or a cocktail—he claims a degree in mixology—and he smokes a pipe. Ned has many of the accoutrements of the 1990s middle-class prosperity, such as a boat ("Thanks for the Boat, Lord II") and a summer beach house. On the other hand, he drives an uninspiring Geo station wagon, with a license plate reading JHN 143 (John 1:43, in which Jesus calls on the disciples to "follow me").

Homer's hectoring notwithstanding, Ned also takes literally Jesus' words in John 15:13: "Greater love hath no man than this, that a man lay down his life for his friends." When Homer faces a triple bypass operation, his neighbor apologizes for not being able to donate his own heart for a transplant. A volunteer firefighter, Ned says a prayer as he risks his life to save Homer from a house fire, almost losing his own life in the process. Homer assumes the fire is God's will, a notion Ned instantly rejects. As the fire spreads to Ned's house, the instantly ungrateful Homer observes that, for all his piety and churchgoing, God is not sparing the Flanderses' roof from fire. Suddenly, a small wisp floating above the Flanders home becomes a rain cloud and douses the blaze. Just to make certain the lesson from above is clear, a rainbow frames Ned's house.

Flanders is altruistic enough to build a bomb shelter large enough for both his and the Simpson families. As a comet approaches Springfield, Ned invites his neighbors to join him. But so many other friends and neighbors force their way in that the shelter becomes too crowded, and one person has to leave. Nominated by Homer as the most useless individual in the group, Ned is ejected, a verdict he cheerfully accepts. In the event he goes mad as the comet approaches, he asks Todd to "shoot Daddy if he tries to get back in."

Like any sitcom neighbor, Homer borrows things from Flanders, ranging from a TV tray, power tools, and a new sprinkler, to a camcorder—which he has no intention of returning. Once, this practice puts Ned in technical violation of the Eighth Commandment, when he steals back his own barbecue. Homer, who covets much of what he has not already borrowed or stolen from the Flanders household, also covets his wife Maude from time to time, which causes her to make certain her blouse is buttoned to the neck whenever he is around. At times, Homer's view of his neighbor can become quite dark. "Life is just one crushing defeat after another," he says, "until you just wish Flanders was dead."

Flanders interacts with Homer on what appears to be a daily basis. However, it takes him eight years to invite members of the Simpson family into his home, a touch of suburban verisimilitude that reinforces the premise. Inside the recreation room, Homer notices the odd mixture of Ned's life: a tap featuring imported beer and a copy of Leonardo da Vinci's *Last Supper.* He owns a Shroud of Turin towel, which is later stolen, and a large collection of Bibles and holy writings, including the Septuagint in Aramaic, the Vulgate of Saint Jerome, the Living Bible, a Samaritan Pentateuch, Solomon's Song of Songs, and the "Thump-Proof Bible." Typically, it is on this first visit that Homer's feelings of inferiority lead him to make a lewd compliment about Maude that Flanders finds insulting. Angrily, and uncharacteristically, Ned orders his neighbor out of his house. Guilt-stricken, he consults Reverend Lovejoy and then asks Homer for forgiveness. "You are my brother and I love you," he writes in a note. "I feel a great sadness in my bosom." Bart and Homer totally miss the message and guffaw over the word "bosom."

There are times when Flanders's response to Simpson appeals for Christian charity is, at best, qualified. Homer and Bart, believing (incorrectly) that they have leprosy, come to Ned for help. At first, he panics and slams the door. But thinking (correctly) that this response is not Christian, Ned dons a high-tech biohazard suit and invites them in, acknowledging at the same time that the Flanders house is "not really set up for lepers." Homer asks if they are being shunned, which is manifestly close to the truth. No, says Ned, they are being sent to a better place—the leper colony on the Hawaiian island of Molokai, at the Flanderses' expense.

Stripped of its Simpsonian excess, it is the kind of solution familiar to many modern believers. Just think about how our society treats elderly parents, severely disabled children, and the mentally disabled.

Ned Flanders has undergone three major crises of faith, each of which has shaken the belief that is central to his life. The circumstances range from the surreal to experiences shared by many.

1. Love. For all his unrequited neighborly love, too much gratitude from Homer turns out to be a deadly thing. Again, prayer plays a central role as a plot device. No sooner does Homer pray for a ticket to a sold-out local football game than Flanders knocks on the Simpsons' door with an offer to take him. Ned buys him refreshments and even gets him the game ball (the quarterback had been converted through the efforts of Ned's Bible group). Homer decides that he has been unfair to his neighbor, in light of his many kindnesses, and he determines to show his love. Alas, the love is the oppressive, smothering variety, and before long it is Ned who is praying—for the strength to survive Homer's friendship.

Feeling trapped, Ned dreams of climbing the church tower, singing "Bringing in the Sheaves" while assembling an assault rifle and picking off people below—all of whom have Homer's face. He wakes, distraught, telling his startled wife that he thinks he hates his neighbor, something he must know is wrong and unchristian. Still, the next day he makes an excuse to avoid Homer and drives off with his family. In his haste to shake Homer, Ned is stopped for speeding by Springfield Police Chief Wiggum, who loudly (and erroneously) accuses him of driving under the influence of drugs—just as a church bus full of horrified members rolls past the scene. "Where's your Messiah now?" the chief asks in his best Edward G. Robinson accent. It's a good question for Flanders, who has rejected Homer's sincere, if irritating, efforts to be a good neighbor. For a man who puts his faith at the center of his life, where *is* his Jesus now?

On Sunday, Ned gets his answer. While driving to church, he is anxious about appearing at the one place, except for his home, where he feels most welcome and part of society. Maude assures him that the church is "a house of love and forgiveness." Sure enough, as Flanders enters the sanctuary people in the pews whisper that he is evil and "the fallen one." Reverend Lovejoy announces that the sermon topic is "What Ned Did." Distressed, Flanders has difficulty recognizing the irony of his situation. He is being condemned for something he did not do—taking drugs. But he is suffering for what he did do, which was to reject Homer's sincere neighborly love and gratitude. Ned then compounds this sin by cursing

Homer for whistling through his nose during silent prayer, further inflaming the congregation against him. The role reversal is nearly complete, as Homer defends Ned, describing him—correctly—as a kind, wonderful, caring man who has "turned every cheek on his body" in the face of Homer's insults. "If everyone here were like Ned Flanders, there'd be no need for heaven. We'd already be there."

Reverend Lovejoy is convinced, acknowledging that Ned is owed an apology. Flanders has clearly learned his lesson and later thanks Homer for being a true friend. Homer reverts to type, telling him to get lost, and all is right again in the world.

2. Loss. A hurricane—an unusual occurrence in Springfield—bears down on the town. Typically, Ned again invites the Simpsons to share his shelter, only to be rebuffed by the neighbors, who prefer their own cellar to his company. Miraculously, the storm spares every house on the street *except* the Flanderses', which is reduced to rubble. Then looters single out the Leftorium, his business at the mall, for looting. Because Ned believes that insurance is a form of gambling, the losses are uncovered. His friends and neighbors come to his aid by rebuilding his home. Unfortunately, and despite their best intentions, the workmanship is shoddy and the new structure collapses immediately.

In the face of these trials, Ned takes the traditional, if not instinctive, path, going to his pastor, the intercessor. He tells the minister that he is beginning to feel a little like Job. Rather than sympathizing, Lovejoy suggests that Flanders is being melodramatic. The minister dissembles when Ned asks directly if God is punishing him, referring him to a book by Art Linkletter—hardly a source of theological solace. Unsatisfied, Ned goes directly to the source, praying, "Why me, Lord? Where have I gone wrong? I've always been nice to people. I don't drink or dance or swear. I've even kept kosher just to be on the safe side. I've done everything the Bible says, even the stuff that contradicts the other stuff." So, in the words of Rabbi Harold Kushner, why *do* bad things happen to good people? When Ned finds no satisfactory answer in his faith, he blows his top, denouncing his friends and going on a rampage that ends only when he drives himself to Calmwood Hospital, a mental institution, seeking a secular explanation and relief.

3. Love and loss. In early 2000, following a dispute over money with Maggie Roswell, the actress who provided the voice for Maude, the series writers killed Ned's wife in a freak accident, knocking her from the top of an auto racing stadium by a barrage of tee-shirts fired by air cannons. Although Homer is accidentally responsible, Ned blames himself, and is crushed to be bereft of his beloved "Popcorn Ball." After the funeral, the Simpsons do their best to comfort him and his boys by hosting a reception at their house. As guests come and go, Ned runs through a gamut of grieving emotions, sitting on the couch looking shell-shocked. Later, Moe the bartender makes a flattering but totally inappropriate remark about Maude, provoking a beating from Ned. Later, Flanders sits on the back swing with Homer and states the obvious, that he will just have to work through his own grief.

But Ned wouldn't be Ned if he didn't turn to God in his time of greatest need. Months later, still desolate, he prays, "Lord, I never question your will, but I'm wondering whether your decision to take Maude was, well, wrong—unless this is part of your divine plan. Could you please just give me some sign, anything?" Instead, there is only silence. Disappointed and angry with God, who has always been his rock, Ned turns a framed, bedside picture of a hoary, white-bearded God (albeit a Catholic one, not unlike the one in Michelangelo's *Creation of Adam* in the Sistine Chapel) to face the wall. The next morning, Sunday, he sleeps late and tells Rod and Todd to go to church with the Simpsons—an act so out of character that the boys back out of their father's bedroom, gasping. Ned vows not to attend church that day and says he might not go the next day as well, telling God he is not kidding.

In the scene immediately following, Flanders is speeding to church, repeating apologies for his momentary lapse of faith. He walks into the sanctuary to find a Christian rock group performing. The beautiful lead singer, later described as the "Christian Madonna," seems to be addressing him: "If you think [God] doesn't care, or maybe that he isn't there, it's not too late to see how wrong you are." Ned, still standing in the aisle, is transfixed. This is the sign he prayed for. Outside the church after the service, he introduces himself to the singer, saying, "My name is Ned Flanders and I'm here every week—rain or shine!"

In May 2001, three months after a Bible-based theme park called "The Holy Land Experience" opened with great fanfare in Orlando, *The Simpsons* aired an episode in which Ned builds a "Christian amusement park" in memory of Maude. Like the Florida park, "Praiseland" is a tax-exempt attraction built with donated funds and volunteer labor, including that of the Simpson family. Ned's goal is to create "A shining beacon for the Lord," since he is convinced that "faith and devotion are the wildest thrill rides of all." But "King David's Wild Ride" turns out to be an enforced listening session of the entire book of Psalms. A pop-up game called "Whack-a-Satan" has no bat because, as Ned explains to a bewildered child, "You can stop Satan with your faith."

Customers soon lose interest and begin streaming toward the exit. Ned concludes that his memorial to his beloved wife is a failure, that his efforts to create an amusement park have resulted in a "bemusement park." Suddenly, a hidden gas leak at the foot of Maude's giant statute creates the illusion of a miracle, causing those who approach to speak in tongues and have comforting visions of heaven. Homer and Bart are quick to capitalize on the phenomenon. The entrance fee to the park does not include miracles, says the father; the son pipes up, "The power of Christ compels you to give Ned an extra ten bucks."

Ned objects, saying it would be wrong to exploit a divine manifestation, until he is convinced that the money could be used to help poor orphans. Even that justification is not enough to keep the park open when he realizes that the manifestation is not divine, and could be dangerous. Not even Homer's plea that Praiseland "has touched an entire town with its inspiring message" can keep Ned from padlocking the place.

Maude's death prompted Frederica Mathewes-Green, an author and former columnist for *Christianity Today* magazine, to write a love letter on Beliefnet.com to the suddenly available widower, called "Ned Flanders, My Hero." She wrote, "Ned is endlessly cheerful because he is pure in heart. He treats everyone around him with generosity and kindness, and can't imagine they wouldn't treat him the same way. He is incapable of cynicism or contempt," unlike most residents of Springfield. While he may be a fool, she observed, he is the kind of fool who makes the world a better place. Flanders, Mathewes-Green wrote, is Christlike, "a beam of light in a depressing little town" and the nicest person on the show.[4]

Not every academic observer is so unambiguous in praising Ned. Flanders's portrayal is "a cheap shot at fundamentalists—which is why I like it," says Landry. Yet, at the same time, Landry says, Flanders's portrayal illustrates "the virtues of hard work and honesty. Flanders is very successful, with well-behaved children, an excellent marriage. He's not portrayed as a real nut. I mean, he's got a beer keg in his basement."[5] The Flanders family is portrayed "fallibly but sympathetically," says Michael Glodo, professor of Old Testament and preaching at Reformed Theological Seminary. "They are simple, sincere, earnest—a good package of virtue, especially in a postmodern culture where cynicism and irony and satire are the prevailing sentiments."

As Michael Weiskopf's *Washington Post* stereotype of evangelicals fades, another equally derogatory and inaccurate one may be emerging to replace it. In February 2000, a family named Scheibner was profiled on the cover of the *New York Times Magazine*. The cover line read "Inward

Christian Soldiers: Fundamentalist families like the Scheibners are no longer fighting against the mainstream—they're dropping out and creating their own private America." In the article, author Margaret Talbot describes a family of nine fundamentalist Baptists, esconced in Pennsylvania's Lehigh Valley. On the surface, the Scheibners are similar to the Flanders. There is no sports gear in the home because parents Stephen and Megan believe athletic competition is not Christlike. There are Christian board games that Rod and Todd Flanders might enjoy. Stephen Scheibner is a pilot for American Airlines and a commander in the Naval Reserve who, like his wife, found his Christian faith in his teens. But, apart from voting and paying taxes, he and his family have consciously opted out of a culture they believe is evil. Talbot, citing the Scheibners' plans to move to Maine and start a church, argue that they are typical of a modern counterculture being constructed by conservative Christians who, at the urging of activists like Paul Weyrich, are giving up on a hopelessly depraved society.

Yet the Scheibners may be more of a caricature than the Flanders family, whose members are fully engaged in the world. "We will exaggerate some of Ned's beliefs as a form of comic relief," says *The Simpsons'* Mike Scully. "I think everybody knows a family like the Flanderses." Stripped of their comedic excess and hyperbole, how fairly do Ned and his family represent evangelical Christianity to the world? As a committed Jew, raised in a Northeastern suburb, I may not be the best judge. Or maybe I am. For the past seven years, I have reported on the evangelical movement—locally and nationally—for the *Orlando Sentinel* newspaper. More to the point, fate and my Central Florida suburb put me into close contact with a family I see as a real-life Flanders family. Until I raised the issue with them, they had no basis for comparison; they didn't watch the show and did not allow their children to watch.

Dan and Lorraine Hardaway are an attractive couple in their early forties. Each experienced some degree of dysfunction earlier in life before turning to Jesus. Dan, who has reddish blond hair and blue eyes, works full-time for Campus Crusade for Christ in Orlando. Lorraine, whose auburn hair frames a face brightened by a toothy smile, is a stay-at-home mom. Their four children, who range in age from seven to fifteen, are as good-natured as Rod and Todd Flanders but considerably more worldly. The college-educated couple belongs to Northland Community Church in Longwood, Florida, a nondenominational, evangelical megachurch. They sing in the choir and listen to a contemporary Christian radio station in their cars and at home, and they hold conservative beliefs on social issues, although they disagree with some extreme positions and approaches of well-known leaders of the Christian right.

For the most part, they grapple with the same things our family does: balancing their stretched budget and busy schedules, deciding what television show or computer game is appropriate for the kids. They don't allow their children to watch *The Simpsons*, but, like their neighbors, they have made an accommodation with Beanie Babies, Pokémon, and, after much soul-searching and consultation with Christian friends, the *Harry Potter* books. With their agreement, I frequently use them as a source, a sounding board, and a pipeline to ground-level believers for my newspaper reporting.

Are the Hardaways typical of evangelical Christians, as typical as the Flanderses? It's hard to say. We have gotten to know them pretty well in recent years. Our children attend the same public elementary school, are part of the same scout troops, and often attend the same birthday parties, which means we are often in and out of each other's houses. They are sophisticated and generally open-minded, and never press their religious or political views on us or on our children. It is apparent, though, that they draw strength from their Christian faith, which they try to apply to every aspect of their lives. I met them before I started watching *The Simpsons*, but I cannot watch the Flanders family without thinking of the Hardaways.

So I showed them an early draft of this chapter and loaned them some tapes from the series and asked them what they thought. "All in all, it would be flattering to be associated with Ned Flanders, based on what I know about the person and how he lives out his faith," said Dan. "There's an element of unconditional love in his life that accurately portrays Christianity." There are Christians who might be put off by some of the idiosyncrasies associated with the character, like "nerdy behavior," he added.

Lorraine agreed that, as a family of believers, they are much closer to the Flanderses than to the Scheibners. "How else are people going to see Jesus' teachings lived out unless they see them in our lives? It's very important that we're part of the world, that others can see the difference he's made and the truth we believe he taught and shared."

Five

The Church and the Preacher: "We Don't Have a Prayer!"

The Hollywood Film Production Code of the 1930s mandated,

> No film or episode in a film should be allowed to throw ridicule on any religious faith honestly maintained. Ministers of religion in their characters of ministers should not be used in comedy, as villains, or as unpleasant persons. The reason for this is not that there are not such ministers of religion, but because the attitude toward them tends to be an attitude toward religion in general. Religion is lowered in the minds of the audience because it lowers their respect for the ministers.

While the code is long gone, the concern remains today. "When clergy are depicted on entertainment programming, their commitment to religion is either ignored completely, or is ridiculed," according to Jim Trammell, of the University of Georgia. "I am concerned that televised messages could influence false expectations and impressions of religiosity. Audiences whose only models of organized religion or spirituality are those depicted on television are perhaps more likely to assume such models are precise. Further, although spirituality is more closely regarded as a personal experience rather than a social function, the fact that television programs have been shown to influence audiences' perception of the social norms has particular ramifications for one's perception of spirituality." In *The Simpsons*, organized religion "is rarely depicted as helping to solve spiritual problems at all, another indicator of the inadequacy of the church."

And at first glance, it may seem that the portrayal of the Reverend Timothy Lovejoy and of Springfield Community Church in *The Simpsons* do stand the Hollywood Code on its head, to the exact effect feared by early industry censors. Although not a leading character in the series, Lovejoy is a major supporting player, presiding at most of the town's weddings and funerals and, in one *Simpsons* comic book, performing an exorcism when

Lisa is possessed by the spirit of the pop singer Madonna. His name notwithstanding, this minister does not love joy. Because he is a foil in the series, personifying many of the failings of organized religion and Christian conservatism, he is usually portrayed as a shallow, intolerant, "pan-denominational windbag," in the words of Steve Tompkins, who wrote for the series in the 1990s. As such, Lovejoy is a much less rounded character than the other prominent Christian in the series, Ned Flanders. Like other characters in the series, however, the minister has had an impact on the culture: There is a popular Norwegian rock group called "Reverend Lovejoy."

Sam Simon, who with Matt Groening and James Brooks shaped the show at its creation, was "very adamant that we not make [Lovejoy] a cartoony, hypocritical preacher," recalls Al Jean, a longtime writer for the series who became executive producer and "show-runner" in 2001. "He wanted a realistic person who just happened to work as a minister." Thus, the minister *is* hypocritical and occasionally venal, but he is not evil or immoral, merely human. Lovejoy has an interior life that includes a troubled family and a hobby—electric trains—and even a sense of humor. In a lighter moment, the minister snaps Homer in the rear with a towel when they end up in the winning locker room after the Super Bowl. He jogs with George Bush when the former president moves to Springfield, and he is the author of a cookbook, *Someone's in the Kitchen with Jesus*. Lovejoy mixes socially with his parishioners, and he drinks, but not to excess. He once had idealistic dreams for the ministry until, after decades in the pulpit, he came down with a classic case of preacher burnout. His sermons are boring, and he knows it. For the most part, the pastor provides an example of what a minister should *not* be.

What is fascinating about Springfield Community's congregation is the absence of significant internal strife and the overall support it gives its spiritual leader. In every congregation I have covered as a journalist (or been a part of as a member) there has been a "clergy party" and an "anti-clergy party." Often, this division, or other issues such as biblical interpretation or the music of worship, creates factions and divisions and, sometimes, splits. I have come to believe that the reason this occurs so frequently and can lead to so much bitterness and intense infighting is the depth of feeling people have about spiritual matters. I think it may also be a function of the powerlessness people experience in other spheres of their lives: work, home, school, government bureaucracy, and the political system. This is an era of church "shoppers" and church "hoppers." In their congregations, they can fight as hard as they like and, if things don't go their way, they can walk away and join another church down the street or around the corner. Regardless of how disappointed people in Springfield are with Lovejoy, they don't fire him or leave the church.

The minister is an instantly recognizable and ludicrous character, with his jet-black pompadour and unctuous speaking voice. His office is that of a generic pastor, with painted cinder blocks on one wall and glass windows on the other. The décor includes a "praying hands" sculpture on the bookshelf, and on his desk a set of three swinging, clacking metal balls. Lovejoy is so certain where he is going when he dies that, after a disastrous meal at the Simpsons, he tells Homer that he will see him in hell—"from heaven." The pastor's clerical garb makes it hard to pin down his denomination, probably by the writers' design. His standard preaching attire is a plum shirt and tie, under a white robe with deep purple borders. He has been known to use sunscreen for anointing oil. In informal settings, he wears a black shirt and a white clerical collar, sometimes over black shorts. A *Simpsons* comic book suggests that in hot weather he wears only boxer shorts and garters underneath his robe. Like many of his colleagues, this preacher is both a writer and a broadcaster. His pamphlets include "Hell, It's Not Just for Christians Anymore" and "Satan's Boners." He cohosts a radio call-in show on Sunday nights with a rabbi and a priest, called "Gabbin' about God," sponsored by Ace Religious Supply, whose motto is, "If we don't got it, it ain't holy." Once, he invited a Mennonite minister to preach in his pulpit. (Groening's father was a Mennonite.)

Lovejoy is politically active, mostly on the local level. The minister belongs to two groups, Citizens for Moral Hygiene and Citizens for Tamer Television, and is a fixture in most mob scenes. He supports Springfield's ill-fated monorail but denounces the town's biosphere as the devil's playground. In addition to his battered Karman Ghia, he drives a Book (Burning) Mobile, and in one episode leads a movement to destroy merchandise of the local children's television show host, Krusty, whom he describes as "the clown prince of corruption." At Easter, he refers to a chocolate bunny as a graven image. Lovejoy heads a drive to rid the town of its lone burlesque house when he learns that Homer has sent Bart there to work off a debt. Together with Ned Flanders, the preacher calls on the Simpsons to discuss the matter. Homer assumes their purpose is evangelistic. "Everything is about Jesus," the minister says, except this, which is about what Bart has been up to. Later, Lovejoy is in the crowd bent on destroying the burlesque house where, to his embarrassment, he spots his father in an upstairs window. (The critique of the minister can be even sharper in *The Simpsons* merchandise than it is in the television series. A CD-ROM called "Virtual Springfield" shows a book of Ukrainian erotica and a metal box labeled "hush money" hidden in the preacher's lectern.)

In a welcoming essay in *The Simpsons' Guide to Springfield*, Lovejoy explains that the town "has a past steeped in faith and faith-related fund-raising activities."[1] This includes its founding by pioneer Jebediah Springfield, who left his home in Maryland with a band of misguided religious zealots in search of a place they called New Sodom, which later took the name of its founder. Newcomers to town are invited by the minister to worship at Springfield Community Church or, if they prefer, at the local Catholic church or synagogue. "A trip to Springfield can be informative, filling and even fun as long as you plan in advance to pacify our vengeful God . . . by attending church at least once while you are here." They are, however, warned away from local cults, secret societies and, most of all, "from a small group of people who split off from the Presbyterians to worship an Inanimate Carbon Rod." One of the religious academies in town is Springfield Christian School, whose motto is "We put the fun in Fundamentalist dogma."

Springfield Community Church—or the First Church of Springfield as it is sometimes called—is in many ways a quite successful congregation. The church is Springfield's central civic institution, second only to the town's community center. Each Sunday the pews are full. Worshipers represent every economic segment of the community, from Mr. Burns to "Cletus the Slack-jawed Yokel." Children sit with their parents. African Americans, from Dr. Hibbert and his family to Carl, Homer's coworker at the nuclear power plant, are part of the congregation, as is Dr. Nick Riviera, an immigrant. Even Moe Szyslak, the bartender, who identifies himself as a lifelong snake handler and adherent of Santeria, attends. This is, in part, a plot device, and the lack of ecclesiastical competition may help; Springfield Community appears to be the main Protestant church in town. Still, many pastors would be happy to look out on such a Sunday morning vista.

The packed and diverse pews notwithstanding, there are serious problems at the church, problems familiar to many mainline churches in America. Worshipers sleep through services, sometimes with their eyes open. They are rarely moved or even involved in the worship experience. The best advice Bart can give to a newcomer is to sit in the back row of the sanctuary. Often, the pastor himself seems to be going through the motions: he hangs a banner at the church's ice cream social announcing, "A Sundae Service You Can Swallow." On Super Bowl Sunday, the sanctuary is nearly deserted, despite the sign outside the church reading "Every Sunday is Super Sunday." *The Simpsons* "implicitly affirms an America in which institutional religion has lost its position of authority, and where personal expressions of spirituality have come to dominate popular religious culture."[2]

At least in respect to its packed, diverse pews, *The Simpsons'* mainline church reality is at variance with statistical reality. Why, in what is said to be an era of cynicism and skepticism, do millions of this edgy show's viewers accept this representation of faithful church attendance in a cartoon? The series' writers say it is because the faith is consistent with the characters. Faith has always been the belief in things unseen, and in that sense it is irrational.

Yet as America in the twentieth century became a more educated, prosperous, urban, and suburban society, its mainline religious denominations became more rational in their theology. As a result, their religious practices and rituals became more settled, staid, and, in the eyes of many experts, bloodless. There were two significant holdouts to this trend: African-American churches and white Pentecostal congregations, both with roots in the working-class and rural South. These groups favored ecstatic and charismatic forms of worship, soul-stirring preaching and lively music, and throughout the century they continued to thrive.

Beginning in the 1960s, middle-class Americans outside these two traditions also began to seek more emotional release and fulfillment in their faith. They yearned to transcend the rational in their worship—to let go, to embrace an identifiably supernatural God. The result was a dramatic growth of invigorated strains of charismatic and evangelical Christianity—often in nondenominational megachurches—that has also proved attractive to a new wave of Third World immigrants to the United States. By the 1990s, some mainline Christian denominations whose memberships were static or declining recognized that they had to adapt to this change in spiritual consciousness or die. One by one, Catholic, Presbyterian, Southern Baptist, and Reform Jewish congregations, among many others, began to reexamine their practices and, where possible, to incorporate more expressive, mystical, and even ecstatic forms of worship, adding healing services, for example.

People continue to pack a mainline church in Springfield the way they do throughout the nation, and for some of the same reasons. "For most Americans, a preeminent benefit of faith is its capacity to improve individual behavior and personal conduct," according to "For Goodness Sake: Why So Many Want Religion to Play a Greater Role in American Life," a 2001 study prepared by Public Agenda and funded by the Pew Charitable Trusts. "If more Americans were more religious, people believe crime would go down, families would do a better job raising children, and people would be more likely to help each other." So when Bart is caught shoplifting a violent video game, Homer asks him, "Haven't you learned anything from that guy who gives those sermons at church? Captain Whatshisname?"

Most often in the series the debate about whether church is necessary takes place in the Simpsons' family car on Sundays, including one morning when Bart and Lisa announce they are contemplating converting to paganism. Bart's use of bad language in raising the question of why he has to go to church causes Marge to snap. "You just answered your own question with that commode mouth," she says. "Besides, you kids have to learn morals and decency and how to love your fellow man." How many parents, unsure of their own beliefs and their own moral leadership at home, drag their children to church with the same goal in mind, to "get a little goodness in them," in Marge's words?

The First Church of Springfield occupies an open city block near the center of town, on the edge of a run-down industrial and commercial area. It is a low-slung, weather-beaten, brick and stucco building, dominated by a sloped, two-story sanctuary lined with faux stained glass windows. There is a paved parking lot next to the building, surrounded by a chain link fence, where a yellow church bus is usually parked. The preferred parking spot reserved for the "parishioner of the month" is usually occupied by Ned Flanders's car. In front of the main entrance of the contemporary structure, which is flanked by boxes of foliage, is a marquee that changes weekly, with black letters on a white background. The sign features a variety of messages, ranging from halfhearted and self-conscious efforts to be hip— "God, the Original Love Connection"—to those more in keeping with the pastor's view of theology and the role of the church. The more illustrative include: "Sunday, the Miracle of Shame," "No Shirt, No Shoes, No Salvation," and "Private Wedding: Please Worship Elsewhere."

Frequently, the signs serve to undermine what Lovejoy is saying in the pulpit, in the process highlighting the hypocrisy of the church, the preacher, or organized religion. Take gambling, for example. Lovejoy has gone back and forth on this moral dilemma, which has divided congregations across the country and brought churches into conflict with political leaders. He occasionally denounces gambling from the pulpit, but during one of these sermons the marquee outside the church advertises that the church offers the "Loosest Bingo Cards in Town." In fact, according to a *Simpsons* comic book, the bingo committee of the First Church of Springfield has exclusive rights to any gambling activities in the community, except for those operated by Native Americans. Other church signs in the show have promoted the congregation's Monte Carlo night and a "retreat" to Reno, Nevada. As the pastor explains it, "Once something's been approved by the government, it's no longer immoral."

Inside the church, which is too financially strapped to afford (or too far north to need) air-conditioning, the red-carpeted sanctuary appears to seat 100 to 150 worshipers—typical in size among American churches, according to a 2001 study by the Hartford Institute for Religious Research and Hartford Seminary—with a center aisle dividing the rows of wooden pews. Lovejoy preaches from a lectern in the middle of a wide, otherwise unadorned stage about four steps above the floor. A blue banner with a white dove of peace hangs from the lectern, which is flanked by simple floral arrangements. To the far left of the stage is a pipe organ. The liturgical music is normally traditional, and the organist, Mrs. Feesh, seems to play on automatic pilot. But Springfield Community is not immune to the "music wars" that have swept the nation's churches, dividing congregations over traditional and contemporary styles of worship.

Bart has strong feelings on the issue, once burning pages from a hymnal to build a "holy fire" for a Hindu wedding. One Sunday, hoping to enliven the repertoire, he and his friend Milhouse print up a sheet with a new "hymn," which they distribute to worshipers. "From God's brain to your mouth," Bart promises gleefully. "Get them while they're holy!" The boys title the hymn "In the Garden of Eden" and credit it to "I. Ron Butterfly"—the latter probably a dig at L. Ron Hubbard, the founder of Scientology. The congregation dutifully begins to sing the 1968 rock classic, "In A-Gadda-Da-Vida" by Iron Butterfly, and the church begins to rock with sweaty enthusiasm. Homer nudges Marge, reminding her of how they used to make out to this "hymn." A beach ball bounces across the pews and, as the soaring, seventeen-minute song ends, tiny flames flicker, and the exhausted Mrs. Feesh collapses onto her keyboard. Lovejoy suddenly realizes that the music sounds a lot like rock and roll. After the service he punishes Bart by making him clean the organ pipes "that you have befouled by your popular music." Yet even the minister succumbs to the power of contemporary music, inviting both a Christian rock group and a barbershop quartet (which included Homer) to perform during services.

Springfield Community is a full-service church, like many in America. There is a Sunday school for children, where young people ask questions like why God causes train wrecks and where an exasperated teacher can ask, in response, "Is a little blind faith too much to ask?" Bart has been expelled and, before he is readmitted, he is frisked for weapons. His teacher admits that the Bible teaches forgiveness, but she asks why he wants to return. While he was gone, she reminds him, "You were happy, we were happy, everybody was happy—particularly the hamster."

The church offers everything from groups dealing with alcohol abuse, Alzheimer's, and marriage counseling, to picnics and a weekly waffle breakfast. There is a thrift shop whose motto is "Nobody Beats the Rev," where the volunteer clerk, Principal Skinner's cranky mother Agnes, is quick to tell Bart, "Buy something or get out." In some of these settings, Lovejoy is portrayed as callous and judgmental in ways ministers are not supposed to be. After being tossed out of the house for a typical act of boorishness, Homer figures he has a natural ally in the minister. "Reverend Lovejoy will make Marge take me back," he confides to Bart. "He *has* to push the sanctity of marriage or his God will punish him." Not necessarily. On this occasion and again at a marriage retreat, Lovejoy suggests Marge divorce Homer rather than attempting to salvage their union. When Homer confesses at a church-sponsored alcohol abuse meeting that he was so desperate for beer that he "ate the dirt under the bleachers" at a football stadium, Lovejoy replies, "I cast thee out!" Lovejoy visits area prisons to minister to inmates, albeit in his own misanthropic way. Attempting to comfort a Death Row inmate about to be executed, who complains that his last meal was filched, the preacher says, "Well, if that's the worst thing to happen to you today, consider yourself lucky."

Like other major characters, Lovejoy has had crises of faith, some of which he overcomes and some he does not. He reacts differently in the face of incipient disaster. A hoax involving a fake angel (see chapter 3) convinces the pastor and all of Springfield that the Day of Reckoning has come, prompting him to don his robe and urge people to be calm but also to be afraid. When Homer forgets to reprogram the computer at his nuclear power plant for Y2K turnover, he causes a universal meltdown that seems to end the world: People go to church, where Lovejoy tells them that Judgment Day has arrived but that it is not too late to repent of their sins, in particular the wearing of "miniskirts and Beatle boots." In another episode, as a comet approaches Springfield, Homer admits that "it's times like this I wish I were a religious man." The next shot is of Lovejoy, ostensibly the man of God, running down the street in a frenzy, shouting, "It's over, people! We don't have a prayer!" Yet when a caller to his radio show asks whether, with all the suffering and injustice in the world, he ever wonders if God really exists, the minister answers with a simple "No."

The church, in the minister's eyes, is synonymous with sacrament, and he is threatened when the two are separated. In a vision of her future,

Lisa's wedding is suddenly called off, and Lovejoy tells her that "it never would have happened if the wedding had been inside the church with God instead of out here in the showiness of nature."

There have been at least three more serious challenges to his role in the community, and, significantly, each represents a major challenge facing mainline denominations: cults, New Age beliefs, and Pentecostalism.

1. The cult. Passing through the Springfield Airport one day, Homer falls into the clutches of a cult called the "Movementarians," who invite him to a free weekend at a local resort. The group believes a great spaceship will transport them to a cosmic paradise called "Blisstonia," which is reminiscent of the "Heaven's Gate" cult, whose Southern California members committed mass suicide as they waited to be transported to outer space. With their veneration of a great, all-knowing leader, the Movementarians also bear some resemblance to Scientology, a fashionable cult in Hollywood founded by science fiction writer L. Ron Hubbard. Like them, the Springfield cult's sacred writings include texts such as "Arithmetic the Leader's Way" and "Science for Leader Lovers," and, like the Scientologists, their deadliest weapons against critics are their lawyers.

Other members of the Springfield community are caught up in the cult, including the entire Simpson family. "When I join an underground cult, I expect some support from my family," Homer tells them. Marge, one of the show's strongest Christian believers, resists joining, but Bart volunteers that the cult and church are pretty much the same thing; the cult simply offers a different place to be bored on Sundays and does nothing to change their daily lives. This is yet another attack on the mainline worship experience, except that the seductive nature of many cults is that they offer much more of an emotional connection than traditional Judeo-Christian denominations—even if it is counterfeit and manipulative.

At the cult's wooded compound, Springfield's gullible residents are subjected to real cult practices, including hypnotic repetitions of chants, six-hour meetings glorifying the leader, and attack therapy sessions. Marge is not taken in and makes a daring escape. Naturally, she goes to the church and the minister for help. She finds Lovejoy, his congregation shrunk to a handful who have resisted the cult, denouncing the Movementarians from the pulpit. Typically and inadvertently, he undercuts the denunciation by highlighting the similarities between "legitimate religion" and cults. "This so-called new religion is nothing but a pack of weird rituals and chants designed to take away the money of fools," Lovejoy says. "Let us say the Lord's Prayer forty times, but first, let's pass the collection plate." The collection is so meager that the minister considers setting fire to the church ("again") to collect the insurance money.

Lovejoy agrees to join Ned Flanders and Willie, the elementary school's strong-willed janitor, to kidnap and deprogram Simpson family members from the cult's compound. After the minister's attempts to subdue Homer with a baseball bat lead to no discernible effect, Lovejoy becomes convinced that the devil has given Homer superhuman strength. The janitor seizes the bat from the minister, dismissing him as a "noodle-armed choirboy." In the Flanderses' basement, where the family is taken, Homer is so resistant to traditional forms of deprogramming that the minister resorts to a more basic approach. He tells Homer that "our commandments" require him to accept a glass of beer, which has been forbidden by the cult. Freed by the taste of forbidden beer, Homer returns to the compound to denounce the cult, causing Lovejoy to shout "Hallelujah!"

The sudden appearance of the cult's leader, hovering in what appears to be a giant spaceship, shakes the minister's faith. Lovejoy panics at the sight, believing that the cult is "the real deal." He rips off his clerical collar, throws it on the ground, and stamps on it. Just as suddenly, the spaceship comes apart and is exposed as a fake, leaving the leader to flee in what turns out to be an ultralight helicopter that uses his followers' bulging moneybags for ballast. Lovejoy realizes he has abandoned his religion too soon, muttering that he should have stuck with the Promise Keepers, the evangelical men's movement famous for stadium and coliseum rallies. Flanders notices the minister's collar on the ground and asks Lovejoy if it is his. Embarrassed, the minister retrieves it lovingly, wondering aloud how it got there.

2. New Age. Brad Goodman, a self-help guru and infomercial star whose psychobabble videotape has helped ease communication in the Simpson household, comes to Springfield to host one of his "Inner Child" seminars. Most of the community turns out, including the Simpsons. Bart's wisecracks get him called to the stage, where Goodman lauds the boy as an example of healthy, unrepressed behavior. He hails Bart's dictum, "I do what I feel like," as a perfect expression of the permissive, situational ethic. The town's residents are urged to act the same way, leading Bart to believe that this advice has turned him into a god. Even Christians like the Flanders family and Lovejoy are caught up in Goodman's feel-good hysteria. The minister preaches a sermon entitled "Be Like Unto the Boy," complete with readings from the "Book of Bart." (How familiar must this seem to church members who have seen their pastors embrace one fashionable therapy or another?) A "Do What You Feel" festival dissolves into anarchy, however, with two women dressed in togas holding aloft a gold statue of Goodman. "God is angry," Lovejoy decides. "We've made a false idol of this Brad Goodman."

3. Pentecostalism and charismatic worship. A college reunion prank gone awry leaves Homer with a bucket filled with superglue stuck on the top half of his head. Bart drills holes through the metal so his father can still drive, but the car skids off a rural road and through a cornfield, ending up at the "Brother Faith Revival." The service is exhilarating, an old-fashioned tent revival complete with folding chairs, sawdust on the floor, and a cross illuminated by an outline of light bulbs. Dressed in dazzling white, Brother Faith and his evangelical ministry are African Americans who take exuberant joy in worship. They sing and they dance and they exalt the Holy Spirit, urging worshipers to check out John 2:11, where Jesus turns water into wine at the wedding feast in Cana. Brother Faith is not a fake and, as Bart observes, "he dances better than Jesus himself!"

Once, in the rural South, faith healers were said to put a sign outside their tents reading "no broken bones"—for obvious reasons. Brother Faith is not so intimidated, and he successfully lays hands on the dislocated elbow of Cletus, the hillbilly, and shouts, "the power of faith compels you—heal! Take that, Satan!" Next up is the bucket on Homer's head, but this time Brother Faith cannot perform the miracle by himself, so he asks for a "holy helper." Bart, of all people, is chosen. Sure enough, with Brother Faith's help, they remove the bucket from Homer's head. After the revival, as Brother Faith is packing up his snakes, Bart asks how he *really* got the bucket off Homer's head. The evangelist explains that the power came from God, who gave some of the power to Bart. "Really," the boy says, "I would think he would want to *limit* my power." Brother Faith assures him that he too was a hell-raiser as a child until he saw the light and changed his wicked ways. He recommends the same choice for Bart. At first, the boy declines at what is clearly a profound invitation, using the logic of many other pragmatic nonbelievers: "I think I'll go for the life of sin, followed by a presto change-o deathbed repentance." That is not "God's angle," Brother Faith says. "Why not spend your life helping people instead? Then you're also covered in case of sudden death."

Back at Springfield Community Church that Sunday morning, Bart is exposed to his usual brand of Christian worship. Lovejoy drones on with a typical sermon, "Life in Hell"—which is also the title of *Simpsons'* creator Matt Groening's counterculture comic strip. The minister takes as his text Paul's letter to the Corinthians, which he manages to convey as a chain letter gone wrong, until he notices that Bart is squirming in his seat. Foolishly, he asks the boy if he is bored, and Bart answers honestly that he is. "I'm doing the best with the material I have," the minister says, referring to the Bible, although he might just as well be referring to traditional theology and worship. Thinking back on his recent experience in

Brother Faith's tent, Bart says that church can be fun, a notion that seems so patently absurd to the rest of the congregation—including the faithful Flanders family—that they burst out laughing. "No, really," he says. "It can be a party, with clowns and lasers and miracles. A real preacher knows how to bring the Bible alive, through music and dancing." Bart's monologue is about as trenchant a critique of mainline Protestantism as one is likely to hear in the mass media. Is worship about substance or simply style? Perhaps he's just talking about "seeker-friendly" congregations like Willow Creek Community Church near Chicago.

Thinking over Brother Faith's advice, Bart decides to give religious revival a try—in a big way—by becoming a backyard evangelist, complete with a cape, a plan to work miracles, and a distinctive exhortation: "Satan, eat my shorts!" Using an exterminator's tent, he starts drawing big crowds, most from Springfield Community. Back at the church, only the faithful Flanderses are in the pew. Lovejoy wonders whether it might be time to "fight razzle with dazzle," but the best he can do is a fractured electric guitar version of "Michael, Row the Boat Ashore." It is, alas, hopeless.

For Lovejoy, the most poignant crises come from within his home—where a copy of *The Last Supper* hangs prominently—and from within his congregation. His family life is a trial. Helen, his sharp-faced wife, is portrayed as a judgmental, antisexual shrew, much like Dana Carvey's Church Lady on *Saturday Night Live*. She describes Michaelangelo's statue of David as "filth" because "it graphically portrays parts of the human body, which, practical as they may be, are evil." (Far-fetched? In 2001, people in the small, central Florida town of Lake Alfred demanded that a replica of the masterpiece displayed outside a shop in the business district be draped.) Bart's use of the term "butt" causes her to cover her ears. She is also, as her husband acknowledges, an incurable gossip. After falsely maligning Marge, she pledges, "From now on, I'll use my gossip for good instead of evil." Every Sunday she can be found outside the church with her husband, dutifully greeting parishioners.

The couple's fifth-grade daughter, Jessica, is a classic PK (preacher's kid). While characteristically overdrawn, her story is likely to strike familiar chords among other clergy parents and children. Bart hears the girl, who has just arrived from boarding school, read the scripture one Sunday morning and is instantly smitten. Thinking it is the best way to come on to a minister's daughter, he tries a new persona, a good boy, although it is an awkward fit. "I don't think God's words have ever sounded so plausible," he says after the service. Lisa tells her brother that his chances with Jessica are slight, since "she's a sweet, kind reverend's daughter, and you're the devil's cabana boy."

Things are not always what they seem. Jessica, who now attends Springfield Elementary, takes pity on Bart when he earns three months' detention and invites him to the Lovejoy house for dinner. The meal is not a success. Bart's efforts to come across as a model of good behavior unravel and, in the midst of an off-color joke, the minister tosses him out the door by his ear. Outside, however, a surprise awaits. Telling her father she is going to her room to pray, Jessica slips out and catches up to her suitor. She tells him that he's bad, and she likes him for it. Bart says that she is his ideal first girlfriend—smart, beautiful, and a liar. They share a kiss—and a minor crime spree of vandalism and antisocial behavior.

Yet Bart is soon shocked and unsettled to learn that he is outclassed by the amoral Jessica, and with Lisa's encouragement he determines to break off the relationship at the next opportunity. That comes at church on Sunday, where the sermon topic is "Evil Women in History, from Jezebel to Janet Reno." Bart sits next to Jessica and tells her he wants to stop seeing her because "you're turning me into a criminal when all I want to be is a petty thug." The minister's daughter agrees to change her ways—as she is slipping the collection money into her purse. She allows Bart to be blamed for the theft, telling him later that no one will believe that "the sweet, perfect minister's daughter" would do such a thing. Lisa comes to her brother's rescue the next Sunday at church and exposes Jessica as the thief.

Despite the discovery of the collection money under his daughter's bed, Lovejoy cannot accept the truth, and claims that Bart framed his daughter. This is too much, even for Jessica. The theft, she tells her father, was a classic cry for attention. She reminds the disbelieving pastor that she was expelled from boarding school for stealing from the school chapel's collection, for fighting, and for building a pipe bomb and exploding the toilets. Lovejoy will not hear this—literally—and sings "Bringing in the Sheaves" to drown out his daughter's confession. "Come on, Dad!" she pleads. "Pay attention to me!" Sometimes comedy isn't pretty. The only response the minister can muster to punish the wayward girl, who is no demon seed, is by making her scrub the church steps, which she cons the ever gullible Bart into doing for her.

Theft apart, finances are an ongoing problem at Springfield Community Church. The minister preaches tithing on the gross—not the net—and when the offering is insufficient, he is not shy about sending the long-handled pole and woven wooden basket around again. He urges members to give as if the person next to them is watching, and threatens them with an audit. Lovejoy claims his salary is so low (perhaps taxed by his daughter's private school tuition) that he has to borrow his Bible from the library. He implies that meager collections inspired him to set a fire in the sanctuary in order to collect the insurance and that, unless things improve, he is contemplating doing it again. On the plus side, he does take care to tally the offering with the door to his office open, using a change counter. The congregation is so desperate for funds it accepts ads for the church bulletin from Fat Tony, the local crime boss.

A deeper problem for the church is Lovejoy's sense of mission. The newly minted minister arrived in Springfield in the 1970s, driving a Volkswagen Karman Ghia and listening to the Doobie Brothers' "Jesus Is Just All Right" on the radio. With the 1960s over, Lovejoy felt he was in his element, living in a time when "people were once again ready to feel bad about themselves." He called parishioners like Ned Flanders "brother" and invited them to "rap" with him. But by the 1980s he stopped caring and found that, given the atmosphere of the time, no one noticed.

A mere ten years later, Marge notices. Concerned about her family's dogged resistance to attend church and the pastor's failure to meet the spiritual needs of the congregation—mostly in the form of widespread sleeping during service—she goes to visit the pastor. "Sermons about 'constancy' and 'prudissitude' are all well and good," she says, "but the church could be doing so much more to reach out to people." Church, she says, "shouldn't be a chore. It should help you in your daily life." Lovejoy replies that Marge is naïve and idealistic, just as he was when he began his ministry, and that his failures have worn him down. She tells him he shouldn't let a few bad experiences sour him on helping people; he insists he should. But, stung by the criticism of his service to the congregation, he challenges Marge to volunteer and—admitting she is motivated in part by guilt—she agrees.

Marge starts her church work by cleaning up, sweeping the aisles and putting the collection plates in the dishwasher. At first, Lovejoy is grateful for the help, thanking Marge for giving him more time to study and enabling him to discover "a form of shame that has gone unused for seven hundred years." He asks her to answer the church's advice line, which brings her more unsettling news about the pastor. As the "Listen Lady," she learns from Moe, the bartender, that Lovejoy was not encouraging when he called earlier with a problem. With her compassion and common sense, she soon becomes a more and more popular counselor than the preacher. People praise her during Lovejoy's sermons and brush past the minister to speak with her after services. Marge starts to call the pastor "Tim," and treats him like a secretary. Lovejoy sinks deeper into despair. "I am a shepherd without a flock," he prays. "What have I done to lose them?"

The minister preaches that "the Lord will hear your lamentations and give solace to your spirit," and God soon gives evidence that he has heard

Lovejoy's own lamentations. Help comes in the form of the saints pictured in the church's stained glass windows (who are imaginatively if improbably named), who come alive and suggest some answers. Thinking the voices are those of disrespectful parishioners, Lovejoy asks, "Could we please not yell out things in church?" The saints respond in kind. They ask what the minister has done to keep his flock, telling him he must inspire their hearts with his bravery. He interrupts and says he has recarpeted the vestibule, which one of the saints calls "the lamest reply I've ever heard. . . . You're just lucky God isn't here." Hmm. The pastor's devastation is nearly complete.

Marge receives a call on the advice line from Helen Lovejoy, herself despondent, asking for advice to perk up her husband, who has sadly retreated to his basement where he runs his electric train set. Marge suggests that he will bounce back after a few days off. When he returns to church, he finds that the Listen Lady is over her head with a problem. Ned Flanders has been abducted from work by a group of thugs and abandoned in a pit of carnivorous baboons at the Springfield Zoo. Lovejoy races to the scene and, making use of his model railroading expertise on the zoo's kiddie train, engineers a heroic, acrobatic rescue of his most faithful parishioner. "Say your prayers, you heathen baboons!" he says, fighting off a counterattack. Flanders thanks his pastor effusively, but Lovejoy passes the credit to Marge, who "taught me there's more to being a minister than not caring about people." The congregation is enthralled as their pastor recounts the rescue in his Sunday sermon, cribbing liberally from "The Charge of the Light Brigade." As he reaches the climax of his story, Homer exclaims, "That's religion!"

Absent such dramatic tales, Lovejoy's sermons are a major issue, for him and the congregation. Typically, his message is along the lines of, "May we burn in foul smelling fire forever and ever," seasoned with a regular plug for his radio show. Jarred awake during one of the minister's eulogies, Homer shouts, "Change the channel, Marge!" Lovejoy's main complaint from the pulpit, one not unfamiliar in some mainline denominations, is that his parishioners are smug. "Today's Christian thinks he doesn't need God. He thinks he's got it made. He's got his hi-fi, his boob tube, and his instant pizza pie." The scripture passages he uses, when not mangled for comic effect, tend to be obscure, arcane, bloody, or simply meaningless selections from the Old Testament, or depressing readings from Lamentations. To wake people, he sometimes resorts to desperate measures, including sound effects like ambulance sirens and bird calls, and even his own rendition of the song, "The Entertainer." Once he offers a baby-sitting discount for anyone who can recall the theme of the sermon he had just finished preaching, but the congregation stares blankly and no one responds with the correct answer: "Love." A sermon about the Samaritan woman at the well, inexplicably advertised out front as "Something about the Virgin Mary," is disrupted when Homer revs a newly won Harley outside the church. Lovejoy gives up, saying "What the heck," and dismisses the congregation, who cheer and stream out of the sanctuary. Homer's excited reaction to another sermon turns out to be a response to the football game he has been listening to with earphones. He admits to the pastor that when he is not sleeping during the sermon he is mentally undressing the female parishioners. Sometimes he even eats. "If God didn't want us to eat in church," he says, "he would've made gluttony a sin."

Kenneth Briggs, former religion reporter for the *New York Times* and a longtime *Simpsons* fan, sympathizes with the pastor: "When you look out at that congregation you get some sense of how difficult it would be to focus that lot on anything." Lovejoy, he said, personifies "the wounded servant. He's not a buffoon." Yet, with a straight face, Lovejoy can tell Bart and Lisa, whom he mistakenly believes are thinking about converting to Judaism, not to make a rash decision, since "the church is changing to meet the needs of today's young Christians." Not this church, however.

Beyond Springfield's congregation and its minister, organized religion in general is a target of many of *The Simpsons*' heartiest satiric wallops. "*The Simpsons* implicitly affirms an America in which institutional religion has lost its position of authority," according to the book *God in the Details*, "and where personal expressions have come to dominate popular religious culture."[3] Mr. Burns, the town's richest man and its most sinister character, warns children at the elementary school in a motivational talk that religion is one of the "demons you must slay if you wish to succeed in business. When opportunity knocks . . . you don't want to be sitting in some phoney-baloney church or synagogue." Bart, taken by his parents to a military school, desperately pleads to be taken home. "I'll do anything!" he says. "I'll find religion!" Before one of the annual Halloween specials, Homer cautions "some crybabies out there—religious types mostly—who might be offended" by the segments to come. The best thing about watching Sunday football on television, he says in another episode, is that it "gets rid of the unpleasant aftertaste of church." Marge tells her husband that "Church shouldn't be a chore. It should help you in your daily life." Well, Homer replies, "It should, but it doesn't." Lisa likes the time right after Sunday service because it represents the longest period before she has to return to church.

The targets are not confined to residents of Springfield or to the series' main narrative. Norman Vincent Peale's birthplace is destroyed in one throwaway sequence. In another, while Homer is dangling naked from a hot air balloon, he drags his rear end along the soaring glass steeple of a church in plain view of the congregation. The building is very reminiscent of the Reverend Robert Schuller's congregation in Orange County, California. "Now, let us thank the Lord for this magnificent Crystal Cathedral, which allows us to look upon his wondrous creation," the minister prays, as Homer slowly slides by. "Now quickly!" the pastor says, suddenly changing course. "Gaze down at God's fabulous parquet floor. Eyes on the floor . . . still on the floor . . . always on God's floor."

Bart and his friend Milhouse find a copy of *Mad* magazine (in many ways a forerunner of *The Simpsons'* brand of humor) with a folding page designed as a riddle. The puzzle asks, "What do televangelists worship most?" Bart—for once the innocent, or at least the straight, man—says God, and his friend guesses Jesus; when folded properly, the answer is money. The boy's grandfather, Abe Simpson, justifies their attempt to defraud residents of the local retirement home by telling Bart that if they don't take the old folks' money, "they'll just send it to some televangelist."

The Western missionary experience is the subject of an episode in which Homer, trying to avoid paying a prank pledge to public television, flees aboard a Christian relief flight to a small island in the South Pacific. Ill-prepared to be a missionary, he is assured by his bright-eyed and clean-cut predecessors as they depart that they have already made a good start by ridiculing the islanders' beliefs, teaching them some English, and giving them the "gift of shame." After distributing Bibles, Homer's next contributions to their cultural devastation are alcohol and casino gambling, to predictable effect. As "God's messenger," he also provides his own admittedly distorted view of Judeo-Christian faith, although he is stumped when a question that recurs in *The Simpsons* is asked by one of the islanders: If God is all-powerful, why does he care if he is worshiped? When the islanders balk at Homer's suggestion that they build a chapel, he snaps, "Either grab a stone or go to hell." The church is built, and the islanders then discuss how often they must attend services to avoid going to hell. Every Sunday for the rest of their lives, one says, while another laughs and asks for a serious answer. Clearly, this is an overdrawn portrait of the Christian missionary experience. Yet for anyone who has studied the experience of, say, eighteenth-century Franciscans in California or

American Protestants in Hawaii in the nineteenth century, this episode includes painfully recognizable elements.

Reverend Lovejoy and the First Church of Springfield must be doing something right. Knowing the failures and weaknesses of the man and the institution does not keep people from returning week after week for solace and inspiration and calling when they are in trouble. Like Woody Allen's definition of marriage, it is the triumph of hope over experience. Kenneth Briggs, who now teaches at Lafayette University, defends *The Simpsons'* overall treatment of Christianity. "I don't see anybody taking any cheap shots. It gives mainline Protestants a fair shake," he told me. "That group is almost constantly maligned or ignored. It's easy to ignore them. This one does give them a fair shake."

Six

Heaven, Hell, and the Devil:
"I'd Sell My Soul for a Donut"

In his version of *Doctor Faustus*, the famous tale about a man who makes a pact with the devil, German writer Thomas Mann described hell as a "soundless cellar, far down beneath God's hearing." Pope John Paul II declared in 1999 that hell is not a physical entity. "Rather than a place, hell indicates the state of those who freely and definitely separate themselves from God," he told a Vatican audience. It is not "a punishment imposed externally by God" but the natural result of an unrepentant sinner's decision to be apart from the divine.[1] Jews do not dwell on the specific nature of hell, called *Sheol* or *Gehenna* in the Old Testament, but view the underworld in a general sense as a dreary, dark, and noiseless place.

In recent years, a vigorous debate has emerged within the evangelical community on the nature of hell. Since the late 1980s, a dozen books about hell have appeared on the subject, debating a provocative and, thus far, minority position that at Judgment Day, nonbelievers will be obliterated rather than forced to suffer eternal torment in hell. Philip E. Hughes resigned as president of Westminster Seminary to write a book supporting this view, called the "annihilationist" view. Even Billy Graham, one of the world's greatest Protestant evangelists, has questioned the existence of the fires of hell. Most evangelicals, however, hold the traditional view of hell that is embraced by *The Simpsons*. Heaven, for some reason, does not provoke the same intense speculation and drama as its alternative, although Homer attempts to capitalize on an end-of-the-world scare in Springfield with a commercial enterprise by warning that "No one gets into heaven without a glow stick."

Characters on *The Simpsons* have their own expectations and opinions when it comes to the hereafter. Although comic on the surface, they often mask serious theological concerns and controversies. Maude Flanders says she hopes that there will be *Us* magazine in heaven. Grandpa Abe Simpson wants to go to "rich man's heaven." Another portrayal of heaven shows founding father Ben Franklin playing air hockey with rocker Jimi Hendrix. Bart's teacher, Edna Krabappel, upon finding herself in hell in a *Simpsons* comic book, observes that at least eternal torment in the underworld "beats teaching." In a Halloween fantasy episode of the show, Homer chokes to death on a piece of broccoli and is surprised to find himself before Saint Peter, who is playing solitaire at the pearly gates. His first reaction is to shout down to earth exultantly to his pious neighbor, Ned Flanders, that he got there first. However, in order to pass through the gates, Homer is required to do one good deed in the next twenty-four hours, which he does. Saint Peter, however, doesn't notice the accomplishment, so Homer lands in hell. Near death after a heart attack in another episode, Homer regains consciousness and tells the doctor he had a vision of "a wonderful place filled with fire and brimstone, and there were all these guys in red pajamas sticking pitchforks in my butt."

The nature of heaven and hell is a topic that comes up often at Sunday school at Springfield Community Church. Unlike many mainline Protestants—and the pope—characters in *The Simpsons* believe unquestionably in a very literal interpretation of both concepts. If a person has been good, says the teacher, Ms. Albright, he or she will go to heaven, where "you get to do whatever you like best." This, of course, runs counter to Protestant theology, in which salvation comes through grace and not works. Still, the hair-splitting children want to know where God draws the line for admission. The teacher's call is "yes" for righteous ventriloquists but "no" for their dummies, "no" for cavemen, and a toss-up for robots with a human brain. Bart raises the question, in deceptively simple fashion, about bodily resurrection, which echoes some of Christianity's early theological debates. He wants to know if a good person who loses a leg in a fight will be reconnected with the limb in heaven. Ms. Albright replies yes, the body will be made whole. For the children, the teacher's most disturbing ruling, concerning the nature of the soul, is that animals won't be going to heaven. This thought literally dumbfounds Homer when Bart passes along the news on the way home from church. "I can understand how they wouldn't want to let in those wild jungle apes," he says, "but what about those really smart ones who live among us, who roller skate and smoke cigars?"

Hell exerts an equal, if not greater, fascination for the children in Sunday school. It is, Ms. Albright explains, a terrible place: "Maggots are your sheet, worms your blanket. There's a lake of fire, burning with sulfur. You'll be tormented day and night, forever and ever. As a matter of fact, if you actually saw hell, you'd be so frightened you would die." Martin, one of Springfield's brighter children, takes the obvious message from his teacher's description. "So what you're saying is that there's a downside to afterlife," he says, and asks how to "steer clear of the abode of the damned." Again, the teacher's answer is "do good works and avoid sin" rather than "accept Jesus." Bart wonders if hell might not be something you would get used to, like water in a hot tub, and is assured it is not.

Reverend Lovejoy's visions of the torments of hell are at least as vivid as the Sunday school teacher's and would be familiar to worshipers in the most primitive of backwoods churches. Trying to get the children to confess to a prank, the preacher has them repeat what is obviously a familiar litany of what will happen to them if they fail to come clean. The consequences, they acknowledge, include going straight to hell, where they will "eat naught but burning hot coals and drink naught but burning hot cola. . . . Where demons will punch me in the back. . . . Where my soul will be chopped up into confetti and strewn upon a parade of murderers and single mothers. . . . Where my tongue will be torn out by ravenous birds." The exercise has the desired effect. Bart's friend Milhouse gets the minister's message, is appropriately terrified, and turns Bart in.

There is some speculation about whether Bart is himself demonic. His teacher at Springfield Christian School, where the boy goes after being expelled (again) from public school, warns the other students to avert their eyes from him because the troublemaking boy might take on other manifestations. Bart gets a closer look at hell in another episode when, while recklessly skateboarding, he is hit by a Rolls Royce carrying his father's boss, Montgomery Burns. The boy seems to be dead, and his spirit rises skyward from his body, riding a celestial escalator. A heavenly voice warns Bart to hold on to the handrail and not to spit over the side—which he immediately does, sending him straight to hell. The underworld tableau he finds is a variation of Hieronymous Bosch's *Garden of Earthly Delights*. Bart introduces himself to the devil in typical fashion, asking, "Who the hell are you?" The devil replies that the boy has earned eternal damnation for a lifetime of evil deeds and that spitting over the handrail just clinched it. But Satan checks his computer and finds that a mistake has been made, that Bart is not expected for almost a hundred years. "Boy, is my face red," the devil says. Departing for the world above, Bart asks if there is anything he can do to avoid returning to hell. Yes, the devil says, but it would mean changing his life in a way he wouldn't like. Instead, the devil instructs him to "lie, cheat, steal, and listen to heavy metal music," which Bart enthusiastically agrees to do.

In a Halloween segment, Bart cheerfully volunteers that he would be willing to sell his soul for a Formula One racing car, which the devil tells him can be arranged. The boy changes his mind in time to avert disaster, and his mother tells him to stop pestering Satan. But on another occasion, Bart takes the prospect of a soulless existence much more seriously. His revelation follows a debate among three children on the nature of the soul. Bart says he does not believe the soul exists, that it is just something people have made up to scare children, "like the boogie man or Michael Jackson." His friend Milhouse disagrees, explaining that every religion believes in the soul, that it is strong enough to swim away if you die in a submarine or roll on wheels if you die in the desert. He also tells Bart, correctly, that people once believed the soul could escape the body during a sneeze. That is the reason we say "God bless you," Milhouse continues, to squish it back in the body. Sister Lisa, ever the voice of enlightenment, argues that the soul is "the most valuable part of you," the only one that lasts forever. Whether or not it is physically real, she says, "it's the symbol of everything fine inside us." (The humor in the scene notwithstanding, bear in mind that this discussion is taking place in an animated sitcom, not on a Bill Moyers special on PBS.)

Bart determines to test his thesis of the soul's nonexistence by selling his to Milhouse for five dollars, writing out the deed on church stationery and immediately spending the money on a set of colorful dinosaur sponges. Suddenly, his life begins to change dramatically: Automatic doors don't open when he approaches, his breath does not produce condensation on the door of a frozen food compartment, he sees no humor in his favorite television cartoon show, and he takes no joy from pranks. He realizes that his essence has departed. Lisa reminds him of his error by saying grace before dinner that pointedly asks blessings for "every soul in Christendom." Bart gets the message. He tries to buy his soul back from Milhouse, only to learn that the price has gone up to fifty dollars, which he does not have. That night, he dreams of his friends cavorting with their beloved souls while he has none, and he awakes screaming. Returning to his friend to plead for his soul in the middle of the night, Bart is told that Milhouse has sold it to the creepy guy who owns the comic book store. At dawn, the owner tells the boy that it has been sold again to a buyer he will not identify.

In crisis, Bart turns to prayer again, and again on his knees. "Are you there, God?" he asks plaintively. "It's me, Bart Simpson. I know I never paid too much attention in church, but I could really use some of that good stuff now. I'm . . . afraid. I'm afraid some weirdo's got my soul and I don't know what they're going to do with it! I just want it back. Please?" he says, weeping. With that, his soul miraculously floats down from above. But the intervention is not entirely divine, and the explanation for it is not directly from the Judeo-Christian tradition. Lisa tells him she went into her piggy bank to buy back her brother's soul. You know, she tells him, "some philosophers believe that nobody is born with a soul—that you have to earn one through suffering and thought and prayer, like you did last night."

Homer has an even closer call with eternal damnation. Daydreaming—as usual—at his workstation at the nuclear power plant, he wakes to find that his coworkers have made off with all his precious donuts. "I'd sell my soul for a donut," he exclaims, and the devil suddenly appears to offer the deal, in the person of Ned Flanders ("It's always the one you least suspect," he says). Taking a stab at fairness, Satan wants to explain the ramifications of the deal, but Homer cuts him off, asking if he has the donut or not. He takes the devil's fiery pen, signs the agreement, and begins to gobble the cruller. According to the deal, the instant the donut is consumed, Homer's soul will belong to the devil. In an unexpected and uncharacteristic display of wit, he saves a tiny piece of the donut and, in so doing, all his soul. Infuriated at being outwitted, the devil turns into a fearsome beast—to the strains of Mussorgsky's *A Night on Bald Mountain*—and hurtles back to Hades in a ball of fire.

There are limits to Homer's self-control, as there are to his intelligence. That same night he wanders sleepily into the kitchen, reaches into the refrigerator, and finishes off the last morsel of the donut. Instantly, the devil is back to collect his prize. Homer's noisy resistance to being dragged to hell attracts the rest of the family, and quick-thinking Lisa demands a fair trial. The devil agrees to a midnight hearing the next day, insisting on taking her father to hell until then. Life in hell is not a pleasant one, as Matt Groening has made clear for years in his comic strip. First, Homer is hacked to pieces and fed into a sausage machine. Then his head is used as a bowling ball by a demon, striking spiked pins. There is a room called "Hell Labs: Ironic Punishments Division" (a crib from Dante's *Inferno*) in which Homer is strapped to a chair and force-fed donuts. Alas, the irony is lost on the gluttonous prisoner, who exhausts his robotic metal tormentor before the device exhausts his appetite. "I'm smarter than the Devil," Homer concludes from the experience, still facing an eternity of hard time.

Homer's trial that night in the Simpson family living room is an adaptation of Stephen Vincent Benet's "The Devil and Daniel Webster." Locked in a flaming cell, Homer has little to say in the proceeding. As in the famous story, the devil here stacks the jury with infamous malefactors, including several of Benet's originals such as Benedict Arnold and the pirate Blackbeard. Among *The Simpsons'* additions to the panel is Richard

Nixon, who addresses Satan as "Master." The devil presents what seems to be an open-and-shut case, and the Grim Reaper is about to flip the switch on Homer. He is saved only when Marge offers as last-minute evidence their wedding picture, on the back of which the groom has written a pledge to give his soul to her forever. The unambiguous message? Traditional family values: true love and marriage will save your soul.

But what happens when the Simpsons' marriage itself comes under siege, as it has from time to time in the show's run, or when Homer and Marge are divided over a moral issue? Is there enough individual religious faith to sustain them and help them make the right decisions?

Seven

Moral Dilemmas: "Dad, We May Have Saved Your Soul"

Characters in *The Simpsons* face moral dilemmas, large and small, on a regular basis. They often fall short when confronted by these challenges: Bart lies and steals, almost reflexively; Lisa sometimes does not honor her father; Homer covets Ned Flanders's wife and those of his neighbors' possessions he has not already borrowed; even saintly Marge becomes addicted to gambling. On the big issues, at least when cornered, they do better. Four episodes in particular place major moral dilemmas center stage, one dealing with theft and three dealing with adultery. In each case, the characters grapple with temptation in a serious way and, in the end, do the right thing. But what is as instructive as the resolution of these dilemmas is the process the characters go through to make their decisions, and the lessons they take from them.

The episode "Homer vs. Lisa and the Eighth Commandment" has the structure of an exquisitely crafted, twenty-two-minute sermon. It could easily have been composed in the finest of seminaries—evangelical or mainline, Christian, Jewish, or Islamic. Good sermons begin with scripture, and this one is no exception. Homer dreams that he is with the children of Israel at the foot of Mount Sinai as Moses returns with the law. He is identified as "Homer the thief," and his friends are a carver of graven images and an adulterer. (The carver of graven images bears a resemblance to Reverend Lovejoy; the adulterer to Jacques, a bowling alley gigolo we will soon meet.) The lives of all three are about to be fundamentally changed as Moses reads the Ten Commandments: Now they are all out of work.

Homer is brought back to the present by the sound of neighbor Ned chasing off a cable television installer who has offered an illegal hookup for fifty dollars, with no monthly payments to follow. The deal sounds so good to Homer that he tracks the man down and is soon plugged in, making the announcement to his family when they return home. Marge is concerned about the arrangement's illegality, but she is distracted when a women's network comes on the screen. As the days wear on, the family becomes increasingly fascinated by the diversity—and triviality—of the world of cable.

At church the next Sunday, Reverend Lovejoy preaches a sermon about the love of possessions and self-satisfaction, making no impression whatever on Homer. In Sunday school, however, the lesson is about the Ten Commandments, and when the teacher gets to "Thou shalt not steal," Lisa makes the connection. She envisions her house falling away, replaced by the fires of hell, where the devil has joined her family on the couch to watch cable programming. Satan invites her to join them, saying there would be no cost—"except your soul!" Returning to reality, she runs screaming from the living room. Later, she confronts her father, who is increasingly fixated on the new television programming. With typical overstatement, Lisa tells him that one reason that the world is a cesspool of corruption is widespread theft, which is a sin. Homer agrees, until his daughter points out that watching television on the illegal hookup is a good example of theft. He is impervious to her arguments and tries to compromise her with programming about her beloved horses. She resists, saying she'd rather go to heaven than watch.

In creating this episode, said writer Jeff Martin, the staff decided from the outset to use "a very strict construction of the eighth commandment," despite the fact that cable theft is "essentially a victimless crime, the kind of thing that many, many good people do." Thus, this apparently benign occasion of sin begins to have wider implications for the family, as it often does in real life. While his parents were out of the house, Bart discovered an adult cable channel that features naked women and is now charging admission for his classmates to watch. Homer discovers them and tells Bart not to watch because the channel is only for "mommies and daddies who love each other very much," an interesting rationale for his libertarian view of soft-core pornography. The rot has clearly set in, and it is spreading.

The next day the cable installer lets himself into the Simpson house and offers to sell Homer some stolen stereo equipment, figuring that someone open to pirated cable would be open to other stolen goods. Homer refuses, but because the cable installer had so easily gained entry into his house, he becomes obsessed with security and installs bars on his windows and a sign saying "No Thieves" on his lawn. "There are thieves everywhere," he explains to Marge, "and I'm not talking about the small forgivable stuff." That would be forgivable stuff like illegal cable television. The message is clear: For every thief there is a victim of theft, buying stolen goods makes you complicit in the theft, and often the perpetrator becomes a victim-in-kind; or to return to the Bible, "A man reaps what he sows" (Gal. 6:7).

Stymied in her efforts to save her father from sin, Lisa goes to Reverend Lovejoy for advice on how to handle the situation at home. She asks if it is stealing for a person to take bread for a starving family. The pastor replies that it would be stealing only if the thief put jelly on the bread, that is, if he or she took more than what was needed for survival. After this bit of sophistry, the pastor gives the girl some good advice, applicable for other children who find themselves in similar straits where their values are out of sync with those of their parents. Lovejoy suggests that she set an example by not watching cable television and that she explain to her family why she has made that decision. There is theological precedent for this approach, a principle in Jewish law called *shalom bayit*, translated as "peace in the home." What this means is that family harmony should prevail whenever possible, with an emphasis on flexibility, without compromising personal integrity. Lisa takes the minister's advice, announces her decision to her father, and pledges to say no more on the subject.

Her campaign has an effect, and Marge begins to waver. She suggests to her husband that they unhook the cable, but he is adamant. A highly promoted heavyweight title fight is coming up and is available only on cable. Homer invites friends and coworkers to the house, which raises even more discomfort. Frantically, he asks Bart to help him hide items that he admits he has stolen before their owners arrive at the house: mugs from Moe's Tavern and a computer from the nuclear power plant. The web of deceit widens. Two police officers come to the door and announce that they have heard Homer has an illegal cable hookup. Homer, fearing he is about to be arrested, blames it all on Marge. Instead, the lawmen say they simply want to watch the fight—more corruption. In a prefight interview, one of the boxers talks about his time in prison, and Homer imagines himself in the same situation, cut off from his family. He gives up.

On the lawn, where Lisa and Marge are camped out in protest, Homer apologizes for interrupting their judging of him. He makes two announcements: He will cut the cable when the prize fight is over, and he is not too fond of his wife and daughter for having driven him to this decision. Unfazed, Lisa says, "Dad, we may have saved your soul." Despite Bart's pleas to reconsider—"tractor pulls, Atlanta Braves baseball, Joe Franklin"—Homer cuts the cable.

Marge has both thrown her husband out of the house and left him a number of times over the course of the series. Yet after ten years of marriage, they appear to have a healthy and loving union, which includes a realistic sexual relationship that ranges from arid to exuberant. It is also apparent that when it comes to thinking about other women, Homer is no angel. He likes skin magazines and he makes lascivious remarks about Maude Flanders—although with no intention of pursuing her. On a wild, drunken binge in Las Vegas with Ned Flanders, the two men may have married cocktail waitresses, matches apparently not consummated. Homer goes to a bachelor party at a local restaurant where Bart uses a mail-order spy camera to photograph him cavorting with a belly dancer. The picture circulates around town, mortifying Marge and getting Homer kicked out of the house. He finishes the episode on the stage of a burlesque show, telling the audience (including Marge) that, "as ridiculous as this sounds, I would rather feel the sweet breath of my beautiful wife on the back of my neck as I sleep than stuff dollar bills into some stranger's G-string."

In each of the episodes that focus on the serious temptation of adultery, neither Homer nor Marge seeks to stray from marital vows. They are, in that sense, typical innocents who run into danger by happenstance, good intentions and, in Marge's case, emotional need.

Homer embarrasses Marge yet again, in this case at the movies, by loudly giving away the ending of a suspense film. His wife shuts him up, to the applause of audience members and to Homer's shame. On the drive home with the kids, Marge fails in her efforts to apologize to her husband, and Homer is still hurt and angry as a result of the public humiliation. He drops the family off and says, angrily, that he's going and "I don't know when you'll see me again." Driving out into the boondocks, he finds a rowdy country-and-western bar. A waitress named Lurleen Lumpkin sings a song she has written, "Your Wife Don't Understand You, But I Do," which Homer later tells her, "touched me in a way I've never felt before." He returns home the next morning, singing the song and affecting a Southern accent. When he goes to his regular tavern he reveals that he has been to another bar, an act of unfaithfulness that shocks Moe, the proprietor. Unable to get Lurleen's tune out of his head, Homer goes to visit the waitress in her mobile home and tells her he wants others to hear it as well. He takes her to a nearby mall, where she records the song on a CD at Lucky Records, for twenty-five cents. The clerk at the recording booth likes it and asks Homer if he can pass it along to his brother, who owns a local radio station.

The plaintive song is an instant hit, captivating listeners in all walks of life. Although Bart is immune, even level-headed Lisa is taken with it: "I can feel her sweet country soul in every digitally encoded bit." Marge recognizes that the situation is getting out of hand and she demands to know from Homer what is going on. He tells her, truthfully, that nothing untoward has taken place. "Nothing," however, includes watching Lurleen try on outfits in her trailer, which he insists is not seamy. When Lurleen calls the house and asks Homer to come over, he asks Marge's permission before agreeing. At her trailer, the singer says that one of the reasons she trusts him so much is that no other man in her life has been nice to her without wanting something in return. Homer does not understand what she is saying, but he agrees to become her manager. She takes him to a store called the "Corpulent Cowboy," where she outfits him in a white-fringed jacket, bolo tie, and Stetson.

Homer, who now calls himself Colonel Homer, returns home after midnight to find a furious Marge, who again wants to know if he is having an affair with Lurleen. Her husband denies it, but admits that he let the singer kiss him several times. Marge says she doesn't want Homer to be Lurleen's manager, something he says is his boyhood dream. He is determined to make her a star. Marge fumes and Homer leaves. But the entire Simpson family now becomes involved in the star-making machinery and, to his wife's chagrin, Homer invests their life savings in the effort. At the recording studio, Marge meets Lurleen for the first time and doesn't like what she sees, starting with the kiss the singer gives her husband and the fact that she is not, as Homer told her, overweight. Lisa accompanies Lurleen on the recording of another love song, "Bagged Me a Homer," but the session is disrupted by the sound of Marge grinding her teeth. The new song is a hit, and the Simpson children become totally involved in Lurleen's burgeoning career by packaging the CDs. At the same time, they are not oblivious to the darker side of success. Lisa says that she never thought she'd see another woman in her dad's life; Bart disagrees, citing Betty Crocker, Sara Lee, and Aunt Jemima.

When Homer arranges a television appearance for Lurleen, she suggests a new song she has written that might "heat things up," called "Bunk with Me Tonight." The lyrics constitute a direct, almost explicit invitation to Homer. Nonetheless, it takes a second run-through before Homer understands what is being offered. He declines the offer and returns home, where the crisis has not passed. Marge tells her sister that she is in a no-win situation and doesn't know whom to root for. If Lurleen's career fails, the family is broke; if the singer succeeds, Marge loses her husband. The climactic event is Lurleen's television appearance. As the Simpsons prepare, Marge says, "You've got a wonderful family, Homer. Please don't forget it when you walk out that door tonight."

In the singer's dressing room, Lurleen makes one more attempt. She locks and bolts the door and kisses Homer, asking if there is anything he needs. At this moment, he tells her, he sees his entire sex life flashing before his eyes—a series of slaps and rebuffs until he meets Marge. He tells Lurleen that all he wanted to do was to share her voice with others and that he has accomplished that. Homer knows what his priorities are: "I'd better get out of here before I lose my family." Just to make sure he knows what he is giving up, he sticks his head back in the room and asks the singer if she was offering to go "all the way" with him, and she nods. Homer sells Lurleen's management contract to a Japanese company for fifty dollars and heads home. Marge is in the bedroom, naked beneath the covers, watching Lurleen's show on television. Homer, abashed, asks his wife if there is room in their bed for a "gad-durned fool." There always has been, she replies as he undresses. Lurleen sings another song for Homer, "Stand by Your Manager," with the last line, "I hope Marge knows how lucky she is." Marge says that she does, and Homer throws his hat onto the camera, turning the screen black. The marriage is preserved and Homer's fragile self-image is restored. If only life were always that simple.

Many adulterous affairs begin at the workplace, experts say. Factors such as the familiarity of day-to-day contact, a sense of common purpose, and business trips can offer a multitude of opportunities for a partner to stray. All of these factors are present in "The Last Temptation of Homer." There is a vacancy in the safety section of the Springfield Nuclear Power Plant, and the Labor Department tells Mr. Burns that it is time to hire the plant's first female employee. This sets up a situation that has been of great concern to stay-at-home wives like Marge Simpson who believe that women in the work place—especially in high-stress, blue-collar jobs like policework, firefighting, and the military—can pose a threat to marriage. Can men and women be coworkers and avoid romantic entanglements?

In typical fashion, the candidate selected for the job at the nuclear power plant is overqualified: Mindy Simmons has an engineering degree and is assigned to work with Homer, who barely finished high school. She is also attractive, and the moment the introduction is made, Homer has a vision of Mindy naked on a clamshell, à la Botticelli's *The Birth of Venus*, a hallucination accompanied by swelling violin music and hovering cupids. Wisely recognizing trouble in the making, he flees his new colleague. After work, Homer notices Mindy leaving on her motorcycle and he is pleased to note that he is not reacting the same way he did when he met her—no visions or goose bumps. After driving off, Homer assumes that his earlier reaction was just a fluke, but his relief is short-lived. He is actually driving in reverse and crashes into a trout hatchery. In the vision that follows, the fish are dancing in a chorus line, singing "Homer loves Mindy! Homer loves Mindy!"

Troubled by his feelings, Homer turns to his favorite source for advice and counseling: Moe's Tavern. He confesses his attraction to Mindy to his friends. They suggest it is infatuation based on physical attraction and that the best way to deflate it is to speak with Mindy and find that they have nothing in common. This strategy backfires. At work the next day, Homer learns that he and Mindy have a lot in common, including an appetite for donuts, watching television, and napping on the job before lunch. "Foul temptress," he thinks, implying that she has cultivated these interests knowing they are identical to his own. Yet he continues to resist, avoiding her for the rest of the day. As he congratulates himself for this victory, he steps into an elevator where he is crammed in with the woman. He does his best to overcome the situation, commanding himself to think unsexy thoughts: Marge's unattractive sisters shaving their legs and his friend Barney, an overweight barfly, in a thong bikini. Failing again, Homer pushes the emergency stop button, forces the door open, and steps out into thin air.

Back at home, he tries to fortify himself by reminding himself of the benefits of a loving family. Alas, the realities of domestic life conspire against him as well. Marge has a cold and the household is in chaos. She gives him a present she has picked up for him at the mall: a tee-shirt of her face, which has come out wrong and makes her look like a grotesque harridan. While watching television together, the couple is bombarded by news and entertainment programming that is a constant stream of debased sexuality and double entendres, sending Homer screaming from the room.

Homer's desperation is deepening. He wants to do the right thing or, more properly, not do the wrong thing. As a last resort, he goes to a phone booth and calls the church's marriage counseling hotline. Confessing his attraction for another woman, he finds the voice at the other end of the "anonymous" line is his neighbor Ned, who immediately recognizes him and suggests a conference call with Marge. (He might have been better off calling Dr. Laura.) In a panic to escape the call and confrontation, he tips over the phone booth and knocks himself out. Unconscious, he has a vision of a guardian angel who, in a play on the movie classic "It's a Wonderful Life," shows him how his life would be if he was married to Mindy instead of Marge. Homer sees that he would be living in a mansion with a butler, happily playing tennis with his coworkers, while Marge—shorn of her inept spouse—would be in the White House. The guardian angel admits the dream is not having the desired effect and drops Homer back to consciousness on the sidewalk.

Clearly, Homer is losing the battle. He is uncharacteristically chipper as he prepares for work, using deodorant all over his body and singing

Barry Manilow's song "Mandy" as "Mindy." Lisa is curious and doesn't take too long to analyze the situation. "Judging from your song, you're infatuated with a woman named Mindy," she says, despite his denial. The encounter with his daughter has an effect, though. Again Homer resolves to distance himself from Mindy because of their "uncontrollable attraction." The breakup speech he had prepared, written on his hand, dissolves into sweat and gibberish. As Homer tries to make himself understood, the exchange is observed by Mr. Burns on a security camera. The plant owner assumes that what he is watching is an example of friendship and teamwork on the job, so he decides to send the pair to an energy convention in Capital City to represent the company. "This is the worst crisis my marriage has ever faced!" Homer exclaims after being told of the honor.

He is not exaggerating. Homer and Mindy are put up in adjoining rooms at the convention. A lascivious bellboy points out the king-sized bed and its possibilities to Homer. "Stop that!" he cries. "I love my wife and family." Mindy is no help. "If it weren't for this wall," she says, "we'd be sleeping in the same bed." When Mindy says she has "a really wicked idea," Homer assumes the obvious and tells her "we have to fight our temptation." She assures him that her idea is to call room service for dinner, which they do. Sitting on Homer's bed, they work on a chili dog from opposite ends and meet in a kiss. Homer recoils and pops his shirt buttons, revealing the tee-shirt with Marge's fearsome visage. He thinks he hears Marge growling and flees the room, only to find the noise is coming from a floor waxer in the hall.

The next day Homer and Mindy are at the nuclear plant's booth, trading insults with outraged convention delegates who accuse them of poisoning the planet and creating another Chernobyl. Tension between the two has dissipated and Homer begins to congratulate himself, which sets up the announcement that they have been crowned King and Queen of Energy, winning a romantic dinner for two at "the sexiest Chinese restaurant in Capital City." The fortune cookie after their cheeseburgers seems to tip the balance. "You will find happiness with a new love," it reads, which Homer interprets as a prediction he will have sex with Mindy. "What's the point?" he asks. "You can't fight fate." (A scene in the back of the restaurant reveals that the fortune was just bad luck. The barrel with the "Stick with your wife" fortune cookies was not used.)

At the hotel, Mindy invites herself into Homer's room, where they sit on the bed again. Homer is overcome and begins to sob, but Mindy reassures him that he doesn't have to do anything he doesn't want to. That, of course, is the moral dilemma. Homer says that he may want to, but then he thinks about his wife and his family. Mindy tells him she understands and urges him to "look into your heart. I think you'll see what you want." They kiss, but only briefly. The next scene shows Homer in the hotel bedroom, Barry White's "Can't Get Enough of Your Love" playing in the background, with the outline of a naked woman who is revealed to be—Marge. He called her to join him, which she has done with enthusiasm.

Marge, the Simpson family's strongest believer, is "my candidate for sainthood," says Kenneth Briggs. "She is the model saint. She lives in the real world, she lives with crises, with flawed people. She forgives and she makes her own mistakes. She's a forgiving, loving person. She is absolutely saintly." Her idea of cursing is that a local prison is a "gosh-darned heck hole." Yet even saints are not immune from the temptation to fall into sin. In the same episode, Marge lies to help a prison inmate, only to have the sociopath reproach her for it. "The Lord will forgive me if it means giving you a second chance," she says, ensuring that her misguided effort at rehabilitation will end in disaster, which it does.

In another episode, Homer forgets Marge's birthday and then compounds the oversight by rushing out to buy her a belated and particularly inappropriate present: a bowling ball drilled to fit *his* fingers, with *his* name inscribed—which he accidentally drops onto her birthday cake. Marge's sisters, Patty and Selma, who have joined the family celebration at a restaurant, suggest she dump her thoughtless oaf of a husband. They remind her that the age of thirty-four is "time enough to start over with a new man." Marge is as crushed by the birthday gift as her cake. When Homer asks how she likes his gift, she screams that it is hard for her to judge since she's never bowled in her life. Her husband says that if she doesn't like it she knows someone who would. That night in bed Marge dismisses Homer's feeble attempts to explain his choice, informing him that she accepts his gift and intends to use it.

At Barney's Bowl-a-rama, she makes an inept effort to get started, brushing aside an attendant's offer of help by explaining that she is just there out of spite. However, she attracts the attention of the bowling alley's sleazy pro, Jacques, who introduces himself and begins to explain the game. He also starts coming on to her, caressing her hands and proffering compliments. Her fingers, Jacques says, are too tender and feminine for the ball she is using. She requires something lighter, more delicate for her tapered fingers. He offers her the use of his own ball rather than the one with the name "Homer" inscribed on it, but she declines. "Many people have senseless attachments to heavy clumsy things such as this Homer of yours," he says. The gift bowling ball is about to become the engine of domestic destruction. Marge accepts Jacques' offer of bowling lessons at a reduced rate, and soon she is bowling strikes. She says he is a good teacher, and he replies, oozing charm, that he is indeed a very good teacher and that "I can teach you everything."

At the Simpson home, Homer is taking up the slack created by Marge's time at the bowling alley. Dinner is usually take-out, but he is still exhausted by the nighttime routine of child care and is shocked when his wife tells him she will be going back to the bowling alley for lessons. This was not part of Homer's plan. Jacques continues his practiced campaign for the affection of a neglected wife by giving Marge a bowling glove that is her size, with her name on it. In marked contrast to her husband's gift, it is meant for her and her alone, and she is thrilled. His lessons become increasingly personal, with much touching and many compliments. "Marge, do you know how beautiful you look in the moonlight?" he asks as he drops her off at home. But I am married, she says. "My mind says stop," Jacques says, "but my heart—and my hips—say proceed." He invites her to meet him away from the bowling alley for brunch, a concept he has to explain to the unsophisticated Marge. At first she says no, then agrees.

Moments later, inside the house, Homer senses that something is wrong, although he isn't certain what it is. They sleep apart from one another on the bed. Lisa, as always, is the first to zero in on the problem. Bart notices that their mom is preparing vastly improved lunches to take to school. This is not a good sign, his sister informs him. It is, she explains, "what the psychologists call overcompensation. Mom is wracked with guilt because her marriage is failing." This is something that happens in homes where the parents no longer love and cherish each other, says Lisa, and there are separate and distinct stages that children in such homes go through. She is in stage three: fear. Bart, lagging a bit, is in stage two: denial.

Jacques takes Marge to brunch at a Cajun restaurant and offers her a mimosa—the name of what is for her an exotic drink—which she mistakes for a pass until he explains what it is. As one might expect, Marge is spotted by Helen Lovejoy, the minister's wife. She explains that she noticed Marge having brunch "with a man who isn't her husband" and had to come over and say hello. Marge stammers, but Helen assures her that she doesn't have to squirm on her account and tells her she will see her at church on Sunday. Jacques launches more compliments, saying her laughter is like music to him, before making his play. He invites her to meet him at his apartment the next day, "away from prying eyes, away from the Helens of this world." The offer is unmistakable.

Marge, the faithful wife and believing Christian, faints. She dreams what the meeeting might bring. It is a rosy vision: she in a ball gown and

Jacques in a tuxedo. They dance through the lavishly furnished apartment at Fiesta Terrace. She notices a glass cabinet filled with trophies she takes to be for bowling; he informs her they are for lovemaking. They sip champagne at the bar and engage in witty and soulful repartee. At this point, Jacques revives her. If this is what adultery will be like, she decides, she is game. She asks if the following Thursday will be all right for the assignation.

The Simpson family is not unaware of what is going on. Homer discovers the bowling glove and is disconsolate, returning it to the dresser and sitting forlornly on the couple's bed. Asked by Bart to toss around a baseball, he says, "Son, I don't know if I can lift my head, let alone a ball." The boy is concerned enough to turn to Lisa, admitting she is right about their parents' marriage, but she says she cannot help because she is mired in stage five: self-pity. Thursday morning arrives and Homer cannot think of what to do to rescue his relationship. As Marge makes sandwiches, her husband tries to reach for her hand, only to grab his lunchbox. Instead, he compliments her on the way she makes peanut butter and jelly sandwiches—the best the inarticulate man can do. As he leaves the kitchen he says, "Good-bye, my wife." Later in the day, at the plant, he sits staring at his lunch, unable to eat, a sure sign of a major crisis.

While driving to Jacques' apartment, Marge sees the spectrum of married life: a wedding, a couple walking with a baby carriage, a family on a picnic, an old couple walking hand in hand and, finally, two gravestones side by side. She comes to a fork in the road, one direction heading to the nuclear power plant, where her husband works; the other to Fiesta Terrace, where her would-be lover is waiting. Marge heads toward Jacques' apartment, then pulls over to the side and turns around. The closing scene is a takeoff on the movie *An Officer and a Gentleman.* Marge walks into the plant and up to Homer, who is completely surprised. She dons a hard hat and he carries her out, to the applause of his coworkers, telling them proudly, "I'm going to the backseat of my car with the woman I love, and I won't be back for ten minutes!"

These three temptations of adultery, though exaggerated to be sure, nevertheless together embody familiar situations that provoke infidelity in the noncartoon world. In each case, the sanctity of the marriage vow is tested fundamentally—and preserved. Another victory for traditional family values.

Eight

The Bible: "I Think It May Be Somewhere toward the Back"

A survey released in late 2000 reported that 86 percent of respondents believed the Bible is relevant in today's world. A slightly smaller majority, 80 percent, said that the Bible could address most of today's problems, although the same percentage felt that the language of the Bible could be confusing. All of these findings are mirrored in *The Simpsons*. Like Ned Flanders, who owns multiple translations, over half the adults surveyed by Zondervan Publishing said they trusted the Bible to get facts correct more than a history book or the local newspaper.[1]

As a child on a Boy Scout trip, *Simpsons'* creator Matt Groening stole a Gideon Bible from a motel and underlined the "dirty" parts, he told an interviewer for *My Generation* magazine in 2001. "Plus, there's lots of stuff that's just weird. For instance, there's a parable about Jesus driving demons into a herd of pigs, and the pigs jump off a cliff. I wanted to know what the pigs did to deserve that."

Characters in Groening's series bring their own widely divergent views of faith and religion to their readings of the Bible, and do not hesitate to use it for their own purposes. The "Rainbow Man," a zealot in a rainbow-colored wig who popped up at various televised sporting events during the 1990s carrying a sign reading "John 3:16," appears in various crowd scenes on the show. Trying to look innocent after doing mischief, Bart pretends to read the Bible—upside down. The show's writers freely mix accurately quoted passages with those they make up, including plausible-sounding gibberish. "And so when Eliphaz came down from Mount Hebron bearing figs, he offered them to Mohem, who you will remember is the father of Sheckhom," Reverend Lovejoy reads, "and to Hazare on the occasion of their matrimony." In *The Simpsons' Guide to Springfield*, the minister quotes from "somewhere in the Bible," possibly "First Thessaleezians," that "blessed is a man who perseveres until trial."[2]

At Sunday services, Lovejoy has a predilection for misinterpretation and choosing inappropriate selections, especially bloodthirsty passages that he claims are from the Old Testament ("With flaming swords the Aramites did pierce the eyes of their fellow men, and did feast on what flowed forth") and meaningless recitations of genealogy. He advises Seymour Skinner, the elementary school principal who has come to him for advice, to read the Bible, but when the preacher is asked what part to consult for guidance, he answers, "It's all pretty good."

However, the advice Lovejoy gives Ned—who is concerned that he has offended his neighbor Homer—from Proverbs 15:1, proves appropriate and effective: "A gentle answer turneth away wrath." On a deeper level, though, the minister has an exceptionally dark view of the Bible's essence, favoring dire, Old Testament judgment to the love, charity, and forgiveness of the New Testament. "Have you read this thing lately?" he asks Marge, holding the Bible. "Everything's a sin. Technically, you can't go to the bathroom."

Lovejoy often relies on biblical citation to support his arguments. When Homer decides to stop going to church, he quotes Matthew 7:26 about the foolish man who built his house on sand. However, the minister can be a little shifty if someone quotes a verse that undermines his own views. After condemning Bart (prematurely and unjustly, as it turns out) for stealing from the collection plate, the minister is brought up short when Lisa repeats one of her favorites, Matthew 7:1: "Judge not, lest ye be judged." The verse might be in the Bible, Lovejoy acknowledges, but if so it is "somewhere towards the back," implying that is has less divine authority. On another occasion, Lisa challenges Springfield's annual "Whacking Day," when residents beat snakes to death. Lovejoy tells her the festival has biblical roots, pretending to read: "And the Lord said, Whack ye all the serpents which crawl on their bellies and thy town will be a beacon unto others," he says. "So you see, Lisa, even God himself endorses whacking." When the girl asks to see where in the Bible it says that, the preacher refuses to show her.

Homer is extremely hazy on many of the particulars of the Bible: He thinks Goliath defeated David and that the story of Hercules and the lion is from scripture. His inattention, leading to misunderstanding, is monumental: He believes God "teased" Moses in the desert, until Marge explains that God actually "tested" the leader. Pressed for a Bible verse to avert a spider's curse, Homer draws a blank, getting no further than "Thou shalt not. . . ." Like Lovejoy, he spouts garbled scripture. As an involuntary missionary in the South Pacific, he introduces Judeo-Christian faith to the natives by reading this selection from the book of Psalms: "God will shatter the heads of His enemies. The hairy crown of those who walk in their guilty ways that you may bathe your feet in their blood." The incomprehensible passage, he says solemnly to the bewildered congregation as he closes the Bible, is "as true today as it was when it was written." Also like Lovejoy, Homer uses the Bible when and how it suits him, justifying gambling on sports to Lisa by telling her that it is permitted in the Bible—"somewhere in the back." When Otto, the stoned school-bus driver, becomes homeless, he is invited by Bart to move into the garage, to his father's chagrin. "I know we didn't ask for this, Homer," says Marge, "but doesn't the Bible say, 'Whatsover you do to the least of my brothers, that you do unto me'?" Yes, Homer replies, "but doesn't the Bible also say, 'Thou shalt not take moochers into thy hut?'" Marge's verse is from Matthew 25:40; Homer's is from his imagination.

To Bart, Homer cites equally spurious biblical authority for afflicting former president George H. W. Bush, who has moved to Springfield, with a plague of locusts. "It's all in the Bible, son. It's the prankster's Bible." Introducing a segment of a Halloween fantasy episode, he claims to be swearing on a Bible—until Marge points out that it is actually a book of carpet samples. Homer tells Lisa, who wants to play ice hockey on a boys' team, that she is going against the Word: "If the Bible has taught us nothing else—and it hasn't—it's that girls should stick to girls' sports, such as hot oil wrestling, foxy boxing. . . ." With Bart, he uses the Good Book as a prop in an attempt to convince Flanders that his wife ordered a gold-embossed Bible before her death, a disgraceful but venerable American con. But Homer recognizes the importance of scripture when it counts. The last thing he does when he thinks he is going to die from eating a poisoned blowfish is to turn to the Bible—in this case a recorded version read by Larry King.

The most detailed representation of the Bible in *The Simpsons* came in the spring of 1999 in an episode titled "Simpson Bible Stories." It is a sweltering Easter Sunday morning, and the Simpsons have gathered at the First Church of Springfield. In the pulpit, Reverend Lovejoy makes no reference to Jesus, crucifixion, or resurrection. (The school chalkboard segment at the start of this episode has Bart writing, "I cannot absolve sins," one of the few clear references to Christianity's most important holiday.) Instead, the minister announces that on this day his congregation is in need of "a hefty dose of the Good Book."

When Ned Flanders calls out from the pew that the noise of the fans are making it difficult to hear, the minister's solution is to switch them off, plunging the congregation into dreamy somnolence. Lovejoy begins his sermon with the book of Genesis, and as he does, the Simpsons nod off and begin to dream, each in turn. In their biblical dreams, family members and their friends assume roles in much the same way as characters do in the movie version of *The Wizard of Oz*. Theologically, the Simpsons' visions are to scripture what "Fractured Fairy Tales" on the *Rocky and Bullwinkle Show* were to the Brothers Grimm. Creator Matt Groening was especially proud of the episode, calling it "our *Prince of Egypt*," although it is anything but DreamWorks' elegant, reverent retelling of Moses and the exodus. Periods and characters from different books of the Bible appear out of chronological order, and events are turned upside down for comic effect. Groening joked before "Simpson Bible Stories" aired that the reason it was written was that executive producer Mike Scully told him the show hadn't been getting enough angry letters.

Genesis. Marge dreams first, of the Garden of Eden. She is Eve, Homer is Adam, and, naturally, Ned Flanders provides God's deep, booming voice, speaking from a cloud. Everything is idyllic: There is no pain or want, the lion lies down with the lamb, and a vivid rainbow hangs in the sky. Even pork, ripped from a willing pig, is kosher. It is "almost like paradise," Marge tells Homer. In additional to his voice, God makes his presence known with a strong right arm, wearing Flanders's signature sweater, and a hand with four fingers. Homer and Marge, wearing fig leaves, fall to their knees whenever they hear the voice from heaven. "You're too kind and wise and righteous," Homer says. Warned that all things are permitted to eat, except for the sparkling tree of knowledge, Homer naturally tries to work the angle to his advantage. He says that such temptation would be easier to resist if he could have a few extra wives.

The couple is then importuned by the serpent, who sounds like Otto the school-bus driver, tempting them to sample "God's private stash." In this version, however, it is Homer's Adam—not Marge's Eve—who is the first to succumb to temptation. "They said it was forbidden," Marge says. "Please stop eating that. God's going to be furious." Homer, his eyes newly opened by knowledge, replies that she is "pretty uptight for a naked chick." She reflects that "it *is* a sin to waste food" and joins him.

Thunder follows, as Marge predicted, and God wants to know if anyone has tasted the forbidden fruit. Homer implicates Marge, who admits that she has. She is expelled from the garden, pleading in vain for Homer to say something in her defense. The world outside Eden is a terrible place, she soon learns, now wearing a dress. Asked by Homer, who is still in the garden, what she is doing, she says, "Toiling—what does it look like?"

Guilt-stricken by his betrayal, Homer decides to sneak Marge back in, believing that "God can't be everywhere at once, right?" He enlists a unicorn to dig a tunnel and, just as Marge rejoins him, they are discovered. God appears again, and again the couple falls to their knees. Wrong again. "This is how you repay me?" the Lord asks, even more angry this time, seeing the last unicorn expire. Homer asks that God not do anything rash and makes a feeble attempt at proto-Christian theology in their defense. He asks, "God is love, right?" but he is in the wrong testament. The couple is expelled, this time for good, to a world of pain and want and misery. But it is also a world of hope and optimism. "I'm sure God will let us return soon," says Marge, with no grasp of the concept of original sin and its durability. "How long can he hold a grudge?"

Exodus. Lisa dreams of the Egyptian captivity, where she is the woman behind Moses, who appears in the person of Bart's friend Milhouse. The Israelite slaves are all children who, when not building the pyramids, jump rope while reciting the genealogy of the patriarchs. Bart, naturally, is a troublemaking slave who infuriates Pharaoh with irreverent graffiti. When Pharaoh, played by Principal Skinner, threatens to slay all the first-born—again—until he finds out who is responsible, Bart is denounced by the burning bush. Making a rare appearance without her signature pearls, Lisa urges Milhouse to tell Pharaoh to let their people go. Pharaoh refuses and is afflicted with a series of plagues. But the frogs the children dump on the Egyptian leader are purchased at the market and do not come from God. Pharaoh finds the amphibians tasty, taking the plague as a message from the sun-god above: "Ra has rewarded my cruelty to the slaves." Lisa tries to explain the subtleties of the divine plan to dim-witted Pharaoh: "It's a plague, you moron!"

Milhouse finally rouses the slaves, telling them their time has come, and urges them to follow him to freedom. At last they are permitted to leave but are then pursued by Egyptian chariots to the shore of the Red Sea. Here, Moses wavers in his faith. "Screw this," he proclaims, falling to his knees and bowing to the sun. "I'm converting. Save us, O mighty Ra!" Lisa bucks him up and he parts the sea, enabling the Israelites to cross to safety. "It's a miracle!" he says, clearly astonished, and drawing the wrong conclusion. "I'm a genius!" he cries. On the other side, Moses asks Lisa what's ahead—a land of milk and honey? After consulting a Torah scroll, she tells him it's forty years of wandering in the desert.

Kings. Lovejoy announces that the next reading will be from the book of Kings, about King Solomon, whose wisdom was "like a drill, boring into the rock of injustice." On the word "boring," Homer dreams that he is King Solomon, judging disputes among the people in a *People's Court* setting. His coworkers from the nuclear power plant, Lenny and Carl, appear as ancient Israelites who dispute the ownership of a pie. The incident is a variation of 1 Kings 3, in which two women claim they are the mother of the same baby. King Solomon orders the infant cut in two and divided between the two claimants. The true mother is revealed when she pleads not to slay the child, and instead to turn it over to the other woman. This time, Homer orders the pie in dispute to be divided and the two disputing claimants slain. Then he eats both halves of the pie.

Samuel. Bart imagines himself as King David, living in Jerusalem in 970 B.C. (although the walled city's appearance seems more like the first century A.D.). It is an action movie sequel to 1 Samuel 17, when as a young man the future king kills Goliath, the Philistine's gigantic champion, with a sling. Years later, King Bart has become an arrogant, sybaritic monarch. He is challenged by Goliath's son, who is played by the bully Nelson Muntz. At first, Bart confuses the giant with Samson, cutting his hair to no effect. "I hope this doesn't get into the Bible," he says. This time around the giant bests Israel's greatest king, knocking him into the next country and seizing the crown. A shepherd recognizes the deposed warrior king and tells him, "I love you 'cause you kill people."

"Goliath II is gonna pay," Bart vows, "and this time, it's biblical." Improbably, the insurgent monarch learns that Goliath II is responsible for the deaths of Jonah and Methuselah, enraging him. Bart climbs the tower of Babel, where Nelson is hiding, and brings the giant down, only to learn that during his exile the Philistine had become a wise king beloved by his Israelite subjects, was known as "Goliath the Consensus Builder," and had constructed roads, hospitals, and libraries. Bart is jailed.

Revelation. The family awakes in church after the service, only to find themselves alone in the pews. It's not the end of the world, Homer says, as they walk out the door. But it is. They appear to have walked into the end of the world. The heavens are raining brimstone and the world is ablaze. The four horsemen of the Apocalypse ride across the fiery sky. Marge realizes what is happening as pure Christian spirits, such as those of their neighbors the Flanderses, kneeling together in prayer, are ascending to the sky. The Simpsons remain firmly earthbound and Marge wonders why they aren't rising to heaven. "Oh right, the sins," she says. Lisa recognizes that the rapture is taking place, and regrets that she has never known true, earthly love. She begins to rise, only to be yanked back by Homer. "Where do you think you're going, young lady?" he asks. This family started together and it will finish together.

The ground near them opens with a ramp to a fiery pit, and the Simpsons descend. At first, Homer is unabashed, saying that he smells barbecue. Then he learns the horrible truth about hell: "They're out of hot dogs, the cole slaw has pineapple, and it's German potato salad!" The closing credits role as the heavy metal rock group AC/DC sings "Highway to Hell."

Much of the reporting I have done about the Bible has involved the issue of inerrancy—the literal, word-for-word truth of scripture. In a classic example of what political scientists call a "wedge issue," conservative Southern Baptists were able to use this theological debate two decades ago to help leverage control of the nation's largest Protestant denomination. My sense is that this debate over the biblical truth of the "Good Book" is largely beside the point to most believing Christians and Jews, who tend to agree that it is divinely inspired and, at the least, a source of practical wisdom and moral instruction. They are more concerned with what is in the book than the manner in which it was transmitted to the world. Like the characters on *The Simpsons*, they return to the Bible for support and sustenance, justification and inspiration. For, as Homer says, it is "as true today as when it was written."

Nine

Catholics: "That's Catholic, Marge . . . Voodoo"

From almost the outset of *The Simpsons*, former education secretary William Bennett had a clear idea of what he was up against and how to deal with it. In the midst of his public flap with the show, he said that there was nothing wrong with Bart "that a Catholic school, a paper route and a couple of soap sandwiches wouldn't straighten out."[1] Is Bart's time at the chalkboard at the beginning of each episode a form of confession or penitence or both? Unlike Bennett, Mark Fischer, an instructor at St. John's Catholic Seminary in Camarillo, California, allowed his two sons to watch the show, although he too had concerns about Bart's behavior. Fischer said he paid closer attention to Homer. "Catholics would say his sins are venial, rather than mortal," he told the *Ventura County Star* in 1999. "He willfully does wrong, but never rejects God or the idea of divine justice. He's simply weak."[2]

Of all the controversies the series has ignited over religion and values, the most serious was with its portrayal of Catholics and the Church of Rome. It was also one of the few cases where Fox Television made the otherwise free-spirited show back down and censor itself—to loud complaints from the executive producer, Mike Scully. The way Catholicism is represented in *The Simpsons* is complicated and subtle, like much of the show's humor, but it has an undeniably hostile, sometimes gratuitous edge to it. At times, the tension between writers and producers and the denomination has assumed some aspects of an intimate, deep-seated family feud. Scully, for example, has described himself as a "lapsed Catholic." Another executive producer and writer, George Meyer, has had an enormous influence on shaping the series over the years, by all accounts second only to the show's three creators. Meyer has also had a problematic history with the Catholic Church. He told an interviewer in the *New Yorker* that as a child he struggled with his parents' strong religious beliefs.

Animus like this has popped up in different forms in the series. Moe the bartender is heard taking a bet over the phone from someone he addresses

102

as "your eminence." Smithers, Mr. Burns's sycophantic assistant at the nuclear power plant, is seen in a confessional. Springfield's most prominent Catholic is Mayor Joe Quimby, a crook, a lush, and a womanizer whose build and accent remind many viewers of Teddy Kennedy. Holy water and its mystical power provide a running gag. Two violent, cartoon-in-a-cartoon characters, Itchy and Scratchy, appear to be reciting a prayer in Latin. At the beach, Ned Flanders is concerned that his son's sand castle looks too much like a Catholic cathedral.

Sometimes these shots come in the form of casual Protestant bigotry. Marge, fearful that Grandpa Abe Simpson is about to die because of a failing kidney, asks Reverend Lovejoy to anoint her father-in-law, to administer what was once called the Last Rites or Extreme Unction, now simply referred to as Anointing. "That's Catholic, Marge," the minister replies dismissively. "You might as well ask me to do a voodoo dance." In an issue of *The Simpsons* comics, Lovejoy is hypnotized by a local thug, who orders him to take the collection money and gamble at an Indian reservation casino—while dressed in a nun's habit. Driving home from church one Sunday, Bart is ravenous with hunger. He asks his mother if the family can become Catholic, "so we can get Communion wafers and booze." Rather than correct her son's caricature of the denomination, Marge compounds it by equating the Vatican with its opposition to birth control. "No one is going Catholic," she says. "Three children is enough, thank you."

Marge's joke, which aired in November 1998, attracted the ire of a New York–based group called the Catholic League for Religious and Civil Rights, headed by William Donohue. Founded in 1973, the organization's goal is to defend the rights of Catholics "to participate in American public life without defamation or discrimination." Patterned after the NAACP and the Anti-Defamation League, the Catholic League is donor supported and nonpartisan, but its board is dominated by conservative activists and intellectuals such as Bennett and Dinesh D'Souza.

The Catholic League is best known for attacking the portrayal of Catholics in various media in recent years, in particular the television shows *Nothing Sacred* and *Ally McBeal*, the movie *Dogma*, and the "Sensations" art exhibit at the Brooklyn Museum of Art. Donohue has charged that these representations are part of a modern wave of Catholic bashing. It is unclear how many of the nation's sixty million Catholics the organization actually represents; it takes out large newspaper ads in major cities to voice its objections, but its individual demonstrations and letter-writing campaigns have never numbered more than five hundred supporters, according to critics. Nonetheless, these efforts were lauded by the late

Cardinal John O'Connor of New York. He said the League played an "indispensable role in defending the rights of Catholics" when "they are unfairly attacked, or the Church is unfairly maligned."[3] There has been a backlash to the League's activities, however, which the organization acknowledges. "We are accused of advocating censorship when all we want to do is eliminate the censorious power of political correctness," according to its statement of purpose. "We are not trying to impose Catholic values on our society to promote Christian ends."[4]

Donohue wrote to Fox regarding the interchange between Marge and Bart, asking, "Can you possibly explain why this dialogue was included in the show?" At first, his complaint seemed to go nowhere with the network. He received a lengthy reply from Thomas Chavez, manager for broadcast standards and practices, which seemed like a polite brush-off. The letter, reprinted in the League's newsletter, *The Catalyst*, read in part:

> In your letter you questioned an exchange in dialogue between Bart and his mother, Marge. Because Bart is starving, he suggests they convert to Catholicism since he is aware communion wafers and wine are dispensed in the Catholic ceremony. Just like other children that are not knowledgeable, Bart sees the wafer merely as food and wine as a forbidden drink. Because many families wait to eat until after they have attended church, it is not atypical that a child would pose a question such as this unknowingly. The writers chose not to have Marge respond to Bart's ridiculous desire to satisfy his hunger with the Sacrament but rather, elected to have Marge respond by stating why she would not be comfortable converting to Catholicism. Her views regarding birth control are obviously contrary to the Catholic Church's belief. While Marge's response may be perceived as short and curt, it also conveys the impression that one's choice of religion is based on more than the religion's rituals.[5]

The League was not persuaded by this response, commenting sarcastically in its newsletter, "Now why didn't we think of that? Just goes to show how thoughtful the Hollywood gang really is."[6]

On January 31, 1999, *The Simpsons* aired an episode that coincided with the Super Bowl, which had been broadcast earlier that evening on Fox. A short segment in the show spoofed both the innovative—but sometimes obscure—commercials aired during the football game and the advertising campaigns by different groups within the Catholic Church to show that the denomination has changed with the times. The "commercial" was based on an old music video showcasing the raucous Texas rock band ZZ

Top, a group known for its beards, dark glasses, and black attire. A car pulls into a windblown gas station in the middle of nowhere. The driver gets out and, seeing no one, honks the horn for service. Out of the station file three buxom, scantily clad young women to provide "service." One lifts the hood suggestively while another slides the gas pump nozzle into the tank in an image too obvious to ignore, but the driver's eyes are riveted to a shiny cross dangling from one woman's quivering cleavage as the rock music soars. What is this all about? The voice-over explains: "The Catholic Church: We've made a few . . . changes." Watching the commercial at home with her mother, Lisa pronounces it "weird."

The Catholic League preferred to call it offensive and complained again to Fox, saying it was the last straw. "We wrote to Mr. Chavez again," the League informed members in the next newsletter, which made the incident its cover story. "We also told him that he'd be hearing from you. So don't disappoint us."[7] The letters evidently poured in and provoked a response at *The Simpsons*. "The joke was an observation on crazy Super Bowl commercials, not a comment on the Catholic Church," Scully told Howard Rosenberg, television critic of the *Los Angeles Times*. "We had the idea for the content of the commercial first. Then we pitched several tag lines. One of the writers pitched the Catholic Church line, and it got the biggest laugh."[8] Obviously, the League didn't see it that way. "We got a couple of hundred letters, and it was very obvious from reading a majority of them that [the Catholic letter writers] had not seen the show. Some of them were from third-graders, all saying the same thing: 'Please don't make fun of my religion.' Which we all know third-graders are very adamant about."[9]

Ordinarily, that would have been the end of the matter for *The Simpsons*. After all, they've drawn protests before and simply ignored them. This time, however, the show was in for an unpleasant surprise. Several months later, the Catholic League contacted Fox again and specifically asked that the word "Catholic" be excised from the voice-over when the episode repeated in September 1999 on the network, as well as in its subsequent syndicated airings. The network agreed, and Roland McFarland, Fox's vice president of broadcast standards, ordered Scully to make the one-word cut or to eliminate all reference to religion. When Scully refused, McFarland offered another solution: Replace the protesting denomination with a Protestant substitute—Methodists, Presbyterians, or Baptists. Scully asked the executive, "What would be the difference changing it to another religion, and wouldn't that just be offending a different group of people?" McFarland explained that "Fox had already had trouble with the Catholics earlier this season," Scully told the *Times*. Given the previous decade's experience—and freedom of expression—Scully was perplexed. "People can say hurtful things to each other about their weight, their race, their intelligence, their sexual preference, and that all seems up for grabs," he said. "But when you get into religion, some people get very nervous."[10]

Rosenberg, no fan of the League's earlier efforts (he called the campaign against *Nothing Sacred* a "fanatical crusade" that "helped drive that achingly noble ABC series off the air"), asked if Fox's actions on *The Simpsons* did not imply that there are "different standards for different religions."[11]

Not surprisingly, the League saw it differently:

> Consider this: All along, we have been told by Fox that none of our complaints were valid because none of the material was truly offensive. But now we have a Fox executive producer disingenuously giving away his hand by protesting why it should be okay to offend another group of people with the same material he initially said wasn't offensive to Catholics! And isn't it striking that Rosenberg is upset with the fact that the double standard—which now, for the first time works positively for Catholics—is a real problem? Never do we remember Rosenberg protesting the double standard that allows "artists" to dump on Catholics while protecting most other segments of society from their assaults.[12]

(Scully and *The Simpsons* were more amenable to making a cut in 2001 when another group, the Media Action Network for Asian Americans, complained about an exchange in which Mr. Burns, the nuclear plant owner, calls Smithers a "Chinaman" while the assistant pulls him in a rickshaw. "There was no malicious intent behind the joke," Scully told the *Los Angeles Times*. "It was supposed to be one of Mr. Burns's typical antiquated expressions." The irony clearly escaped the group, and Scully agreed to delete the term in future airings. "For future runs, we will change the line to offend another ethnic group," he joked.)

The lesson of the controversy for the League was clear: "It just goes to prove what can be done when Catholics get actively involved." It also proved how many Americans feel about censorship, pressure politics, and *The Simpsons*, after Rosenberg's article was reprinted around the country. The League reported that it was itself deluged with critical and sometimes obscene e-mail and letters. And the series has not been hesitant to strike back, although less directly. A 2000 episode purporting to show a "behind the scenes" retrospective of *The Simpsons* has Bart including among the show's merchandise a tee-shirt with his face on it with the message, "Life

Begins at Conception." The League won, but *The Simpsons* fired the final shot, bloodied but unbowed.

Kenneth Briggs says that one reason for the success of the League's campaign may have been that "there is much more sensitivity toward Catholic references because there is still a feeling out in the world that there is a powerful anti-Catholic element in the media. I don't think that's true, but it is the perception." Another explanation for Fox's yielding to pressure from the League, he said, is that "the Catholic Church is perceived to be hierarchical, and hierarchical structures are perceived to be more powerful than egalitarian ones. . . . The Church's hierarchical structure probably gives it, whether intended or not, a degree of intimidation. I find this rather interesting."

The Catholic Church's representation in *The Simpsons* is not uniformly negative and, Scully's protests notwithstanding, the show's writers know when to tread carefully. Catholics are a part of the Springfield community, attending the downtown church, Our Lady of Perpetual Sorrow, whose sign advises would-be thieves and muggers that "Archbishop Carries Less Than $20"—perhaps a small nod to the denomination's commitment to impoverished urban centers. The congregation sponsors an annual Fun-and-Food Fest. Monsignor Kenneth Daly appears with Lovejoy on "Gabbin' about God," a weekly radio program. There is also a parochial school in Springfield, Saint Sebastian's School for Wicked Girls, which is run by nuns.

Pope John Paul II, a universally beloved figure, is often portrayed as a tiny figure, silent but benign. Wearing his miter and carrying his shepherd's staff, he pops up waving from an open car in a ticker tape parade and in unlikely crowd scenes, such as the unveiling of a new car designed by Homer. The closest thing to a dig came in one brief sequence where the Pope is at the Mayo Clinic, apparently being treated for flatulence. In an episode dealing with the apparent end of the world, based on a sign found in Springfield, the news is carried to the Vatican. From an exterior shot of St. Peter's Basilica the scene shifts inside, where the pope is seen sitting on a lawn chair, reading the newspaper *La Stampa*. This pope is not John Paul II, however, but another man wearing glasses. Asked by his aide what to do about the news from America, the pope says, "Keep an eye on it."

On a deeper level, the Catholic Church as portrayed in *The Simpsons* is a reflection of what George Weigel, author of *Witness to Hope: The Biography of Pope John Paul II* and a Catholic League board member, calls "the conventional story line" of the American media. Catholics, he said in a conversation sponsored by the Washington, D.C.-based Ethics and Public

Policy Center, "are probably the most varied, multi-hued religious community in the nation. Yet for almost forty years, the Catholic story has been reported in starkly black-and-white terms."[13] In *The Simpsons*, the Catholic Church is the sum of its least popular stands, such as opposition to birth control. Still, the ubiquitous presence of the small, mute figure of the pontiff, moving through the scenery, acknowledges John Paul II's longevity and—by not attacking or satirizing an otherwise perfect target—his popularity.

Ironically, the Christian theology represented by *The Simpsons*—salvation by works as well as by grace—may come closest to that enunciated by Pope John Paul II in late 2000. Speaking to thirty thousand pilgrims gathered in St. Peter's Square, the pontiff proclaimed that all who live a just life will be saved, even if they do not believe in Jesus. That sounds a lot like Homer Simpson and other characters in the show. John L. Allen Jr., Vatican correspondent for the *National Catholic Reporter*, a liberal weekly, and a longtime *Simpsons* fan, is not troubled by his denomination's portrayal. He says his reading of the series is that "Catholicism as such is not a major target, perhaps reflecting a tad the Ivy League generic Protestantism of the show's writers. . . . I would say Catholicism gets off comparatively easy."

Briggs, who now serves on the board of the *National Catholic Reporter*, agrees. "It's a real big stretch to make *The Simpsons* anti-Catholic; it's anti-hypocrisy. My first impression is how little Catholic content there is in it—and I'm surprised. Everyone takes a shot on *The Simpsons*, so it's common sense that there are little comments here and there. Compared to the general foibles in Lovejoy's life and church, I can't think of how they would stack up to much."

Ten

The Jews: "Mel Brooks Is *Jewish*? . . . Are *We* Jewish?"

O ne night while working on this book, I heard my daughter reading aloud to my wife a story by Isaac Bashevis Singer, the great Jewish writer and Nobel laureate. It was a classic tale that provoked gales of laughter from both of them, and suddenly a thought struck me: *The Simpsons'* Springfield is a lot like Chelm, Singer's celebrated Eastern European village of Jewish fools, buffoons, and dunderheads, except that in Springfield, most of the fools are Gentiles (or seem to be). This transposition is not surprising, given the background and viewpoint of *The Simpsons'* writers and producers. "There have always been a lot of Jewish writers on *The Simpsons*," says longtime writer Mike Reiss. "We bring that comedy to it."

It is also not surprising that Judaism, although a target of satire like other faiths, denominations, and institutions in the series, is accorded considerable respect. As with most Hollywood productions, there is good representation of Jews on the creative side. "Jews play a disproportionate role in several key sectors of American society," including the media, according to Jack Wertheimer, provost of the Jewish Theological Seminary. "Jews have achieved respectability, and Judaism is treated with a great deal of acceptance within American society," he said at a seminar sponsored by the Ethics and Public Policy Center.[1] Despite their atheism or secularism, the Jewish writers on *The Simpsons* represent their faith well. Jewish humor, says Rabbi Harold W. Schulweis, the longtime spiritual leader of Valley Beth Shalom synagogue in Encino, California, "is not just funny—it's philosophical." Comedian Mel Brooks, who appeared as himself in an episode, observes that, for the Jews, "humor is just another defense against the universe."[2]

The many jokes squeezed into each episode of *The Simpsons* weave together two distinct strands of humor: On the one hand, the snarky, iconoclastic nastiness embodied by Harvard University's *Lampoon* magazine; and on the other, the dark, rapid-fire, angst of Borscht Belt *tummlers* ("roisterers") and *shpritzers* ("sprayers") such as Lenny Bruce and Don

Rickles. None is more typical of this Jewish strain of humor than the exchange between Bart's friend Milhouse and Lisa in the Exodus segment of the episode, "Simpson Bible Stories." In this dream sequence, Milhouse is Moses. He has just led the Israelite slaves across the Red Sea, only to learn that what lies ahead is forty years of wandering in the desert. But after that, he asks Lisa hopefully, "it's clear sailing for the Jews, isn't that right?" Lisa, unwilling to break the news of what the next three thousand years holds for the Chosen People, smiles tightly and says, "Well, more or less."

There is an Orthodox synagogue in town, with the improbable name of Temple Beth Springfield (Jewish congregations are usually either "Temple" or "Beth," followed by a Hebrew name), located not far from Reverend Lovejoy's First Church of Springfield. The two houses of worship are so close, in fact, that once the church marquee carried the decidedly non-ecumenical message: "No Synagogue Parking." Without further comment on the subject in the episode, one can reasonably surmise that the incident might have occurred in a year when the Jewish High Holidays coincided with the church's Sunday morning service. This can be a sore point where synagogues and churches are neighbors. Otherwise, relations between Lovejoy and Rabbi Hyman Krustofsky are cordial. The rabbi, bearded and dressed in the black garb of the Hasidim, is a regular on the minister's weekly call-in radio show, "Gabbin' about God." Orthodox rabbis are often wary of such interfaith dialogues, but Krustofsky does not conform to this stereotype. According to *The Simpsons' Guide to Springfield*, the rabbi plays basketball against Lovejoy in the annual "Springfield Two-Man Interfaith Jimmy Jam." Each Friday, according to the same guide, the synagogue offers a regular Friday Sabbath dinner that includes gefilte fish and Manischewitz wine, although this is highly unlikely since such meals are traditionally held in Jewish homes.

Jewish references thread through *The Simpsons*, and they sometimes reinforce stereotypes. The local Jewish hospital is considered the best, if the most pricey, according to an ambulance driver. An unnamed Jewish child can be seen in an occasional suburban crowd scene, called in from the playground to practice his music. There is still an "old neighborhood" downtown, Springfield's Lower East Side, where Jews lived before moving to the suburbs. This is where Krustofsky's synagogue is located and where visitors can dine at restaurants such as Tannen's Fatty Meats and Izzy's Deli. In real life, if there were enough Jews in Springfield, the synagogue would have followed the migration from the urban center to the suburbs, the pattern in most American cities of any size. Thus, the town's small Jewish community is marginalized and often misunderstood in ways that are still common in small Protestant communities in the American heartland. Related problems facing modern American Jewry in such towns—assimilation and how to fit into an overwhelmingly Christian society—are raised in various ways in *The Simpsons*. Thus, we learn that Kent Brockman, the local television news anchor and member of Springfield Community Church, started his broadcasting career as Kenny Brockelstein, and still wears a pendant around his neck with the Hebrew word *C'hai* (life).

This environment gives rise to a kind of unconscious anti-Semitism. For example, Lovejoy keeps the rabbi's address and phone number on his "non-Christian Rolodex." At the elementary school, Principal Skinner is heard fielding an angry call from the superintendent. "I know Weinstein's parents were upset," he stammers. "But, but, ah, I was sure it was a phony excuse. I mean, it sounds so made up: 'Yom Kip-pur.'" The Day of Atonement, the holiest day of the year for Jews, is completely unfamiliar to the school principal. When Homer needs fifty thousand dollars for a heart bypass, he goes to the rabbi, pretending to be Jewish in the only way he knows how. "Now, I know I haven't been the best Jew, but I have rented *Fiddler on the Roof* and I will watch it," he says. All he gets from the rabbi is a dreidel. In another episode, while visiting New York City, Homer mistakes several Hasidic rabbis—black-clad and bearded—for the Texas rock group ZZ Top, who favor the same attire, plus sunglasses. Finally, Bart works a sympathy scam in the shopping mall wearing a yarmulke, pretending that his bar mitzvah cake has just been smashed.

Just as Ned Flanders and Reverend Lovejoy embody Protestant Christianity on *The Simpsons*, the character Krusty the Clown represents the Jews. The host of a popular children's show on the local television station, Krusty was introduced during the 1989–1990 season in a short for *The Tracey Ullman Show*. Series creator Matt Groening, who wrote the episode, said in an interview that Krusty came as "a sudden inspiration on the part of a couple of writers" for the show. Groening told *TV Guide* that the braying, self-centered clown, who always appears in brightly colored hair, red nose, and makeup, was based on a clown named Rusty Nails in Groening's hometown of Portland, Oregon. Rusty Nails "was actually a very nice Christian clown who showed old Three Stooges shorts. But I couldn't get past the idea that this was a nice clown with the scariest name possible."[3] Writer and producer Mike Scully has similar memories. "For my generation, Krusty is every Saturday-morning TV clown. Everybody had a Krusty in their town." Cast member Dan Castellaneta, who does Krusty's voice, says he used the voice of Bob Bell, who played Bozo the Clown on Chicago's WGN-TV for many years, as a model for his characterization.

Krusty's show on *The Simpsons* features live gags and routines before an audience of kids, along with violent cartoons starring a cat and mouse named Itchy and Scratchy. Commercials promote a full line of Krusty merchandise: posters, lunch boxes, cereal, and appliances of dubious utility and reliability. There is a chain of fast food restaurants featuring Krusty Burgers and a disreputable summer camp where overweight kids can avail themselves of his "exclusive program of diet and ridicule." In 2000, Krusty released a biography, *Your Shoes Are Too Big to Kick Box with God,* ghost written by novelist John Updike. And Krusty is Jewish, *very* Jewish. His picture forms a stylized Jewish star on his dressing room door. Yet Dalton, Mazur and Siems, in *God in the Details,* see Krusty as "a gross caricature of a stereotypical secularized Jew corrupted by wealth and fame" who "dislikes children (and) finances his lavish debt-ridden lifestyle by overmarketing his own image unabashedly."

Krusty and Judaism are the center of a 1991 Emmy-winning episode entitled "Like Father, Like Clown." The show's premise is a reworking of the 1927 movie classic, *The Jazz Singer,* which starred Al Jolson and was made again, with considerably less success, in 1953 (starring Danny Thomas) and in 1980 (starring Neil Diamond). The film tells the story of a Jewish cantor who disowns his son because the young man chooses to be an entertainer. Rabbi Lavi Meier and Rabbi Harold Schulweis, a leading thinker of Conservative Judaism in America, served as "special technical consultants" on *The Simpsons* version. The two rabbis' expertise and guidance is apparent throughout the show, which ranks in religious significance with episodes such as "Homer the Heretic" and "Lisa the Skeptic." Unlike most *Simpsons* episodes, there is no subplot in "Like Father, Like Clown," which means the full twenty-two minutes are devoted to a single narrative.

Schulweis said he was not a fan of *The Simpsons* when someone from the show called and asked if he would be willing to look at a draft of the script. He agreed to help, and said he was surprised to find how genuine it was. "I thought it had a Jewish resonance to it. It was profound. I was impressed by the underlying moral seriousness." The show's writers, he said, "have a Yiddish spark in them." Schulweis said he made some corrections to the script, and then he told the show's writer a Hasidic story about the honored role of the jester, called a "badchan." Such a person, who brings joy and happiness, would have a share in the world to come, the sages said, because "God loves laughter." When the episode aired and Schulweis's name appeared on the closing credits, the impact in his congregation was immediate and profound: "I became an instant hero among my young people. I was cool."

In the episode, members of the Simpson family are so oblivious to Judaism that they are shocked to discover that Krusty is Jewish. Having been invited to dinner, the clown is asked by Marge to offer a grace before the meal. Apologizing for being rusty, Krusty folds his hands (not a Jewish practice) and proceeds to recite the traditional blessing over bread, the "hamotzie," in Hebrew. Homer bursts into laughter, calling the blessing "funny talk." Lisa corrects her father, recognizing the language and making the connection that Krusty is Jewish. Naturally, Homer is shocked at the notion of a Jewish entertainer, only to be informed by his daughter that many show business people are Jews: Lauren Bacall, Dinah Shore, William Shatner, and Mel Brooks. The revelation that Brooks (whose humor is in fact nothing if not Jewish) is Jewish dumbfounds Homer. Suddenly, Krusty collapses into tears, as a clarinet plays European klezmer music. Reciting the blessing—the "bracha"—brings back painful memories involving his father, he tells the Simpsons.

The clown reveals to family members that his real name is Herschel Krustofsky and he is descended from a long line of rabbis, ending with his father, Temple Beth Springfield's Rabbi Hyman Krustofsky. Krusty's story flashes back to his youth, when his father—voiced in an unmistakable Yiddish accent by comedian and former rabbi Jackie Mason—was a respected leader of the Lower East Side's Jewish community, dispensing all manner of wisdom on issues both profound and trivial. A man asks if he should finish college, and the rabbi answers that "no one is poor except he who lacks knowledge." A woman with an infant in her arms asks whether she should have another child. The rabbi says that she should, that another child would be a blessing. But when a man asks whether he should buy a Chrysler, Rabbi Krustofsky requires him to rephrase the query as an ethical question, the approach favored more recently by Dr. Laura Schlessinger, another Orthodox Jew with a penchant for giving advice. Asked whether it would be "right" to buy a Chrysler, the rabbi says it would, "for great is the car with power steering and Dyna-flow suspension."

As sometimes happens in clergy households, however, the rabbi's wisdom does not extend to his own family. Young Herschel, who wears a yarmulke on the street, yearns to go into comedy to be a clown: "I want to make people laugh," he says. Because a clown is not a respected member of the community, the rabbi forbids the boy to consider such a career. Life is not fun, the rabbi says—life is serious. "Seltzer is for drinking, not for spraying," the father admonishes. "Pie is for noshing, not for throwing." He threatens to give his son "such a *zetz*" (a hit) if he pursues his ambition rather than becoming a rabbi like his father.

But, Krusty tells the Simpsons back at their dinner table, "the Lord works in mysterious ways." The father's threat does not deter the boy, who gets his first laugh imitating his father in his yeshiva class, and the rabbi's efforts to extinguish his son's love of comedy fail. Soon, Krustofsky discovers his son in the bathroom, squirting himself with seltzer, prompting the rabbi to cry out, "*Oy gevalt!*" (O, horrors!).

Time passed. Older, but still unabashed, the young man donned what would be his trademark Krusty the Clown costume and makeup and accepted a paying gig entertaining rabbis at a Talmudic conference in New York's Catskill Mountains—his first big break. The act, which featured Israeli folk music and colorful balloon sculptures of a Star of David and a menorah, was a hit, even with his unsuspecting father who was in the audience. To compound the irony, as Krusty performs, Rabbi Krustofsky brags about his son to a colleague, saying he was first in his yeshiva class and voted "most likely to hear God." The fellow rabbi accuses Krustofsky of being so proud of his son that he exaggerates. No, insists Krustofsky, "a rabbi never exaggerates. A rabbi composes. He creates thoughts. He tells stories that may never have happened. But he does not exaggerate!"

Just then, a rowdy rabbi in the audience gets carried away with the clown's performance and squirts Krusty with seltzer, dissolving his makeup and revealing his true identity. His father is crushed and shouts "*Oy vey is mir!* ("Woe is me!"). He denounces his son, saying he has "brought shame on our family! I never want to see you again, you clown!" A joke within a joke follows, in typically brilliant *Simpsons* fashion, reminding knowing viewers of the episode's cinematic reference. "Oh, if you were a musician or a *jazz singer*, this I could forgive," the rabbi proclaims. But not this, and from that time on the clown has not seen or spoken with his father. Despite the twenty-five-year estrangement that has followed, Krusty tells Bart that he thinks about his father almost all the time—"except when I'm at the track. Then I'm all business." Similar estrangements, provoked by less profound differences, are common in the Jewish community, rabbis today will testify.

After completing his tale, Krusty leaves the Simpson household, telling the sympathetic family not to worry about him, because he is a survivor. Yet he is in fact tortured by the memories and wanders the rainy streets of Springfield after midnight. He passes a newsstand where his eyes fall on a magazine called *Modern Jewish Father*, featuring a bearded father and young son happily working together in front of a computer, an image that causes him to burst into tears. All this reminiscence and rambling prompts Krusty to try to reestablish contact with his father. He phones the rabbi at home, yet he cannot speak. "Hello, hello?" Rabbi Krustofsky says, awakened from sleep. "Anybody there? What's this? I hear the phone ring and suddenly there's nothing. I'm listening and there's no talking. Hello, mister, who are you? Why would they call if they don't want to talk to you?" The rabbi hangs up, and the next day Krusty continues to disintegrate, this time on screen during his show. After a violent cartoon that includes tender scenes between a mouse and a cat and their respective fathers, Krusty weeps.

Lisa and Bart, watching in horror on their couch, decide they have to intervene to bring father and son together. Through Reverend Lovejoy, who shares a radio show with Rabbi Krustofsky, they get his address and pay him a visit. The children knock on the door of his book-lined study. He is studying from a scroll, muttering words including, "*rebonno shel olam*" ("Master of the universe"), a reference to God. The rabbi asks what he can do for his "young friends," and the two children tell the rabbi they want to talk about his son. Repeating a line from countless plays, movies, and television shows about parents and alienated children, Rabbi Krustofsky says, "I have no son!" and slams the door in their faces. Bart, clearly his own father's son, takes the statement literally and assumes, "We came all this way and it's the wrong guy." Krustofsky opens the door to explain that his comment was metaphorical—and then slams the door again.

The next airing of "Gabbin' about God" on KBBL-AM (K-babble? The broadcast tower sometimes seems like the tower of Babel in Genesis 11, with its "confusing tongues") offers another opportunity to approach Rabbi Krustofsky on the subject of reconciliation. First, Krusty calls, but again he is unable to speak. "Anybody there?" the rabbi asks. "I hear breathing but I don't hear talking. . . . Some people got nothing to do but call people and hang up. There's all kinds of *mishegoyim* in the world." "*Mishegoyim*" can be translated "crazy Gentiles," but the voice at the end of this particular line belongs to a distraught Jew. Bart then calls the show, identifying himself as "Dimitri." He asks all three religious leaders, "If a son defies his father and chooses a career that makes millions of children happy, shouldn't the father forgive the son?" The priest and the minister say he should, but the rabbi goes ballistic. "No way! Absolutely not! Who screens these calls? Who's in charge here? There's nobody in charge here!"

Bart and Lisa are undeterred. The boy goes to Springfield's Lower East Side to a shop called Yiddle's that specializes in "practical jokes, magic tricks, and medical supplies." He buys a fake beard, eyebrows, and earlocks, and a set of black clothes, white fringes, and a broad-brimmed hat favored by Hasidic Jews. Thus disguised, the boy slips into a circle around the rabbi, who is in the park, in the midst of a discourse on the nature of philanthropy, as more Jewish music plays. Krustofsky quotes the medieval philosopher Maimonides, that "the best charity is to give and not let anybody know." (Or, as Jesus puts it in the Sermon on the Mount, "When you give to the needy, do not let your left hand know what your right hand is doing, so that your giving may be in secret. Then your Father, who sees what is done in secret, will reward you" [Matt. 6:3–4].) A man in the circle questions this view, just as the ancient rabbis did, wondering if the public example might not encourage others to give to charity. Before the debate can continue, Bart interrupts, saying, "speaking of charity," shouldn't Krustofsky forgive his son? The rabbi rebuffs him. "Don't you understand that my boy broke my heart? He turned his back on our traditions, on our faith and on me." He exposes Bart's disguise, denounces him as a "little *pisher*" (squirt) and tells him to go away.

Lisa suggests they try to outsmart the rabbi by using another approach to bring father and son together. First, they call the rabbi and pretend to be the Nobel Prize–winning author Saul Bellow, requesting a meeting at Izzy's Delicatessen. Then they call Krusty, impersonating former French president François Mitterand, and request a meeting at the same place and time to present the clown with the Legion of Honor, another sly reference, this one to the unfathomable popularity in France of another Jewish comedian, Jerry Lewis. Disaster ensues at the restaurant, which we soon learn is Jewish but not kosher. The rabbi is offended and storms out after seeing a Krusty the Clown sandwich on the menu, which consists of ham, sausage, bacon, and mayonnaise on white bread—as Gentile a combination as can be imagined.

Lisa won't quit and tells her brother that the way they have been approaching the problem is all wrong. "What's the one thing rabbis prize above everything else?" she asks. (She might just as well be asking, "What's the one thing Jews value above everything else?") For comic relief, Bart guesses, "Those stupid hats?" The correct answer is "knowledge," and Lisa pledges to "hit him where it hurts—right in the Judaica." Easier said than done. They don't know it yet, but the good-hearted, well-meaning Simpson kids are in way over their heads. At the Old Springfield Library, Bart and Lisa begin their research. While her brother focuses on Bible pop-up books, Lisa dives into weightier fare, including the Babylonian Talmud, *The Big Book of Chosen People*, *Views on Jews*, and *Jewishness Revisited*. Using Lisa's crib note, Bart returns to the rabbi's study and, before he can be driven off once more, asks if the Babylonian Talmud does not say, "A child should be pushed aside with the left hand and drawn closer with the right." Krustofsky agrees. "Then doesn't your religion command you to make up with Krusty?" Bart asks. The rabbi easily bats this away, citing the Fifth Commandment (Ex. 20:12), "Honor thy father and thy mother," he tells Bart. "End of story." This round goes to the rabbi.

But this argument is a profound one, according to Rabbi Sholom Dubov of Congregation Ahavas Yisrael in Maitland, Florida. Some talmudic scholars have suggested that when Jesus confronted the rabbis in the first century he too should have been pushed aside with one hand but drawn closer with the other, rather than driven away. One historic strain of rabbinic Judaism that survives to this day—exemplified by Rabbi Krustofsky—characterizes some sins as so unforgivable that the sinner must be abandoned. Other strains, like the Orthodox Lubovitch Hasidim of which Dubov is a part, strive for a more inclusive approach. "For us, that means unconditional acceptance of the person on one hand, and absolute rejection of the bad behavior on the other," he says. "The Talmud says you should be capable of having both feelings at the same time. Unfortunately, some parents and some rabbis, like Rabbi Krustofsky, are unable to adopt this seemingly contradictory approach. "There's no reason why Krusty can't be a kosher clown."

Lisa sends Bart back with what she says is dynamite material, this time from Rabbi Simon ben Eleazer, a second-century talmudic scholar. This time the forum is a steam bath—the *schvitz*—where the learned men gather to discuss ethical issues wearing nothing but towels. "At all times," says Bart, to the approval of other sweating rabbis, "let a man be supple as a reed and not rigid as a cedar." Krustofsky, now addressing Bart as "my learned short friend," replies from the book of Joshua, "You shall meditate on the Torah all day and all night" (1:8). Again, the round goes to the rabbi.

Almost asleep in the library, Lisa is running out of answers, but she tries once more. Bart again attempts to win over the rabbi, interrupting him without success in the midst of a circumcision. He asks if it is not written in the Talmud, "Who will bring redemption? The jesters." Krustofsky says he is not convinced, adding, his blade poised over the male infant, "This is hardly the time or place to discuss it."

Short of learning ancient Hebrew, Lisa has only one long shot idea remaining. Back in the park, Bart engages Rabbi Krustofsky in another Jewish arena, a chessboard. Bart quotes a source he identifies as another "great man," without further citation. "The Jews are a swinging bunch of people," the boy recites. "I mean, I've heard of persecution, but what they went through is ridiculous. But the great thing is, after thousands of years of waiting and holding on and fighting, they finally made it."

This time, the rabbi is clearly impressed. "Oh," he says, "I've never heard the plight of my people phrased so eloquently." He asks Bart if the citation is from a sage like Rabbi Hillel, Judah the Pious, Maimonides, or the Dead Sea Scrolls. The boy trumps the rabbi, telling him the quote is from *Yes, I Can*, the autobiography of Sammy Davis Jr.—"an entertainer, like your son." (Davis, an African American and a convert to Judaism, was known as "The Candy Man," the title of one of his hit songs.) "The Candy Man said that?" the rabbi says, incredulous. "If a performer could think that way, maybe I'm upside down on this whole problem." But of course no Jewish dilemma could possibly be resolved without a healthy dose of guilt and a lament. "Ah, all the years of joy that I've lost. Why? Because of my stubborn ways." He weeps, consoled by Lisa, who tells him it is not too late to make things right.

Meanwhile, still dispirited and listless over his relationship with his father, Krusty is barely going through the motions on his television show. He lights a cigarette while a cartoon rolls. Suddenly Bart and Lisa lead Rabbi Krustofsky through the backstage door. From the shadows, a familiar voice admonishes, "Hey, such a filthy habit." Krusty snaps, "Who asked you?" The rabbi emerges from the shadows and is recognized by his son. They embrace and weep, calling each other "Papa" and "Boychick" (little boy). Krusty brings his father on stage and introduces him to the audience. The clown asks the band to strike up "some reconciliation music," and the two men sing a schmaltzy duet of "Oh, Mein Papa," a 1950s hit by the Jewish crooner Eddie Fisher that is a paean to a beloved father. To seal the bond, the rabbi takes a pie from Bart and hits his son in the face.

"That's a great episode!" says Rabbi Daniel Wolpe of Congregation Ohalei Rivka in Orlando. "I thought the episode was brilliant, first of all, because of the use of real Jewish sources. Second of all, because it was an interesting take on the greatest of contemporary Jewish dilemmas, which is the battle between tradition and modernity." When "Like Father, Like Clown" first aired in reruns, Wolpe—himself the son of a rabbi and then living in Los Angeles—assigned the Hebrew high school class he was teaching to watch, prompting some puzzled phone calls from parents.

The on-camera denouement of "Like Father, Like Clown" was not the end of the story of the Jews of Springfield or of Krusty, their exemplar. The clown remains clearly ambivalent about his religion and heritage. At his fifth "retirement" show, Krusty tells the audience, "I'd like to thank God for all my success, even though I never worshiped or believed in him in any way." In another episode, Lisa accuses him of being ashamed of his Jewish roots, and with some justification. In a kitchen segment of his show, "Cooking with Krusty," the chef surprises the clown with the news that he has gotten Krusty's mother's recipe for a traditional Passover breakfast fare, called "matzoh brie." Krusty snaps, "I don't do the Jewish stuff on the air!"

Like many of his coreligionists, Krusty is extremely conflicted about Christmas. "A Krusty Kinda Kristmas," a television special on which Christmas merchandise is advertised, later gives way to a "nondenominational Holiday Fun Festival," with God as "our sponsor." During the holiday season, Krusty Burger restaurants have menorahs and Stars of David in their windows. A sign in front of Temple Beth Springfield advertises the coming Saturday sermon as "Coping with Christmas," although the "December dilemma" does not usually trouble Orthodox Jews.

Jewish dietary laws are another recurring theme. Given the Simpson family's love of pork products, Krusty was lucky that dinner in "Like Father, Like Clown" was meatloaf. In another episode, a row of rapping rabbis dressed like Hasidim appear on a local television show, "Eye on Springfield," singing, "Don't eat pork, even with a fork." Yet Chunky the Pig is a regular character on Krusty's show. And while pushing his own signature line of sausage and bacon products on the air in the 1980s, the clown suffers a near-fatal heart attack and is saved only by both a triple bypass *and* a pacemaker. A divine message, perhaps?

Krusty has had a checkered career in show business, which took him from work as a street mime in Tupelo, Mississippi, to the self-designated titles of "Sultan of Seltzer" and "Prince of Pies." He is considered to be a god by Bart and the other children of Springfield. But his show has been canceled at least once, and he failed at foul-mouthed stand-up comedy for adults. When he is framed for shoplifting, his arrest sparks a campaign against all of his products, led by Reverend Lovejoy. The minister denounces him as the "Clown Prince of Corruption" and organizes a bonfire of the merchandise. The subtext of the minister's drive is clear, and familiar to students of anti-Semitism: "lascivious Jew." And Krusty, who has a frequently referred-to weakness for pornography, has been ordered to do community service for unspecified offenses. His television biography (portrayed in *The Simpsons* as airing on the WB network, a Fox rival) was titled, "The Krusty the Clown Story: Booze, Drugs, Games, Lies, Blackmail, and Laughter," starring the Jewish actor Fyvush Finkel.

Although he lives alone in an apartment, he is not without honor in his own land. On Springfield's Lower East Side there is a Krusty the Clown Birthplace Tour & Gift Shoppe, known as "the Graceland of Jewish clown fans." During the Gulf War, he was invited on a USO tour to the Persian

Gulf. And he is philanthropic. He goes door to door, collecting money for the Brotherhood of Jewish Clowns. "Last year, tornadoes claimed the lives of seventy-five Jewish clowns," he tells Homer. "The worst incident was during our convention in Lubbock, Texas. There were floppy shoes and rainbow wigs everywhere. It was terrible!"

How unlikely is the premise of such a gathering? Given the heavy burden placed on Krusty—to represent the Jewish people—it is fair to ask, Are there *really* Jewish clowns? Of course there are, just as there are Jewish bullfighters and cowboys and American army generals. Perhaps the most famous Jewish clown was Max Patkin, known as the "Clown Prince of Baseball" and a member of the Philadelphia Jewish Sports Hall of Fame. The rubber-faced, double-jointed comic began as a minor league pitcher but became famous for dressing as a ball player and imitating real athletes on the field. Patkin, who died in 1999 at the age of seventy-nine, had a cameo role in the movie *Bull Durham*.

There is, in fact, a national (if informal) organization of mostly amateur and part-time Jewish clowns, called "Clowns for Judaism," founded in 1999 by Bruce and Kim Bayne of Colorado, both of whom have clown forebears. Their Web site is "dedicated to reaching out to Jewish families through Jewish humor" and "incorporating Jewish heritage into public performances." Bruce Bayne performs under the name of "Poppy Hamentashen" and teaches kindergarten at Temple Shalom in his home town. Perhaps because the issue is too close to home, or too painful, no one from the discussion list would comment on Krusty's portrayal.

Yiddish expressions, usually voiced by Krusty, abound: *tucchus* (butt) and *yutz* (empty head), *plotz* (burst), *bupkes* (nothing), *ferkakteh* (execrable), *schlemiel* (bungler), and *schmutz* (mess). The clown refers to his long-lost daughter as "my lucky little *hamentaschen*," a reference to triangular pastry eaten on the holiday of Purim. Other Yiddish words and puns and double entendres also pop up. Springfield's miniature golf course is sometimes (but not always) called "Sir Putts-a-Lot." The Yiddish word *putz* means penis. Krusty's middle name is "Schmoikel," which sounds like the diminutive of another Yiddish term for penis. "What's a good Jewish word Krusty can use here?" Gentile writers would ask Mike Reiss. And it usually would be Gentile writers who would seek such words. "Not even a majority of the stuff comes from the Jews."

There are other in-jokes that were obviously written by Jews for other Jews. A casino boat travels from Springfield beyond the territorial limit to allow activities forbidden by U.S. law. In a fleeting shot, a man in a tuxedo, under a canopy, is seen marrying a cow in what is clearly a Jewish wedding ceremony—then the groom smashes with his foot a glass wrapped in a napkin.

The Jewish content of *The Simpsons* inspired one fan, Brian Rosman, a health policy researcher at a Brandeis University think tank, to create a web site that features still shots from "Like Father, Like Clown" under the heading, "Jewish Life in Springfield." It also uses Homer Simpson to help Jewish viewers with the observance of Lag B'Omer, the counting of the sheaves between Passover and Shavuot, the Feast of Weeks, and a bilingual pun on Homer's name. Rosman believes that

> *The Simpsons* does the funniest, most authentic parodies of Jewish life among all the comedy shows on TV, certainly compared to shows that are considered more "Jewish," like *Seinfeld*. *The Simpsons* demonstrates a more intuitive understanding of American Jewish history, Jewish religion and culture, and Judaism's place among all the other varieties of belief and identity in America. I only wish there was more Jewish content on the show, because when they do it, they do it very well.

Actually, there may be more than Rosman realizes. Apart from Krusty, *The Simpsons* from time to time suggests an underlying element of what might be called "crypto-Judaism." In one of the opening chalkboard sequences, Bart writes, "I am not the reincarnation of Sammy Davis Jr." While watching the "Rapping Rabbis" on television, Homer asks Marge, "Are we Jewish?" Sight gags in the series also extend this conceit. A menorah—the Hanukkah candelabra—is seen in the Simpsons' family storage closet, without comment on how or why it got there. Several other characters in the show, ostensibly *not* Jewish, can be read by their names and their view of life as otherwise distinctly Jewish: Homer's father, Abe; and Marge's twin sisters, Selma and Patty Bouvier. In manner and disposition, Abe, a child immigrant from "the old country," is every *alta kaka* (old fart) sitting around a swimming pool in Miami Beach, complaining about his declining health and the ungrateful younger generation. His absent wife, Penelope Olsen, Homer's mother, is a '60s radical and free spirit whose anti–germ warfare activities forced her underground for twenty-five years. Her Scandinavian name notwithstanding, she *could* be Jewish; she fits the profile. The Bouvier sisters are also familiar types: sharp-tongued unmarried aunts and sisters-in-law, their dialogue taken directly from the late Selma Diamond or Fran Leibowitz or Sandra Bernhard. And according to Matt Groening's *The Simpsons Uncensored Family Album*, Montgomery Burns's sister, Cornelia, has five grandsons named Bernstein: David, Levi, Moshe, Murray, and Saul.

So, latent or blatant, is the portrayal of Jews in *The Simpsons* on balance a positive one, likely to encourage understanding among society at large? The rabbis seem to think that it is, although not entirely without qualification. Rabbi Steven Engel of the Congregation of Liberal Judaism, a Reform temple in Orlando, says, "For Jews, humor has always been as reflective as our holy writings and sacred liturgy in expressing our feelings, concerns, aspirations, and in bringing to light the realities we face. Our general understanding is that humor has contributed to our ability to survive as a people. There is no question that *The Simpsons'* Springfield in many ways accurately reflects the feelings, concerns, aspirations, and realities of contemporary Jews. It is certainly funny stuff and does make people laugh. But is it good for the Jews? I suppose that depends upon who is doing most of the laughing, why they are laughing, and to whom the laughter is directed."

Eleven

Miscellaneous: "Hindu! There Are 700 Million of Us!"

In the episode "Homer the Heretic," Springfield's multifaith volunteer fire department mobilizes to save the Simpsons' home—and Homer's life. Reverend Lovejoy explains to Homer that God was working through his friends and neighbors, including Ned Flanders, a Christian, and Krusty the Clown, a Jew. But the minister comes up short when he points toward the other firefighter, Apu Nahaasapeemapetilon. After a nonplussed pause, the minister characterizes the convenience store operator's religion as "miscellaneous." This level of ignorance is too much for the normally mild-mannered Asian immigrant. Apu explodes: "Hindu! There are 700 million of us!" Corrected, Lovejoy replies with condescension, "Aw, that's super."

Despite a surge of immigration from the Indian subcontinent and a growing interest in beliefs outside the Judeo-Christian traditions, most Americans are as in the dark about Hinduism as Reverend Lovejoy. A few aspects of the faith have penetrated Springfield's consciousness: Lisa patronizes a New Age store called Karma-Ceuticals, which features a shrine to Vishnu and a *Kama Sutra* poster, and where the owner offers the traditional Hindu greeting, "Namaste." There is a Hindu priest in town, Sadruddin Mabaradad, host of an exercise show called "Yoga Party" on the Springfield television station and author of the ghost-written *The Unsinkable Sadruddin Mabaradad*. "Just let your head flop back and forward," the priest tells viewers. "Your neck is a well-cooked piece of asparagus." (Incidentally, Sadruddin is typically a Muslim, not Hindu, name.)

For other residents of the town, Apu is their introduction to Hinduism. *Simpsons* creator Matt Groening, a fan of obscure Indian music, initially suggested that the operator of the Kwik-E-Mart come from the subcontinent. "With Apu, that kind of character has not been seen on U.S. TV," Groening told a British magazine. At first, writer-producer Al Jean told *TV Guide*, "we were worried he might be considered an offensive stereotype."[1] Apu in the series was named for a character in a trilogy of Indian films made in the 1950s by famed director Satjayit Ray. In one episode, a photo on the wall of *The Simpsons* character's father is similar to that of the actor who played Apu's father in the Ray movie *Pather Panchali,* one of Groening's all-time favorites.

In many ways, the character *is* stereotypical of Asian immigrants to North America, and a model minority member. Born in Pakistan, Apu migrated with his family to Ramatpur in India and later studied at the Calcutta Institute of Technology ("CalTech"), where he graduated at the top of his class of seven million. In the 1970s, he came to the United States on a student visa to do graduate study in computer programming at the Springfield Heights Institute of Technology (try the initials). During his nine years at the school, he took a job at the convenience store to pay off his student loans, a choice that evolved into a career. Apu often works eighteen hours a day, seven days a week, and, on at least one occasion, worked ninety-six hours straight. He is frequently the victim of shoplifters and armed robbers.

However, not all of the stereotypes Apu embodies are positive. For example, he is apparently a Hindu nationalist: On the shelf in his apartment is a record album entitled "The Concert against Bangladesh," with a mushroom cloud on the cover, obliterating India's poverty-stricken, Muslim neighbor. He refers to Springfield residents with a different area code as "foreign devils." An obsequious shopkeeper, he is known for outrageous overcharging ($1.85 for a 29-cent postage stamp and $4.20 for $2.00 worth of gas) and for selling foods well beyond their expiration dates. "I think he really loves his job and the power that it gives him to frustrate other people," Groening says.[2] As Apu has prospered—offering everything from flavored iced treats called "Squishees," to beef jerky, to *"Playdude"* magazine, to violent video games—he has been able to follow another immigrant pattern, that of bringing to America other members of his family.

Yet next to Marge, Apu is probably the most good-hearted and saintly character on *The Simpsons*, qualities presented on the show as an outgrowth of his Hindu faith and of his Indian culture. At his dinner table, with Homer and Marge as guests, he recites a grace that is clearly a parody of one familiar to the Simpsons: "Good rice, good curry, good Gandhi, let's hurry." Of course, the beloved independence leader Mohandas K. Gandhi, although martyred and worshiped by millions of Indians, is not a part of the Hindu pantheon. On another occasion, Apu swears by the god Vishnu and keeps a statue of Shiva in his apartment, but his continuing allegiance is to a deity less well known in the West—Ganesha.

With four arms, a pot belly, and the head of an elephant, Ganesha is a god who bestows happiness and banishes sorrow—ideal for a character in *The Simpsons*. There are various explanations for how and why he came to have a pachyderm's head: He betrayed his father Shiva; he defended his mother; he lost a race to his brother. Ganesha is popular in the west and south of India and is the focus of a joyous, annual ten-day festival in Bombay. Most statues of Ganesha, such as the one Apu places in a shrine in the Kwik-E-Mart's employee lounge, are two to four feet tall. In his first encounter with the statue, Homer is particularly scornful of Apu's devotion, in much the same way that some evangelical Christians still dismiss Hindus as "pagans" or "heathens." For offering the statue a peanut, Homer is ordered out of the store by the Indian. "No offense, Apu," Homer says, "but when they were handing out religions, you musta been out taking a whiz."

Over time, in small ways and large, and in more than a dozen episodes, Apu articulates essential elements of Hinduism, Indian culture, and the plight of immigrants, including:

1. Vegetarianism. Apu wears a tee-shirt with a red circle and slash, superimposed on a cow, with Bart's slogan, "Don't Have a Cow, Man!" and he secretly substitutes tofu for beef in the hot dogs he sells. The storekeeper is a vegetarian, but he acknowledges to Lisa that it is not easy. The girl lets slip that she includes cheese in her diet, which Apu says he does not, since it comes from an animal. Lisa concludes that he must think her a monster for this lapse. Indeed he does, Apu replies with a smile, in what is a clear distortion of Hinduism. "As any yogi or Hindu will tell you," says yoga instructor Ted Srinathadas Czukor, "we drink milk and eat ghee, yogurt, cheese, lassi, etc. This is why the cow is considered such an important animal in the Hindu culture."

2. Reincarnation. Sideshow Mel, one of Krusty the Clown's television sidekicks, says, "You only live once." Apu pipes up, "Hey, speak for yourself."

3. Meditation. Apu has a secret stairway in the Kwik-E-Mart that leads to a rooftop garden, where, he tells Lisa, "I go when I need some refuge from the modern world."

4. Pluralism. "I learned long ago, Lisa, to tolerate others, rather than forcing my beliefs on them," Apu tells the girl. "You know, you can influence people without badgering them always." *The Simpsons* writers used Apu to take a well-deserved swipe at anti-immigrant hysteria in California, which gave rise to a referendum called Proposition 187 in the 1990s that would have barred the children of undocumented workers from public schools and from all social services. In the episode, it is a proposed local ordinance called Proposition 24, which would expel all immigrants from Springfield in order to pay for patrols to guard against marauding bears.

Homer is all for the measure until he figures out that it will affect Apu. Apu has overstayed his student visa by years, although the merchant has done everything he can think of to fit into American society, including going bowling and learning to square dance.

Things get out of hand when an anti-immigrant mob gathers outside the Kwik-E-Mart in support of Proposition 24. Apu attempts to placate the mob by feeding his statue of Ganesha Yoo-Hoo, a chocolate milk drink. "If you help me out, I'll give you the rest of the bottle," he explains to the deity, demonstrating that bargaining with the divine is not confined to the Judeo-Christian tradition. (Even for well-informed Indian viewers, there are inside jokes on *The Simpsons*. Six months earlier, in India, a craze swept the country as some Hindus claimed a "milk miracle" in which a Ganesha statue appeared to be drinking milk from a spoon. "The milk-drinking episode was witnessed by hundreds of thousands of people in dozens of nations," says Acharya Palaniswami, editor-in-chief of the U.S. monthly magazine *Hinduism Today*.)

When Apu's offering to the Hindu deity fails, the convenience store operator panics. He replaces his shrine to Ganesha with a periodicals rack, featuring magazine covers of movie actors Tom Cruise and Nicole Kidman, both prominent Scientologists. "Who needs Ganesha when I have Tom Cruise and Nicole Kidman to guide me?" he tells Homer. Still, his betrayal provokes a tearful flashback to his departure from India, where his parents urge him, "Never forget who you really are." Apu admits that, in an attempt to fit in as an American, he has turned his back on his faith. "I cannot deny my roots and keep up this charade," he says. "I only did it because I love this land, where I have the freedom to say, and to think, and to charge whatever I want!" In the end, Marge realizes that Apu has been in the United States long enough to qualify for amnesty, which enables him to take—and pass—the citizenship test.

5. *Assimilation*. A member of the Brahmin caste (a Brahmin would never be a shopkeeper in India), Apu faces similar challenges to maintaining his minority faith when it comes time to marry. Like Jews who become Episcopalians and Koreans who become Baptists, the immigrant must decide what road to take. In the U.S., many modern immigrant parents still prefer arranged marriages, although they are more willing to make the process seem voluntary. Apu's mother arrives from India, wanting to know why he says he cannot marry the young woman to whom he was betrothed when he was eight (sealed with the promise of a dowry that includes ten goats, an electric fan, and a textile factory). Her arrival affords her an opportunity to explain to Bart and Lisa the meaning of the red dot, called a gopi or bindi, on her forehead.

The main reason Apu does not want to marry is that he has been having the time of his life playing the American field after starring in Springfield's Charity Bachelor Auction. A plot to convince Apu's mother that he is already married—to Marge—fails. Apu protests that one in twenty-five arranged marriages ends in divorce, but he eventually agrees to the match, to be held in the Simpsons' backyard. Upstairs before the ceremony, Apu worries about the custom of not seeing his future bride until the wedding ceremony, and wonders if the whole world has gone mad. Homer, Mr. Diversity, blames it on "your screwy country."

Alas, there is no Hindu priest (perhaps Mabaradad is out of town), so Reverend Lovejoy agrees to be drafted to conduct the ceremony. After all, as the minister observes, when it comes to performing a wedding, "Christ is Christ," and anyway Lovejoy has consulted a Hindu Web site to customize the service. The wedding goes forward, with Apu wearing a turban and riding an elephant, heralded by trumpets and guests wearing floral garlands. Homer attempts to break up the ceremony the best way he can think of, by dressing as Ganesha, complete with elephant head. He shouts that Ganesha is angered by the wedding and that all present will die unless it is called off, but he is subdued by an Indian guest and stuck up in a tree until the ceremony is completed. To his delight, Apu finds his bride Manjula beautiful and witty, and is reconciled to the match. The couple walks around the sacred fire hand in hand.

The course of the love that follows is not without interruption, as Homer and Marge learn when they are invited to the Nahasapeemapetilons' book-filled apartment for dinner. A fight erupts between the Indian spouses, and the Simpsons excuse themselves. As they leave the apartment building, a copy of the *Kama Sutra* comes flying out the window and lands at Homer's feet, provoking his interest in at least one aspect of Indian culture. For the most part, however, Apu is known to be so devoted to his wife that all the other husbands in Springfield fear he will make trouble for them on Valentine's Day.

In another episode, Homer sets off a series of events that culminates in a TV exposé of Apu's shady practices at the Kwik-E-Mart, and the merchant is stripped of his franchise. At first he is angry at Homer for causing this misfortune, but he realizes that his Hindu faith requires that he make amends to his customer. "I blamed you for squealing," Apu says, "but then I realized, it was *I* who wronged *you*." It is up to the Indian to work off his karmic debt to Homer, who shocks Apu by pointing out that "karma can only be apportioned out by the cosmos." There is but one way the matter can be resolved and Apu restored to his rightful place at the Springfield Kwik-E-Mart: Homer must accompany him to the chain's headquarters in India and plead his friend's case. As one might expect, when the pair arrives at the airport in India they encounter young Christian proselytizers rather than the Hare Krishnas familiar to American travelers. In any event, the debt is forgiven, and balance returns to the universe.

Like Catholics and Protestants, some Hindus have objected to their portrayal on *The Simpsons*. In the mid-1990s, Southern California Hindus protested the representation of Ganesha. The president of the Federation of Hindu Associations, Prithvi Raj Singh, called Fox Television to complain. A spokeswoman returned his call, Singh told *Christian Century* magazine, offering the network's standard response. "She said it was not a planned attack on Hinduism. . . . 'The show treats other religions humorously too,' she said."[3] Unlike the Catholic League and Media Action Network for Asian Americans, however, the Hindu group was not able to force *The Simpsons* to knuckle under.

With the help of *Hinduism Today*, I informally surveyed attitudes toward *The Simpsons*. What I found was that Indian immigrants and adolescent and teenage children of immigrants—especially orthodox Hindus—were generally offended by Apu and his stereotype. They also have specific complaints about what they feel is doctrinal error and distortion. "Hindu kids growing up in America have enough trouble adjusting during middle and high school, and they don't need *The Simpsons* fueling teasers with misinformed jokes about Hinduism," Amit Chatwani, a Princeton University student, said. "I think that Hinduism is trampled to add more laughs to the show. People who don't know anything about Hinduism watch the show and with the idea of a 'goofy, sacred elephant statue' that is Lord Ganesha. This skewed view then becomes their only knowledge of Hinduism."

By contrast, American converts to Hinduism, steeped in our culture of irony, seemed amused and unfazed by the portrayal of their faith on the series. "Unlike Hindus, *The Simpsons* have no sacred cows," said Fred Stella, an actor and yoga instructor from Michigan who identifies himself as an Italian-American adherent to Hinduism. "But more than making fun of Hinduism, the writers tend to mock people's perception of Hinduism. They do the same with Christianity."

Ty Schwach, an orthodox Hindu from Los Angeles, said that the humor involving Hindus and Apu "seems quite clearly to be poking fun more at the stereotypical ideas and preconceived notions of mainstream America regarding the Indian culture. The incidents involving Apu always leave me feeling a sense of respect for him and the way he responds to the provincial notions of his neighbors and friends who truly know very little about his culture and religion."

Bo Lozoff of the Human Kindness Foundation in Durham, North Carolina agreed. "I like the way *The Simpsons* makes no effort to pretend that elements of Hinduism, like Ganesha, seem sensible. I trust that perspective, because we know where we stand with each other," he said. "What I enjoy about the show's religious plurality is that the bottom line gets back to the actions of the adherent and not the trappings of his or her religion that can seem weird or blasphemous to outsiders."

There are exceptions to the division between American and Indian Hindus—those Indian immigrants to the United States who said they see beyond the errors and the caricature. "Sure, it skewers us," said the Indian-born novelist and journalist S. V. Date, author of the satires *Deep Water* and *Smokeout*. "But *The Simpsons* skewers everybody, and in the process, it's obvious that it likes us, and that's what makes it okay."

Kartik Mohan, an animator from Bombay studying at the School of Visual Arts in New York, said he is a huge fan of *The Simpsons* and watches episodes repeatedly and learns many by heart. "I don't think there is anything the least bit offensive about their treatment of the Hindu religion or their depiction of Indian people over and above the general irreverence towards all people and norms that makes the show so uniquely funny." He acknowledged that "there are a number of hot-headed Hindu fundamentalists who are defensive about their status as a newly emergent, highly successful immigrant group in the United States and are all too eager to take offense at anything even obliquely derisive of our culture."

Vikram Rangala, a Hindu who has taught a course on spirituality in popular culture at the University of Florida, said he is also a huge fan of the show, which he considers "the best television show on the air." It is "supportive of religion and even spiritual itself," although it does require "a depth of understanding beyond stereotypes."

For Acharya Palaniswami, the editor of *Hinduism Today*, this double-edged response to *The Simpsons* is entirely understandable: "It is often difficult for good, religious people to smile at their faith's foibles. That's natural. Religion is a serious matter for the devout, and when things they hold precious are held up to humorous scrutiny or even ridicule, they are offended. Among Hindus, such offense is not unknown, but Hindus are more forgiving and perhaps a little more at ease with disdain and ignorance than most. Largely due to an innate ethic of tolerance, Hindus can and do personally enjoy Homer's stupidity and narrow-mindedness toward their religion, and Apu's unctuous money grubbing. They've seen it before, and endured less good-hearted ridicule—probably daily if they live in Memphis or London."

Palaniswami stresses that humor can signal cultural receptivity: "Hindus in America don't yet understand that ridicule is actually part of the process of acceptance of minorities here, that once a minority has become prominent enough to attract ridicule in fictional pieces, be it cartoons, movies or TV shows, that is part of a process of education. It does seem strange, even cruel, but the creation of 'stock jokes' about a minority is part of letting them in, so to speak, welcoming them into the great melting pot.

"Still, Hindus will cringe knowing that *The Simpsons* is seen by millions of Americans who don't have a clue about the ancient and profound Hindu beliefs and customs. At least when characters go after a Christian or a Jew, most in the audience have a sense of the reality that writers are mining for humorous nuggets. They know about Christian beliefs and the people who follow Christianity, mainstream and fringe. When it comes to the Hindu references, the uninformed audience sees only the denigration, the inflated tale, the twisted view. They have met a dozen Indian spice-or-sari store owners, but probably have not been introduced to a single Indian neurosurgeon or high-tech CEO.

"Hindus will note the factual failings of the writers, who would do well to consult more with those who know. . . . Most Hindus will enjoy the fact that karma and reincarnation are subjects for today's films and cartoons, reflecting the fact that the West is intensely interested in and believes in these fundamental Hindu principles. They will smile to see Apu rejecting Lord Ganesha, then coming back, just as so many Indians abroad have done, coming to America the Beautiful, Land of Money, then later rediscovering their faith."

What would the editor of *Hinduism Today* have Homer Simpson understand about the "miscellaneous" Hindu faith?

"Tell Homer there are a billion Hindus in the world; one-sixth of the human family living on Earth today. Tell Homer that in Hinduism it's okay to be a heretic, an agnostic, a disbeliever. Tell him there is no eternal hell in Hinduism, and that all spiritual paths are honored and encouraged. Tell him Hindus believe every single soul will ultimately reach God, not just the saintly ones, not just the chosen believers of this Christian denomination or that Muslim sect. Tell him Hindus learn the value of nonviolence from childhood and have spread the principle to the far corners of the Earth. Tell him all that, and you might one day find Homer going back to India for good."

Twelve

The Creators: "Humor Is in Indirect Proportion to One's True Belief"

Over the lifetime of *The Simpsons*, hundreds of writers, producers, and animators have helped shape the show, beginning with creators Matt Groening, James L. Brooks, and Sam Simon. Others, including George Meyer, John Swartzwelder, John Vitti, Bill Oakley, Josh Weinstein, Mike Scully, Ian Maxtone-Graham, Al Jean, and Mike Reiss have left their mark on the series and scores of scripts. Through his attorney, Susan Grode, Groening told me that he wanted to encourage critical studies of the show like this book. However, Grode said that because Groening sees *The Simpsons* as a collaborative and sometimes collective effort, the show should speak for itself, and he declined further comment.

More than anyone else associated with the show, Groening has been the subject of innumerable interviews and feature stories, but he has rarely spoken about the role of religion in his own life and the show, apart from his comment to *Mother Jones* about the portrayal of God. He told one British journalist that he considers himself a "crusader against injustice in my own little way. Of course, I'm not advocating the religion of 'Simpsonism,' although judging by the fanatics it is almost religious in nature. We cater to obsessive fans."[1] At various times, Groening has said he patterned the character of Bart after himself, the cartoon strip character Dennis the Menace (but not the television version), and after the character of Eddie Haskell in the television series *Leave It to Beaver*. Haskell, he told a television interviewer, "was the bad kid, and he got away with stuff, and I liked that. I thought, 'Eddie Haskell should have his own show and when I grow up, I'm going to do my own show and it's going to star Eddie Haskell or a version thereof.' Hence, Bart Simpson."[2] Springfield, he said, was named for the hometown in another early television show, *Father Knows Best*.

The cartoonist grew up in a middle-class home in Portland, Oregon, the son of Homer and Marge Groening and the brother of four siblings, including sisters named Lisa and Maggie. He told *My Generation* magazine in 2001 that his relationship with his father—who was himself a cartoonist, filmmaker, and advertising executive—was "contentious." Homer Groening was raised a Mennonite and spoke German until he attended school, his son told the magazine. Matt recalled in numerous interviews that his was by and large a happy childhood; he favored *Dr. Seuss* books and, as an aspiring eleven-year-old cartoonist, began imitating Batman comics. He did get into periodic scrapes in elementary school that landed him, like Bart, in the principal's office.

His career as a Boy Scout foundered on his refusal to cut his long hair and the trip on which he took the Gideon Bible from his motel room, thinking it was free. "The scoutmaster screamed, 'You stole this Bible on top of everything else?'" he recalled. "So I prayed to God and said, 'I know you'll forgive me for not believing in you.' . . . Basically I was a pagan." Groening made good grades in high school and was elected student body president. He also spent a lot of time in his room, listening to rock music and perusing magazines famous for their cartoons—*The New Yorker*, *Esquire* and *Punch*—and read a book that impressed him, Walter Kaufmann's *Critique of Religion and Philosophy*. "I had a strong sense of bitterness and self-pity," he said in an interview with Richard von Busack in 1986, published in *MetroActive* magazine in 2000.

The teenager continued to do good deeds, even without the Boy Scout merit badges. For a time he worked in the kitchen of a convalescent home. But he was rejected when he applied to Harvard in the mid-1970s. Instead, he went to Evergreen State University in Olympia, an experimental, progressive college where he was editor and cartoonist for the campus daily, *The Cooper Point Journal*, and a friend of the artist and cartoonist Lynda Barry. He enjoyed his time at college and returned the favor by situating the Simpsons household on Evergreen Terrace.

Early influences on his comic art were polar opposites: Charles Schulz, creator of *Peanuts*, and the ribald, 1960s undergound cartoonist R. Crumb. Groening moved to Los Angeles in the 1980s, recalling that he lived in "a seedy Hollywood apartment." He did a variety of odd jobs and hawked his original comics until he launched his alternative comic strip, "Life in Hell." One of his strips was entitled, "What Not to Say During Moments of Intimacy," and included this one: "O My Lord in Heaven, forgive me for this vile sin I am about to commit." For nearly a decade, he worked on the strip in his garage, "lonely and socially backward," he told *TV Host* magazine in 1989.

In the late 1980s, award-winning film and television producer James L. Brooks, a fan of *Life in Hell*, tapped him to help develop cartoon vignettes—which would later become *The Simpsons*—for *The Tracey Ull-man Show*. It was a good match. Brooks had also produced *The Mary Tyler Moore Show* and *Taxi* for television and made the Academy Award–winning *Terms of Endearment, Broadcast News*, and *Jerry Maguire* for the big screen. Brooks said in a broadcast interview that he believes that "tele-vision is probably one of the last stands for writer control. A writer can still control his work almost utterly on television."[3] Groening, who by some media accounts has had his ups and downs with Brooks since they began working together, gave much of the credit for the series' success to the producer. "It was his clout that allowed the show to be made without compromise," the cartoonist said.[4] Neither Brooks nor Groening nor anyone else present at the creation was prepared for the worldwide phe-nomenon *The Simpsons* became. Over the years since, Groening has played a diminishing role in the show's day-to-day production, telling interviewers he sticks his nose in the door every so often and keeps an eye on his characters. "Matt is good at keeping the writers honest," said Mike Scully. "If he thinks Homer is becoming too insane, he'll pull us back."

In 1999, Groening launched another animated comedy for Fox, *Futu-rama*, set in the year 3000, where one target of satire was the "Church of Robotology." Here again, Groening took a shot at Scientology, which is ironic in light of the fact that Nancy Cartwright, the voice of Bart Simp-son, is an outspoken Scientologist. In a 1997 interview with National Pub-lic Radio, Cartwright said that once she started practicing the religion in 1989, her reaction was, "Oh, God. This is cool." She said that Scientology is different from other faiths: "not like a real religion . . . you don't pray." She said she found both a spiritual life and a husband when she discovered Scientology. The writing of Scientology founder L. Ron Hubbard "totally makes sense to me," she said, and in her autobiography, *My Life as a 10-Year-Old Boy*, she describes Hubbard as a "humanitarian," although she makes no other mention of Scientology in the book. One of the show's writers told me that producers vetoed an episode-length swat at Scientol-ogy in fear of the group's reputation for suing and harassing opponents. Other character voices part ways with the parts they play. Harry Shearer, the voice of Ned Flanders and Reverend Lovejoy, said in an interview with the online magazine *FilmForce* that these two parts no more reflected his personal spiritual and theological views "than doing the voice of Otto (the stoned school bus driver) has affected my choice of intoxicants."[5]

Groening's interview with *Mother Jones* was one of the most incisive and revealing of his moral moorings. In both *The Simpsons* and *Futurama*, he said, he has tried to use the guise of light entertainment to wake people up "to some of the ways we're being manipulated and exploited" by modern

American culture. *The Simpsons'* message, in particular, is that "your moral authorities don't always have your best interest in mind. Teachers, principals, clergymen, politicians—for *The Simpsons*, they're all goofballs, and I think that's a great message for kids."[6] In a more recent interview with the Spanish language newspaper *La Opinion* in Los Angeles, he said that the show was "secretly educational, not for giving sermons or giving lectures about morality. *The Simpsons* is good for children because it's about learning how to tell a story."[7] Despite the series' underlying support for marriage, family, and values, Groening's wife, Deborah, told the *Seattle Times*, "Republicans and religious fanatics don't always get Matt's intentions. . . . [They] keep trying to convert Matt because they're worried he's going straight to hell—the real hell."[8] And, at one point, the burly, bearded father of two acknowledged that he did not permit his own elementary school age sons to watch *The Simpsons*.

Without live, aging actors and their egos to deal with, *The Simpsons* has evolved into a writers' medium. "As a writer," said Mike Scully, an executive producer who joined the show in 1993, "you really get spoiled on *The Simpsons*. I tell all our younger guys to enjoy this while it lasts, because you'll never have it this good again from a creative standpoint." Groening admitted that if he hadn't help create the series he probably wouldn't have been hired to write for it. "It's next to impossible to break into the inner circle unless you went to Harvard with one of those eggheads," he said, later referring to them as "Harvard-grad-brainiac-bastard-eggheads."[9] Richard Appel, a graduate of Harvard and Harvard Law School, left a job with the United States Attorney's office in Manhattan to write comedy in Los Angeles, where he joined other members of the Harvard *Lampoon* on *The Simpsons* in the 1990s. "It's like there's a conveyor belt now of people coming out here," he told the *New York Times* in 1997.

Typical of the writers who have shaped the series from the beginning is George Meyer, who started writing for the show in 1989 and wrote the episode "Homer the Heretic." Raised in Arizona, the oldest of eight children in a Catholic household, he was an A-student in school, on the speech team, editor of the school paper, and was an Eagle Scout. At Harvard, he was elected to head the *Lampoon*, the fabled humor magazine. After graduation, he was accepted to medical school but gravitated to comedy writing, working for David Letterman and *Saturday Night Live*. Scully called Meyer "the best comedy writer in Hollywood." The myriad of writers, producers, and consultants listed at the end of each *Simpsons* episode makes it nearly impossible for anyone outside the show to know (or recall) who was responsible for what joke or what plot twist. Much of the credit, most agree, goes to Meyer.

"I felt I was a happy kid," Meyer said in a 2000 *New Yorker* profile, which was written by David Owen, his Harvard roommate and longtime friend. But, as a Catholic, "I did feel that I was made to shoulder a lot of burdens that shouldn't have been mine—such as the frustrations of older women wearing nun costumes. People talk about how horrible it is to be brought up Catholic, and it's all true. The main thing was that there was no sense of proportion. I would chew a piece of gum at school, and the nun would say, 'Jesus is very angry with you about that,' and on the wall behind her would be a dying, bleeding guy on a cross. That's a horrifying image to throw at a little kid. You really could almost think that your talking in line, say, was on a par with killing Jesus. You weren't sure, and there was never a moderating voice."[10]

Another import from the Letterman show—and former *Lampoon* president—was Jeff Martin, who wrote for the series for three of the early seasons. Martin also came equipped with considerable knowledge of evangelical Protestantism. He is the son of William Martin, the author of *A Prophet with Honor: The Billy Graham Story* and *With God on Our Side: The Rise of the Religious Right in America*, and professor of the sociology of religion at Rice University. "We were active in church when the boys were growing up," said William Martin, a graduate of Harvard Divinity School. The family attended a Church of Christ in Massachusetts and, later, a moderate Southern Baptist Church in Houston, which he described as being "ecumenical, with evangelical roots." Family ties were also strong, William Martin said. "Nearly all of our relatives are actively religious, and Jeff saw a very positive representation of that tradition." His son "grew up recognizing that there were a lot of healthy and positive aspects to it, seeing the good sides of sincere, positive, true belief."

Martin admitted that he and his wife were skeptical about Jeff's move from the Letterman show to *The Simpsons*: "When he told us he was going to California to write an animated show about a loser working-class family, we thought, 'This is a bad career move.'" But at Rice, being the father of a writer for *The Simpsons* has turned out to carry considerable cachet, he said. "I get lots of mileage out of it." He never missed an episode and, early on, found himself providing informal script consultation to Jeff. "He would call about scripture or reference or phrase or a song—some technical point."

For his part, Jeff Martin said, "I knew I could always call my parents" for background information on religion, in addition to calling on his own memories. "My extended family contains many, many people who have an abiding faith that sustains them." Not surprisingly, he liked writing for the Flanders family. "Their religion obviously gives them a great deal of happiness and guidance, and the writing staff has respect for that. Ned is a truly nice man." But Jeff said he had a particular affinity for the two boys, Rod and Todd: "I'd have them singing songs I learned in Vacation Bible School when I was a kid."

As an industry, comedy writing is dominated by Catholics, Jews, and atheists, which made Martin a valuable resource in creating episodes of *The Simpsons*. In the months-long process—which is at once cooperative and competitive—script ideas are proposed, outlined, written, rewritten, and polished, often by more than a dozen writers and producers on a single episode. "I was in a minority as a Protestant, but I wouldn't say anyone deferred to me. It wasn't a case of me being an expert, although I suppose I did have more hands-on experience with a Protestant service." Martin moved on from *The Simpsons* to become cocreator of another animated series about a family, *Baby Blues*, which airs on the WB network.

Steve Tompkins, a veteran of three seasons with the series during the mid-1990s, was another writer who brought a Protestant perspective to *The Simpsons*. His insight is valuable because he is also a distinctive voice for religious values in Hollywood's high-powered world of animated comedies. Most of the writers on the show "were atheist Jews or atheist Christians, and only two of us were churchgoing Christians when I was there." Yet, when Tompkins and I first spoke, for a short article in *Christianity Today* magazine, he admitted to being wary of being identified as a Christian in print, in part because the label can be the kiss of death for a comedy writer. "The two are seen as antithetical," he said, sounding perplexed by the notion that a self-described class clown like himself should have to choose between the kingdom of heaven and a successful writing career. "I do believe that Jesus is the Son of God, that he was crucified and that he rose again." Tompkins was raised an Episcopalian in an upscale Massachusetts town, where he attended the same church as the novelist John Updike. As a child, he recalled watching *Davey and Goliath*, an early animated show produced by the Lutheran Church that used biblical themes, before going to church on Sundays.

Tompkins drifted from faith in his twenties, like many young people. While writing for *The Simpsons*, he had what he called a "reconversion experience," one he emphasized was unrelated to his comedy writing. Because he had not fallen out of faith, Tompkins hesitated to call it a born-again experience: "A little slice of me made itself known again. When that happened it *informed* my life, but didn't *transform* my life."

In the fall of 2000, Tompkins showed clips from *Simpsons* episodes while speaking at Fuller Theological Seminary in Pasadena, California, on a program entitled, "Does God Have a Sense of Humor?" as part of the school's "Reel Spirituality" series. He admitted that writing for Homer, Marge, Bart, and Lisa was a challenge. "There were some rabid atheists at *The Simpsons*," he said, yet it was not as much of a challenge as believers might think. "If you look at *The Simpsons*, no matter how twisted the story, no matter how profane the jokes, goodness wins, goodness prevails. No matter how much those writers pride themselves as being atheists, probably deep down, they're not. They have love for humanity, and they love those characters." (Like many Christians, Tompkins equates believing in God with loving humanity, and assumes that not believing is the same thing as not loving humanity. Atheists, who sometimes prefer the term "humanist," say they act in a moral and humane way because it is the right thing to do, not because they are bound by some supernatural set of beliefs.)

Tompkins too is a graduate of Harvard University and the *Lampoon*, and so was well equipped for the vigorous cut-and-thrust of *The Simpsons'* writing regime. "You pride yourself on being able to pitch jokes on any subject, no matter how blasphemous or sacrilegious," said Tompkins, who has also written for comedies such as *In Living Color* and *Everybody Loves Raymond*. "Whatever your religious beliefs might be, the process doesn't injure your personal spirit at all." In fact, he said, being able to participate fully in this raucous "room" can inoculate writers from concerns that they are pushing a particular agenda.

"At *The Simpsons*, you are reined in," Tompkins said. "You can't stick your neck out and do anything that's overtly religious on its face. You must undercut it. There's a gag reflex in comedy writers to undercut any honest religious sentiment. It is easier to pass a camel through the eye of a needle than it is to make a comedy writer quote scripture with a straight face." The key, he said, is "respecting the faith of the characters because it's true to the characters. I think that's what's going on in the best moments of *The Simpsons*. Marge's faith is respected because that is a huge part of who she is as a character. Homer has no faith, so we use him to tromp over Marge's faith, or whatever needs to be done comedically." At times, the show does seem to engage in "blasphemy for blasphemy's sake, an omnidirectional assault on all that's sacred." It helps, he says, that "no one really takes its blasphemy seriously. The things that should be mocked are mocked, and the things that shouldn't be mocked are mocked."

Tompkins worked on several *Simpsons* episodes that dealt with religion, the church and faith, including the one in which Ned, like the Bible's Job, has his faith tested. "There is a tremendous amount of affection for Ned" among the writers, he said. That episode, "Hurricane Neddy," used as its comedic premise a faithful Christian singled out for devastation, and "how a person behaves in times of crisis." Still, he insisted that, for the most part, he is a secular writer. "I had no ax to grind at *The Simpsons*. I believe the quality of humor is in indirect proportion to one's true belief. The more those beliefs are put in, the less funny it gets. The characters on *The Simpsons* do not represent the writers' faith." This is in contrast to *Touched by an Angel*, where, he said, "the stories those show-runners are creating really represent the way the world should be, could be." *Touched by an Angel* takes a more direct approach, using its content to communicate the message, Tompkins said, a conscious choice which works well for that show. "*The Simpsons* doesn't do that. The mark of good writing is letting the message be true to the characters, to honor their beliefs and keep them sacred to the character."

Ian Maxtone-Graham is an articulate representative of nonbelievers on *The Simpsons* staff, and he confirmed Tompkins's observation about the show's frenetic writing and rewriting process. This is especially true when it comes to the matter of credits for writers. "The titles don't mean much," he said. "Everyone's in the room and pretty much everyone moves up the ladder to 'co-executive producer.' Then there are the 'consulting producers' who—it's too complicated. We're all writers. The 'writer' of the episode wrote the first draft. It might be their story; might not. They might keep 80 percent of their jokes and lines. Most likely they'll keep way fewer. To my knowledge, no *Simpsons*' writing credit has been disputed or arbitrated by the Writers' Guild. The first draft guy or gal keeps the writing credit come hell or page one rewrite."

Maxtone-Graham, who has written many episodes, also confirmed Tompkins's description of the theological mix among writers: "There are many, many atheists in that room." A graduate of Brown University, *National Lampoon* magazine, and *Saturday Night Live*, Maxtone-Graham grew up in New York in an Episcopal family but never attended church. "I don't believe in God particularly," he told me, "although I always enjoyed Christmas carols. You don't need to believe in all the religious details to have it work. You don't have to believe in a higher power."

Music has been a path to spirituality of a sort for Maxtone-Graham. He helped write the popular "Hanukkah Song," cowritten and introduced by Adam Sandler on *Saturday Night Live*, as well as a Kwanzaa song for that show. In the early 1990s, Maxtone-Graham also wrote new lyrics for the classic "Silver Bells," which was sung by Glenn Close, who was hosting the holiday *SNL*, in her opening monologue. The Academy Award–winning actress was accompanied by about a dozen residents of her hometown in upstate New York.

"It was in the middle of a huge blizzard in New York," he recalled. "These poor guys—none of them performers—had come down to sing on national television. I had spent several hours teaching them the song, and I conducted them, quite inexpertly. Everyone was nervous, but they did a hell of a job, and the audience loved it. At the end of the song, they dropped artificial snow onto the stage, and the effect was just magical. A colleague came up to me and told me it had made her cry. It was a deeply moving experience, one of the greatest I have ever had as a writer. It was a hugely emotional moment for me. And I'm sure that's what got me interested in writing 'religious' songs."

After joining *The Simpsons*, Maxtone-Graham made a study of Christian rock music. His nonbelief notwithstanding, Maxtone-Graham wrote the episode in which Maude Flanders dies, including the moving, contemporary Christian rock song that sets up the dramatic reconciliation between Ned and his faith. This preparation helped him understand the characters' religious life. "It seems like a natural, everyday thing that they go to church," he said, "but they are not slavishly devoted to organized religion. They like the routine of going to church. And that's probably the way most people feel. They all have their skeptical moments."

It was while writing for *The Simpsons* that the skeptical Maxtone-Graham developed his own serious interest in religion and in the Bible. He stumbled across the book *Gospel Truth: The New Image of Jesus Emerging from Science and History, and Why It Matters*, by the journalist Russell Shorto. In part, Maxtone-Graham said he liked the book, which relies on the scholarship of the Jesus Seminar, because the author does not come from "a religion-hating background." He was so impressed with the work that he loaned it and gave it as a gift to other *Simpsons* writers. Before long, he was reading *Jesus: A Life* and *Paul: The Mind of the Apostle*, both by A. N. Wilson. "I was fascinated by the truth behind the New Testament. It turned me into a Bible know-it-all, but it didn't make me more or less religious. I admire many of the things Jesus said, but I'm not religious. I never was."

In writing about religion for the series, he said, "there is an attempt to universalize things without losing the Middle American flavor of their church, to leave it open to many intelligent people who are atheists." Thus, in writing about Flanders's crisis of faith following Maude's death, the viewer can interpret Ned's return to the church as God's answer to his prayers, or, for skeptics, that Ned simply found the inner resources to cope with his loss. "It seemed to have a message that works for both sides," Maxtone-Graham said.

Mike Reiss is one of those "Jewish atheists" on the show's writing staff. "I know Jewish culture," he said. "I was bar mitzvahed, but I've never been a believer. It's a rich culture full of interesting quirks, yet sometimes I wish Jewish kids would go to karate class rather than Hebrew school." Reiss grew up and attended synagogue in a Connecticut city that was home to only fifty Jews out of a population of fifty thousand. He went to Harvard, where he roomed with future *Simpsons* writer Al Jean, who would become his longtime writing partner. Both worked on the *Lampoon*, where Reiss said Jewish and Irish students tended to congregate.

His atheism notwithstanding, Reiss said, "I don't know any show that covers religion like *The Simpsons* does. The very best episodes are the ones that take a big, big issue like religion and look at it, and turn it upside down and examine it from all angles. We know there's no one answer to these things. It's one of those really big topics we come back to a lot, and I'm glad we do." If *The Simpsons* seems to favor religion, he said, it's more of a case of "being nice by accident . . ." As writers for the series, we go to church partly for mockery and comic value, for its ripe comic potential. Homer is always punished for his sins, and always punished way out of proportion. But there has always been a basic humanity to the show, and sometimes that manifests itself religiously."

Not that there aren't limits, even for an atheist, he said. "Every writer has built-in boundaries, a taste level that they won't cross. I consider myself one of the most conservative guys. The name 'Jesus' comes in as a punch line every so often. The show has gotten more sacrilegious as time has gone on. There's much more leeway. The cartoon format provides a buffer against these hard issues. The best live action sitcom couldn't play with religion the way *The Simpsons* does. You can't beat the cuteness factor, it looks so innocuous." The show's writers have learned through experience that viewers are willing to accept jokes and situations if they are presented in an animated form. In a larger sense, humor does not touch the same nerve with the faithful as drama. *The Last Temptation of Christ,* a serious attempt at portraying the Gospel, attracted far more Christian protests than the outrageously blasphemous *Monty Python's Life of Brian.*

In 2000, Reiss wrote a children's book called *How Murray Saved Christmas,* in which a Jewish delicatessen owner fills in for Santa Claus. Although there were some obvious Jewish references in the manuscript,

Reiss said that his editor, a Gentile from North Dakota, kept pressing him to add more. It was the same dynamic he experienced when he and Al Jean wrote *Simpsons* episodes together. Everyone assumed that he was the source of any "Jewish" material, when, in fact, as often as not it came from his Catholic partner. "In the writing room, Jewish people are there to provide authenticity—and pronunciation," Reiss said. "It's the Gentiles who get a real kick out of this stuff."

"I consider myself someone who believes in the teachings of Jesus Christ but who is not a huge fan of organized religion," said Al Jean, who returned to the job as *The Simpsons'* show-runner in 2001. "We respect everyone's belief." Jean began working on the show in 1989 and, with Reiss, is credited in over 200 episodes, which provides him with perspective on the way the presentation of religion in the series has evolved. "Often things on the show grow of their own accord," he said. "We didn't set out on the show with an agenda. But very early on we showed characters going to church, and we began exploring that venue, which was obviously very rich. So, for example, we looked at the Ten Commandments as source material. As writers, we are always looking for aspects of life that are undercovered or underrepresented on TV, and religion is definitely one of them." And the frequent inclusion and favorable slant on faith? "It wasn't because of any conscious attempt at the beginning," he said. "We didn't want to take cheap shots. It was a subject that was not explored much in prime-time sitcoms. We're not perfect, but we definitely are very thoughtful and funny. The show is something a family can watch."

Jean acknowledged that there are some taboos in the religion area; crucifixion or resurrection jokes are generally off limits. "People are very sensitive to those things," he said. "Images of Christ on the cross, things like that can't avoid offending a huge group of people. We're pretty cautious about that." Crossing such lines, he said, "would erode all the goodwill the show generates and would undermine the show's moral messages."

While there are people on the staff who may now be irreligious, he said, religion plays a part in *The Simpsons* because the writers were raised in middle or upper middle–class homes where faith and observance were part of their lives. "We're just aiming to depict what we saw as reality. We just want you to believe these are real people. Without a doubt, religion has been accepted in the show because it is reflective of life, but we never forget that comedy is the real point of it all."

Particular care is taken not to single out one denomination or another for praise or pillory, Jean said. "I can't say one faith is right over another."

Salvation by faith is eclipsed by salvation by works for a very simple reason. "As writers, we're always interested in dramatic actions. Works are more interesting to watch than grace."

Over the years, *The Simpsons* has made fun of Protestants, Catholics, Jews, and Hindus. Jean, a Catholic, admitted that Muslims have also been largely off limits. "One reason is, I don't think we've had a writer who was Muslim," noting that there was a chill resulting from the Salman Rushdie affair. "It's a faith where you don't want to offend, because we're not Muslim, and we're not sure what might be offensive."

Why do the writers and creators believe the role of religion in the show has gone unnoticed until fairly recently? "Two or three things can pigeonhole a show," Jean said. "Our pigeonhole was that we were the outrageous show that had no conscience. We got this bad boy image since the beginning, but over the past ten years it has evaporated. We're a little less outrageous compared to *South Park*. People are looking beyond the surface. There is a thoughtful core to the show. We believe in the little guy, the triumph of the family. Our characters are real; they want love and companionship in the end."

Thirteen

Conclusion: Cloaking the Sacred with the Profane?

If you excise the jokes, *The Simpsons* is a tragedy of operatic proportions—repeated failures and frustrations, punctuated by the occasional, wacky, life-affirming reprieve that returns everything to the status quo. And, like any comedy aimed at a mass audience, it is at its roots doggedly conservative. Leon Trotsky, one of the fathers of Russia's Bolshevik uprising, used to characterize a political movement he opposed as being "left in form, right in essence," which is to say that his opponents were revolutionary in appearance but reactionary in nature. With *The Simpsons*, I think it may be a similar case: cloaking the show's sacred essence in the guise of profane storytelling, although there is no evidence that this is a result of any conscious, consistent effort on the part of the show's writers and producers. Longtime writer George Meyer argued just the opposite in the *My Generation* magazine article. "It's like a Trojan horse that gets past people's radar because it's superficially conservative," he said. "The show's subtext, however, is completely subversive and wild."

Whether the series, once considered so antiauthoritarian, is subversive or supportive of faith is largely in the eye of the beholder. Some Christians remain resolutely unconvinced of its value. The Reverend Francis Chan of the evangelical Cornerstone Community Church in Simi Valley, California, told the *Ventura County Star* in 1999 that he once found the show funny, but gave it up. "It portrays Christians as being out of touch with reality. It makes anyone who follows God look like a fool."[1]

The Reverend Clark Whitten, pastor of Calvary Assembly of God in Winter Park, Florida, one of the largest Pentecostal churches in that area, tries not to miss a single Sunday night episode. "It's life, it's hilarious, and it's so insightful into the culture," he said. The Anglican Archbishop of Wales, Dr. Rowan Williams, considered a strong candidate to become the next Archbishop of Canterbury, called *The Simpsons* "a positive example to children" and a show with "a strong sense of family values."

In his study of religion in television series, Jim Trammell of the University of Georgia arrived at a similar conclusion. "Despite the church's depicted irrelevance, despite the depicted wrath of God and the likeable character of the Devil, despite the disrespected devoted neighbors, despite the inadequate minister, despite even the insignificance of spirituality upon one's behaviors, the Simpson family, the show's heroes and representatives of the American family, remain committed to their religion."

Some atheists think *The Simpsons* is so proreligion that it's more like a Sunday school lesson than a sitcom. In a 1995 atheists' Internet discussion group, one member wrote, "The central message of the show, I've noticed, is that only the good people are religious and that those who are not are immoral. Some episodes really hammer the point home. And the true religious fanatics in that show are portrayed as the most moral, ethical people around. I stopped watching in disgust a long time ago." Like the Christians, even the atheists are split on the series. "It's a great show," said George H. Smith, author of *Why Atheism?* and *Atheism: The Case against God.* "I think there's a good balance" on religion, he said. "It's a remarkably well-done show."

This appraisal has not escaped the attention of a growing number of commentators who argue that the show is far more conservative and supportive of traditional faith and family values than you would think. "What I do appreciate about *The Simpsons* is that evil often—if not always—is punished with consequences," said Robert Knight, former director of cultural studies for the Washington, D.C.-based Family Research Council and author of *The Age of Consent: The Rise of Relativism and the Corruption of Popular Culture.* "*The Simpsons* function in a moral universe and, while the show seems to make fun of moral standards, it often upholds those same standards in a backhanded way."

"The show provides elements of continuity that make *The Simpsons* more traditional than may first appear," according to Paul A. Cantor, writing in the December 1999 issue of the journal *Political Theory.* "The show's creators have been generally evenhanded over the years in making fun of both [political] parties, and of both the Right and the Left," providing something to both liberals and conservatives. In essence, Cantor argues that "*The Simpsons* seems to offer a kind of intellectual defense of the common man against intellectuals, which helps explain its popularity and broad appeal."[2]

Take, for example, the characters' hometown of Springfield. Cantor argued in his award-winning paper for the American Political Science Association that, while the show makes fun of small town life, "it simultaneously celebrates the virtues of the traditional American small town. . . . *The Simpsons* is profoundly anachronistic in the way it harks back to an earlier age when Americans felt more in contact with their governing institutions and family life was solidly anchored in a larger but still local community."

In his essay, Cantor suggested that an even more telling analysis would focus on the family. "*The Simpsons* shows the family as part of a larger community and in effect affirms the kind of community that can sustain the family. . . . For all its slapstick nature and its mocking of certain aspects of family life, *The Simpsons* has an affirmative side and ends up celebrating the nuclear family as an institution. . . . Though it strikes many people as trying to subvert the American family or to undermine its authority, in fact, it reminds us that antiauthoritarianism is itself an American tradition and that family authority has always been problematic in democratic America. What makes *The Simpsons* so interesting is the way it combines traditionalism and antitraditionalism. It continually makes fun of the traditional American family. But it continually offers an enduring image of the nuclear family in the very act of satirizing it. Many of the traditional values of the American family survive this satire, above all the value of the nuclear family itself."

Jonah Goldberg reinforced Cantor's take on the series in an article in the *National Review*. Many conservatives share a negative view of *The Simpsons*, based on the controversies generated in the first few seasons, he wrote. "That's regrettable, because it's possibly the most intelligent, funny and even politically satisfying TV show ever." In contrast to previous sitcom hits, which he said were "invariably and predictably liberal," *The Simpsons* "is never predictable; and its satire spares nothing and no one. . . . This even-handedness is noteworthy. Against the backdrop of conventional sitcoms, it makes *The Simpsons* damn near reactionary; if 50 percent of the jokes are aimed leftward, that's 49.5 percent more than we usually get." Yes, Goldberg acknowledged, "Christian fundamentalism get[s] the full treatment," but the satire "is aimed at all of society's false pieties. . . . What should dismay liberals about this is that so many of today's pieties are constructs of the Left. . . . Some important pretensions are being punctured here—but not the usual ones."[3] Targets include liberal Democrats, environmentalism, gun control, and '60s radical sellouts.

Even *The Plain Truth*, a nondenominational magazine affiliated with the Worldwide Church of God, took favorable note of *The Simpsons* in a lengthy article by Barbara Curtis in the January/February 2001 issue of the evangelical magazine. Under the headline, "Are the Simpsons 'Okily

Dokily'?" Curtis answered vigorously in the affirmative. The show was "long-forbidden fare in many Christian homes," she wrote, including her own. "Like most good Christians, I refused to give them the time of day." After giving the show a chance, however, "I was impressed with the grace abounding in the characters' relationships, as well as the intelligence and wit of the writing. . . . There is no other show in TV land that so acknowledges the immediacy of God and the effectiveness of prayer. Peel away the laughter, and you will find *The Simpsons* have a strong foundation in love and faithfulness."[4]

The show's potshots at Christians and their church did not offend Curtis. "When it comes to exposing human foibles, *The Simpsons* is an equal opportunity employer. . . . I'm glad I'm not alone in finding the Christian highlights hilarious. Our weaknesses are, after all, our weaknesses. We all know Neds and Maudes and Reverend Lovejoys—may even *be* them from time to time ourselves. Perhaps the greatest weakness of all is to take oneself too seriously."

If these conservative commentators are correct, how did this happen, and why? Televangelist and Christian Coalition founder Pat Robertson, who told me he much preferred *Touched by an Angel* to *The Simpsons*, suggested that the Great Man Theory of History might explain why the Fox show has turned so positive on faith. "I was somewhat appalled at what I saw of *The Simpsons* initially, and I am frankly not an aficionado of *The Simpsons*. I know Rupert Murdoch, and Rupert's a pretty good guy, and it may be that he has allowed some of these good things to come through in this cartoon. I am delighted if I could see any type of family values being shown in that show."

In fact, the opposite appears to be the case. Murdoch, an outspoken conservative and owner of Fox who bankrolls the *Weekly Standard* magazine, has taken a hands-off position with the show, which takes frequent potshots at him and his network. Characters on *The Simpsons* repeatedly call Fox's programming cheesy, while at the same time taking credit—accurately—for playing a critical role in its financial survival in the early years of the upstart network's existence. The autocratic media mogul has also endured personal criticism from *The Simpsons* on numerous occasions, and Murdoch's good grace has even included voicing dialogue for the unsympathetic caricature of himself on one episode. This self-parody is probably an example of what the Marxist philosopher Herbert Marcuse called "repressive tolerance." Since Fox and its parent company have fattened on worldwide syndication deals for *The Simpsons* and license fees on more than a billion dollars worth of series-related merchandise, it is literally a case of Murdoch laughing all the way to the bank. "As a commercial program," writes Jim Trammell of the University of Georgia, *The Simpsons* simply "follows an entertainment and capitalistic ideology."

There may be another incidental, economic reason for the show's conservative bent and the relatively prominent role played by religion in it: production costs. Harry Shearer, the gifted writer and actor who provides the voice of Ned Flanders, Reverend Lovejoy, and many other characters, offered this explanation. He told me that, in his opinion, "the richness of the religious universe of the show is, I think, a largely accidental byproduct of the fact that, because it's an animated show, the creators decided to fill it with—for television—an unusual number of secondary characters. It's these characters—Ned, Lovejoy, Krusty—who would be economically impossible in a live-action show, whose stories led the writers into normally uncharted territory for sitcoms. So, yes, I'm saying follow the money."

There are other ways to follow the money. In his preface to *A Contribution to the Critique of Hegel's Philosophy of Right*, Karl Marx wrote, "Religion is the sigh of the oppressed creature, the heart of a heartless world, and the soul of soulless conditions. It is the opium of the people." Most social scientists agree that if Marx were writing today he would substitute the word "television" for the word "religion." An article by Associated Press writer Todd Lewan entitled, "How the Talking Box Changed a Village," in the March 2001 issue of *Catholic Digest* examined the impact of television on one of America's most remote communities. The Alaskan village was home to ninety-six members of the Gwich'in people in 1980, when television was introduced there. Until then, the native peoples lived as their ancestors had, their lives circumscribed by the hunt for caribou and telling stories about their culture. Two decades later, Lewan reported, every cabin had at least one television, consumerism had invaded the village, and storytelling was nearly extinct: "Old legends told around campfires could not hold [the children] when Bart Simpson was talking."

Television, what Homer calls his "teacher, mother, secret lover," has transformed Homer's own family into a consumer unit. "They're creatures of consumption and envy, laziness and opportunity, stubbornness and redemption," Matt Groening said in a 1998 talk at the Museum of Television and Radio University Satellite Seminar Series. "They're just like the rest of us. Only exaggerated." His television family is "utterly addicted to TV," and the series is "about watching TV," he told the students. Or, as the authors of *Watching What We Watch: Prime-Time Television through the Lens of Faith* put it: "The message is that the great American viewing public is now watching a show about *themselves*, in front of their own television hearth."[5]

As Clay Steinman, professor of communication studies at Macalester College, noted, most people watch television commercials along with any programs, though this can be defeated by zapping or muting or buying or renting tapes. Thus, the meanings of the programs are intertwined with those of the commercials embedded within them. Indeed, this is what advertisers hope: that the products advertised will gain value by their association with elements of their adjoining programs. "Advertisers are aware that men aged 18–49 make up 40 percent of the audience of *The Simpsons*," writes William D. Romanowski, in *Eyes Wide Open: Looking for GOD in Popular Culture* (Brazos/Baker, 2001).

In *Consuming Environments: Television and Commercial Culture*, Steinman and his coauthors, Mike Budd and Steve Craig, argue that a telling way to analyze shows like *The Simpsons* is to look at the advertisers and their target audiences. Using this criterion, could any program that counted among its regular advertisers in the 2000–2001 season the U.S. Army, Air Force and Old Navy clothing be considered subversive of traditional religious values? "Except for certain shows intended for specific, smaller audiences, 'Don't offend' remains the slogan of the age as far as desired viewers are concerned," Steinman and his coauthors wrote. "That means don't challenge any desirable sector of the audience, don't question conventional wisdom, don't risk driving anyone you want away."[6]

In a backhanded way, Andrea Alstrup, corporate vice president for advertising for Johnson & Johnson, which spends $600 million a year in television commercials, confirmed Steinman's analysis in a June 1998 speech to three hundred advertising executives at a luncheon meeting of the Advertising Women of New York. "Do we really need to continue to support with our advertising a constant barrage of media that appeals to the lowest common denominator of values?" Alstrup asked, according to the March 2001 issue of *Brill's Content*.

Of course, strictly speaking, every episode of *The Simpsons* can be seen as a twenty-two-minute commercial for the show's vast and durable array of licensed merchandise. And the broadcasters don't care how critical viewers are, as long as they continue to watch and see the ads. Clearly, members of the Simpson family spend many more hours worshiping together before the altar of their screen than they do in the pews of their church. In that, they are like most people in the United States, and increasing numbers throughout the world. "To the extent that people take *The Simpsons* as being about real people or being magical or godly," Steinman told me, "they are engaging in contemporary forms of idol—or idle—worship."

Politically, in *The Simpsons'* portrayal of nuclear plant owner Montgomery Burns and others of great wealth and power, "it would appear that the ultimate antagonist is really the competitive, materialistic nature of American capitalism," according to *Watching What We Watch*. The show articulates "a vision critical of the unjust distribution of power in America. . . . *The Simpsons* can continue to skewer the evils of society while not seeming too dangerous."[7] The key word here, I think, is "appear." *The Simpsons* only *seems* to question conventional wisdom and values. For me, the consistent message of *The Simpsons* is this: If you are part of the American working class, your family—and to a lesser extent your faith—are the only reliable defenses against the vagaries of modern life. (For some, "modern life" may mean carpooling, office politics, making ends meet, or anxieties about raising kids in a risky world; for others, it is a convenient euphemism for globalized capitalism.) Or, as the authors of *Watching What We Watch* put it, "The only thing that really matters in life is having a supportive family." As always, Homer says it best: "I guess I'll have to give up my hopes and dreams, and settle for being a decent husband and father."

In this context, religion serves as a palliative, comforting characters in their social futility. *"The Simpsons* represents both a model of and a model for contemporary American society, not only because it reveals contemporary attitudes about religious institutions, morality and spirituality, but also because it functions in the time-honored way of religious satirists," observed the authors of *God in the Details*.[8] "Traditionally, religions have employed humor and satire to bring people together and dissolve their differences," Joseph Bastien wrote in the *Encyclopedia of Religion*.[9]

The Simpsons' gospel is not the fighting faith of the Old Testament prophets or of the confrontational Jesus, both of which sought to rock the boat of unrighteous comfort. At the same time, *The Simpsons'* theology is not one that takes joy in acceptance. Marge, Ned, Lovejoy, and other believers in the series are not like those collaborationist ministers of the early twentieth century who were accused by radicals of preaching "pie in the sky, bye and bye." Their faith is a bulwark, a highly meaningful and relevant refuge. And, as it is for many of us, faith is a last resort against the pressures of the ever faster pace and power of the global market, personal and natural disasters, or whatever significant stresses one might face.

"The question arises as to whether the satirical tenor of the show actually causes viewers to look critically at their culture and their own lives," according to *Watching What We Watch*. "Are audience members likely to agree with the overall message of the series about the importance of having a supportive —if 'dysfunctional'—family to shield individuals from the oppressive forces of society? If so, are we likely to react by trying to change alienating social institutions along more humane and egalitarian lines?"

John Heeren puts the question another way in *The Simpsons and Philosophy: The D'Oh! of Homer.* "Does *The Simpsons* use its humor to promote a moral agenda?" His conclusion is also different: "*The Simpsons* does not promote anything, because its humor works by putting forward positions in order to undercut them. Furthermore, this process of undercutting runs so deeply that we cannot regard the show as merely cynical; it manages to undercut its cynicism too."[10] Steve Tompkins, the former *Simpsons* writer, made that same point to me, explaining the tortuous and sometimes frustrating process by which positive messages regarding religion ultimately make it into the show.

Given the world we live in, and the economic system we live under, *The Simpsons* is about as trenchant, as life-affirming, as socially critical a prime-time situation comedy as we can reasonably expect on a major, commercial television network. So, what impact does television, in particular a show like *The Simpsons*, have on tens of millions of viewers? That question remains open. The Rev. Donald Wildmon, head of the ultra-conservative American Family Association, based in Tupelo, Miss., believes it is considerable. "You may think that Billy Graham is the leading evangelist in America, but he's not. The leading evangelists in America are those people who make the TV programs." Graham himself has written that "television is the most powerful communication ever devised by man." But communications scholar Quentin Schultze of Calvin College disagrees. "Research clearly documents the ineffectiveness of electronic media as agents of religious conversion, yet the popular mythology holds that spiritual battles can be won electronically."

Does the favorable portrayal of God, faith, and religion in *The Simpsons* have any lasting effect? What is the message the show's writers and producers—non-Christians and non-believers, in the main—want to convey? There is a clear contrast between *The Simpsons'* writers and producers and one of the best-known and intentional purveyors of moral values and religious faith in popular culture. The late Charles Schulz used his *Peanuts* characters to communicate his gentle, New Testament faith, along with a darker undercurrent of life's unfairness, from the Old Testament's book of Job. I asked Robert Short—author of the best-selling *The Gospel according to Peanuts* and a pioneer in the study of religion and popular culture—what he thought. In the lectures he gives around the country, often to church groups, he said, "*The Simpsons* always comes up. People seem very impressed with it, with what they find in *The Simpsons*. They look at it as the same kind of thing as *Peanuts*, in another medium. They know

The Simpsons, and they are convinced it is on their side." The people he meets, Short said, believe that the show's writers are more fond of Christian faith and Christianity than they are critical. They feel that the writers seem to be saying that they have no quarrel with the basics of religion, that they "support it in a very subtle way and Christian viewers are appreciative of that, but not surprised." They sense "a genuine admiration and respect."

And what about viewers who don't come to Short's church lectures, namely, the legion of the unchurched? If, as some researchers and many observers have suggested, television can inure impressionable minds to violence through repetition, might not the same hold true for repeated and positive portrayals of faith in *The Simpsons*? Granted, it is just one show, but it is one with millions of devoted adolescent and teen fans who watch the episodes over and over. In this way, Short believes *The Simpsons* can have an impact in the postmodern world.

"It's amazing how God can speak in these out-of-the-way places," Short said. "He can be very deliberate in using a medium like *The Simpsons*. It's the shock of the surprise: The arts get under our skin far more effectively than direct discourse, far more effectively than a sermon. People don't even realize what has been said to them. They like what they hear and see. It makes a deep impression on them. It's a form of indirect communication. Even someone who is a hard case, an agnostic, is probably going to be impressed with the way Christianity is portrayed. It can be cool to find great values there."

The movie industry—television's older sibling—has always been fascinated by its younger rival for a mass audience, and by TV's impact on society. One such examination, *The Truman Show*, posits a ratings hit "reality" series about a totally artificial environment in which everyone except the program's title character, played by Jim Carrey, is in on the conceit. The show's advertisements promise "No Scripts . . . No Cue Cards . . . It's Genuine . . . It's a life." At the film's conclusion, the unsuspecting Truman finally punctures his television-created environment. Just as Truman is poised to escape, the show's developer and director introduces himself: "I am the Creator," he explains, "of a television show that gives hope and joy and inspiration to millions."

Matt Groening probably wouldn't put it exactly that way. In its animated, absurdist form, *The Simpsons* is about as removed from "reality" television as one could imagine. "We try to put real human emotion into it," he told one interviewer. "Most other cartoons, except the Disney films, don't seem to do that. They are just about surface emotion. The [*Simpsons*] has a rubber-band reality. We stretch it way out into the far reaches of human folly, and it snaps back to relative sanity." So, in essence, while not at all dangerous or threatening to the status quo, it is a sweet, funny show about a family as "real" as the faith lives of many Americans. It is a show that does in fact give hope and joy and, yes, inspiration to millions. But mostly, as my wife reminds me, it's funny. And as Homer says, "it's funny 'cause it's true."

A Note on Methodology

The ideal way to analyze an episode of *The Simpsons* is to buy, rent, or record the show and watch it with a notebook in one hand and the remote in the other, running the tape back and forth until no line of dialogue, image, cultural reference, or nuance escapes. With more than 275 episodes, that was not possible for me. Using the resources available, I estimate that I have seen close to 150 *Simpsons* episodes, some of which I purchased, borrowed, or taped. As a substitute or a supplement, the episode summaries on the *Simpsons* Archive Web site (snpp.com) are an excellent source for information, as well as excellent observations and reviews. Less comprehensive—but quite valuable and entertaining—are the brief episode summaries in the *Simpsons* guidebooks published by HarperPerennial and edited by Ray Richmond. With key episodes such as "Homer the Heretic," "Lisa the Skeptic," "Homer vs. Lisa and the Eighth Commandment," and "Like Father, Like Clown," I have been fortunate to make use of all of these resources. Nonetheless, I am certain I have made some mistakes in reporting dialogue or situations, and for that I apologize.

Notes

Where no citation is given, the quotation comes from an interview or personal conversation between the author and the subject.

Introduction

1. Jon Horowitz, "Mmm . . . Television: A Study of the Audience of *The Simpsons*," unpublished paper, Rutgers University, courtesy of the author.
2. Todd Brewster, "How TV Shaped America," *Life*, April 1999.
3. Kurt Andersen, "Animation Nation," *New Yorker*, June 16, 1997.
4. Robert Thompson, quoted in the *Orlando Sentinel*, December 2, 2000.
5. Sharpe James, quoted in the *Star Ledger* (Newark, N.J.), June 20, 1990.
6. William Bennett, quoted in the *Seattle Times*, August 19, 1990.
7. Barbara Bush, quoted in "And on the Seventh Day, Matt Created Bart," *Loaded Magazine*, August 1996.
8. Reinhold Niebuhr, quoted in Conrad Hyers, *The Comic Vision and the Christian Faith: A Celebration of Life and Laughter* (New York: Pilgrim Press, 1981).
9. Hyers, *Comic Vision and the Christian Faith*.
10. Gerry Bowler, "God and *The Simpsons*: The Religious Life of an Animated Sitcom," academic paper presented October 1996 at "The Media and Family Values" seminar at Canadian Nazarene College, Calgary, Canada.
11. William Romanowski, *Pop Culture Wars: Religion and the Role of Entertainment in American Life* (Downers Grove, Ill.: InterVarsity Press, 1996).
12. Beth Keller, "The Gospel according to Bart: Examining the Religious Elements of *The Simpsons*," master's thesis, Regent University, College of Communication and the Arts, 1992, courtesy of the author.
13. Mike Scully, quoted in "The Gospel According to Homer," by Bob von Sternberg, Minneapolis Star Tribune, May 30, 1998.
14. "No Sacred Cows for Groening," Associated Press, April 24, 1999.
15. John Heeren, "Religion in *The Simpsons*," in *The Simpsons and Philosophy: The D'oh! of Homer*, ed. William Irwin et al. (Chicago: Open Court Press, 2001). An early version of this paper was presented at the Society for the Scientific Study of Religion conference in Houston, Texas, in October 2000.
16. *The Door*, November–December 1999.
17. David Dark, "The Steeple and the Gargoyle—Celebrating *The Simpsons*," PRISM, July–August 1997.
18. David Landry, quoted in Bob von Sternberg, "The Gospel according to Homer," *Twin Cities Star-Tribune* May 30, 1998.

19. Paul Cantor, "The Simpsons: Atomistic Politics and the Nuclear Family," *Political Theory* 27, no. 6 (December 1999).

Chapter 1

1. William A. Dembski, *Intelligent Design: The Bridge between Science and Theology* (Downers Grove, Ill.: InterVarsity Press, 1999).
2. "Matt Groening: *The Mother Jones* Interview," *Mother Jones*, March–April 1999.
3. Eric Michael Mazur and Kate McCarthy, eds., *God in the Details: American Religion in Popular Culture* (New York: Routledge, 2000).
4. Abraham Heschel, *The Prophet* (Philadelphia: Jewish Publication Society of America, 1962).
5. David Owen, "Crazy for the Simpsons," *TV Guide*, Jan. 3–9, 1998.
6. Mazur et al., *God in the Details.*
7. Keller, "The Gospel according to Bart."
8. Gerry Bowler, quoted in Douglas Todd, "The Simpsons as TV's Holy Family," *Vancouver Sun*, December 1996.
9. Elton Trueblood, *Humor of Christ* (New York: Harper & Row, 1964).

Chapter 2

1. Lee Strobel, *What Jesus Would Say* (Grand Rapids: Zondervan Publishing House, 1994).
2. Robert Thompson, quoted in the *Ventura County Star,* "The Gospel of Homer," by Tom Kishen, September 4, 1999.
3. Ibid.
4. Strobel, *What Jesus Would Say.*
5. Mazur et al., *God in the Details.*
6. Heeren, "Religion in *The Simpsons.*"
7. Wendy Kaminer, *Sleeping with Extra-Terrestrials: The Rise of Irrationalism and Perils of Piety* (New York: Vintage Books, 2000).

Chapter 3

1. James Lawler, in Irwin et al., eds., *Simpsons and Philosophy.*
2. Aeon J. Skoble, in *Simpsons and Philosophy.*

Chapter 4

1. Gerry Bowler, quoted in Les Sillars, "The Last Christian TV Family in America," *Alberta Report*, October 21, 1996.
2. Michael Weisskopf, quoted in the *Washington Post*, February 1, 1993.
3. Harry Shearer interview in *The Door,* May–June 1999.
4. Frederica Mathewes-Green, "Ned Flanders, My Hero," on Beliefnet.com, February 10, 2000.
5. David Landry, quoted in von Sternberg, "Gospel according to Homer."

Chapter 5

1. Matt Groening, *The Simpsons Guide to Springfield* (New York: HarperCollins, 1998).
2. Mazur et al., *God in the Details.*
3. Ibid.
4. Ibid.

Chapter 6

1. Pope John Paul II, quoted by the Associated Press, July 28, 1999.

Chapter 8

1. "Public Perceptions about the Bible in the Twenty-First Century," survey released by Zondervan Publishing, November 15, 2000.
2. Groening, *Simpsons Guide to Springfield.*

Chapter 9

1. William Bennett, quoted in the *Seattle Times*, August 19, 1990.
2. Mark Fischer, quoted in the *Ventura County Star*, "The Gospel of Homer," by Tom Kishen, September 4, 1999.
3. Cardinal John O'Connor, quoted on the Catholic League Web site (www.catholicleague.org/faqs.htm).
4. The Catholic League statement of purpose, from the Catholic League Web site.
5. Letter by Thomas Chavez, quoted in *The Catalyst*, January–February 1999.
6. "*The Simpsons* Gets Too Cute," *The Catalyst*, January–February 1999.
7. "*The Simpsons* Offends Again," *The Catalyst*, March 1999.
8. "Rosenberg on TV: Fox Does Have Standards—And Double Standards at That," *Los Angeles Times*, June 2, 1999.
9. Ibid.
10. Ibid.
11. Ibid.
12. "Fox Gets Message on *Simpsons*," *The Catalyst*, July–August 1999.
13. George Weigel, speaking at a conference sponsored by the Ethics and Public Policy Center at Prouts Neck, Maine, September 1999.

Chapter 10

1. Jack Wertheimer, speaking at a conference sponsored by the Ethics and Public Policy Center at Prouts Neck, Maine, September 1999.
2. Mel Brooks, quoted in *The Big Little Book of Jewish Wit and Wisdom* (Black Dog & Leventhal Publishers, 2000).
3. Matt Groening, quoted in "Life in Hell," by Alan Paul, *Flux*, September 30, 1995.

Chapter 11

1. Al Jean, quoted in Joe Rhodes, "Flash! 24 Simpson Stars Reveal Themselves," *TV Guide* October 21, 2000.
2. Matt Groening, quoted in Rhodes, "Flash!"
3. Prithui Raj Singh, quoted in John Dart, "TV's Most Religious Family?" *Christian Century*, January 31, 2001.

Chapter 12

1. Matt Groening interview with Andrew Duncan, *Radio Times*, September 18–24, 1999.
2. Matt Groening interview, "Influences: From Yesterday to Today," CBS, August 27, 1999.
3. Ibid.

4. Matt Groening, quoted in "The Making of The Simpsons," by Joe Rhodes, *Entertainment Weelky*, May 18, 1990.

5. Harry Shearer interview, *FilmForce*, April 25, 2000 (www.filmforce.ign.com/chats/harryshearer.shtml).

6. "Matt Groening: The *Mother Jones* Interview," *Mother Jones*, March–April 1999.

7. Matt Groening interview with Isis Sauceda, *La Opinion*, November 30–December 10, 2000.

8. Deborah Groening, quoted in Paul Andrews, "The Groening of America," *Seattle Times*, August 19, 1990.

9. Matt Groening interview with Carina Chocano, Salon.com, January 30, 2001.

10. George Meyer interview, "Taking Humor Seriously—George Meyer, the Funniest Man behind the Funniest Show on TV," by David Owen, *New Yorker*, March 13, 2000.

Chapter 13

1. Francis Chan, in the *Ventura County Star*, "The Gospel of Homer," by Tom Kishen, September 4, 1999.

2. Cantor, "The Simpsons: Atomistic Politics."

3. Jonah Goldberg, "Homer Never Nods: The Importance of *The Simpsons*," *National Review*, May 1, 2000.

4. Barbara Curtis, "Are the Simpsons 'Okily Dokily'?" *Plain Truth*, January–February 2001.

5. Matt Groening, quoted in Walt Davis et al., *Watching What We Watch: Prime-Time Television through the Lens of Faith* (Louisville, Ky.: Geneva Press, 2001).

6. Mike Budd et al., *Consuming Environments: Television and Commercial Culture* (Piscataway, N.J.: Rutgers University Press, 1999).

7. Davis et al., *Watching What We Watch*.

8. Mazur et al., *God in the Details*.

9. Joseph Bastien, "Humor and Satire," in *The Encyclopedia of Religion*, ed. Mircea Eliade (New York: Macmillan, 1987).

10. Heeren, "Religion in *The Simpsons*."

Bibliography

Books

Budd, Mike, Steve Craig, and Clay Steinman. *Consuming Environments: Television and Commercial Culture*. Piscataway, N.J.: Rutgers University Press. 1999.

Davis, Walter T. et al. *Watching What We Watch: Prime-Time Television through the Lens of Faith*. Louisville, Ky.: Geneva Press. 2001.

Dembski, William A. *Intelligent Design: The Bridge between Science and Theology*. Downers Grove, Ill.: InterVarsity Press. 1999.

Dossey, Larry, M.D. *Be Careful What You Pray For . . . You Just Might Get It*. San Francisco: HarperSanFrancisco. 1998.

Irwin, William, Mark T. Conard, and Aeon J. Skoble. *The Simpsons and Philosophy: The D'oh! of Homer*. Open Court. 2001.

Mazur, Eric Michael, and Kate McCarthy. *God in the Details: American Religion in Popular Culture*. Routledge. 2000.

Postman, Neil. *Amusing Ourselves to Death: Public Discourse in the Age of Show Business*. Penguin. 1985.

Romanowski, William D. *Pop Culture Wars: Religion and the Role of Entertainment in American Life*. Downers Grove, Ill.: InterVarsity Press. 1996.

———. *Eyes Wide Open: Looking for God in Popular Culture*. Brazos/Baker. 2001.

Strobel, Lee. *What Would Jesus Say?* Grand Rapids: Zondervan Publishing House. 1994.

Articles

Curtis, Barbara. "Are the Simpsons 'Okily Dokily'?" *Plain Truth*. January 2001.

Dark, David. "The Steeple and the Gargoyle—Celebrating the Simpsons." *PRISM*. July/August 1997.

Goldberg, Jonah. "Homer Never Nods: The Importance of *The Simpsons*." *National Review*. May 1, 2000.

Kisken, Tom. "The Gospel of Homer." *Ventura County Star*. September 4, 1999.

Mathewes-Green, Frederica. "Ned Flanders, My Hero." Beliefnet.com. February 2000.

McKenna, Kristine. "Matt Groening: The Genius Who Controls Bart Simpson (Yeah, Right!)" *My Creation*, May/June 2001.

Owen, David. "Taking Humor Seriously—George Meyer, the Funniest Man behind the Funniest Show on TV." *New Yorker*. March 13, 2000.

Sillars, Les. "The Last Christian TV Family in America." *Alberta Report*. October 21, 1996.

Todd, Douglas. "The Simpsons as TV's Holy Family." *Vancouver Sun*. December 1996.

Von Sternberg, Bob. "The Gospel according to Homer." *Twin Cities Star-Tribune*. May 5, 1998.

Academic Papers and Journal Articles

Bowler, Gerry. "God and *The Simpsons*: The Religious Life of an Animated Sitcom." Symposium on "The Media and Family Values" held at Canadian Nazarene College, Calgary in October 1996.

Cantor, Paul. "The Simpsons: Atomistic Politics and the Nuclear Family." *Political Theory*. December 1999.

Heeren, John. "Saints and Sinners in Springfield: Religion in *The Simpsons*." 2000 meeting of the Society for the Scientific Study of Religion.

Keller, Beth. "The Gospel according to Bart: Examining the Religious Elements of *The Simpsons*." Regent University, College of Communication and the Arts. September 29, 1992. Unpublished.

Trammel, Jim. "The Wages of Sin Is D'oh!: An Analysis of the Portrayals of Religion on *The Simpsons*." University of Georgia, Grady College of Journalism and Mass Communication, December 2000. Unpublished.

Acknowledgments

The reason I usually turn to the acknowledgments page of a book is to see if my name, or the name of anyone I know, is there. If that is what you are doing now, I'll do my best to see that you are not disappointed.

I first found the idea of writing books attractive because I liked the idea of working alone, of having the illusion of control in this small portion of my professional life. In contrast to writing for newspapers, magazines, radio, television, and film—all collaborative projects—this time it would be my show. Or so I thought. It puzzled me when, while searching for my own name in the back of books written by friends and colleagues, I would find page after page of names and institutions and expressions of gratitude.

Well, now I know. Even in a book this short, there are many people to thank. First, of course, I must thank my family. My children, Asher and Liza, got me started on this project, as I explained in the introduction, and since then they have tolerated my telling this story about them over and over again. My wife Sallie—the photographer Sarah M. Brown—has been supportive and encouraging throughout the process, and has assisted me in keeping my head from growing too large to fit through the doorways of our home. My in-laws, Joe and Charlotte Brown, good Presbyterians both, were my two most enthusiastic cheerleaders. Maryland Senator Paul Pinsky, my younger brother and one of my heroes, asked some hard questions and taught me, through his example, to recognize an opportunity and seize the moment.

Peter Brown, my good friend and colleague at the *Orlando Sentinel*, is most responsible for launching this book. What began on one of our regular afternoon walks around the block as a general notion for an essay in his weekly editorial review section became a book proposal thanks to his wise judgment and experience. Our *Sentinel* book editor, Nancy Pate, was never too busy to advise me about the ins and outs of the publishing industry. Old

China hand Fergus Bordewich, a better writer than I will ever be, was a great sounding board and resource.

Brent Bierman, of Knight-Ridder-Tribune news service in Washington, D.C., saw my original *Simpsons* essay and put it on the wire. My Internet friend, David Buckna, of the delightful religious trivia list "Sol O Mann Top 10," was one of the first people to see my *Sentinel* essay on the Internet and to encourage the idea of a book. In the years since then, he was always willing to steer me in the right direction.

I am most grateful to the creators of *The Simpsons* Archive Web site. Their meticulous research was invaluable, in particular their episode capsules. Jouni Paakkinen, Jordan Eisenberg, and Bruce Gomes, among many others, answered hundreds of my questions. When they didn't know an answer, they used their contacts to find it for me. Evan Dunlap, a fan's fan in Orlando, also had some good catches, as did Steve Mathewes-Green.

Even before I was able to sign a contract with a book publisher, Douglas LeBlanc, associate editor of *Christianity Today* magazine, saw the value in the sample chapter I wrote on Ned Flanders, and tirelessly shepherded it to the cover of the February 5, 2001, issue. I know he had to convince a lot of people that it was the right kind of story for the publication, not to mention that it had been written by a Jew who was well outside the evangelical community.

Gail Hochman, a longtime and long distance friend and supporter, did me a very large favor on very short notice that I will never forget. Jill Schwartz, my neighbor and friend, and Cecil Ricks, of Costa Mesa, California—the finest employment lawyers on two coasts—also helped me when I needed it. My editors at the *Orlando Sentinel* were gracious in granting me two book leaves and supporting my work.

The academic community, both religious and secular, was extremely helpful. Professors were willing to walk this C student through some very complex concepts and analyses, and to allow me to pilfer their scholarship for my own purposes. They include Quentin Schultze and Bill Romanowski, both of Calvin College; my good friend from *Duke Chronicle* days and Columbia J-School, Clay Steinman, of Macalester College; John Heeren, of California State University at San Bernardino; Michael Glodo, Lyn Perez, and Matt Lacey (the latter two also neighbors), all of Reformed Theological Seminary in Oviedo, Florida; Eric Michael Mazur of Bucknell University; Gerry Bowler of Canadian Nazarene College; David Landry of the University of St. Thomas; Tom Rainey of Evergreen State College; and Paul Cantor of the University of Virginia, who also copied some of his own tapes for me. In a category of his own was Martin Marty, the godfather of America's religion writers and the dean of academic observers of church life.

I benefited greatly from the advice of my journalist colleagues around the country, such as S. V. Date of the *Palm Beach Post*, and my cousin, Linda Loyd, of the *Philadelphia Inquirer*. I also benefited from some colleagues whose excellent work on this subject I have cited in the text, but never met, such as Les Sillars of the *Alberta Report*, Douglas Todd of the *Vancouver Sun*, Bob von Sternberg of the *Twin Cities Star-Tribune*, Paul Andrews of the *Seattle Times*, and Tom Kisken of the *Ventura County Star*.

In particular, I wish to thank my colleagues in the Religion Newswriters Association, as collegial and supportive a group of journalists as one is likely to find. These include Gayle White of the *Atlanta Constitution*, Cary McMullen of the *Lakeland Ledger* (Florida), Ken Garfield of the *Charlotte Observer*, Yonat Shimron of the *Raleigh News & Observer*, David Briggs of the *Cleveland Plain-Dealer*, Patricia Rice of the *St. Louis Post Dispatch*, John Dart of the *Christian Century*, and Adele Banks of Religion News Service.

Several other friends read this manuscript and offered many valuable suggestions, including another old friend from Duke, Rusty Wright, whose renewed acquaintance and friendship helped shape this manuscript. John Valentine, of the Regulator Bookshop in Durham, was an early and enthusiastic encourager of my work. Mark Andrews, a *Sentinel* colleague, offered some keen insights and made the kind of good catches editors often do, and *Sentinel* film critic Jay Boyar made some excellent suggestions. Darren Iozia, also of the *Sentinel*, came through with copies of vital tapes. Rob Waters, of the *Raleigh News & Observer*, the best newspaper editor in the world, provided some of the same wise counsel he has been giving me for the past fifteen years (this time I took it). Durham novelist and dear friend Laurel Goldman had acute observations, whenever I was able to decipher her handwriting.

The leaders of Central Florida's religious community have taught me much about Christianity, from left to right, mainline to evangelical. Often they have kept me from embarrassing myself in print by taking my phone calls at inconvenient times. I have learned a great deal from them. In particular, I wish to thank these pastors: Jim Henry of the First Baptist Church of Orlando; Howard Edington of the First Presbyterian Church of Orlando, the "Heart of the City"; Clark Whitten of Calvary Assembly of God in Winter Park; Joel Hunter of Northland Community Church, Distributed, of Longwood; John Dalles of Wekiva Presbyterian Church in Longwood; and good neighbor Reid McCormick of Emmanuel Episcopal Church of Winter Park. Also, Bishop Norbert Dorsey of the Catholic Diocese of Orlando and Bishop John Howe of the Episcopal Diocese of Central Florida, and, especially, Bill Bright, founder of Campus Crusade for Christ.

National leaders of the Southern Baptist Convention, whom I have come to know and respect despite our many differences—political as well as theological—were also of great assistance, challenging me when and where I needed to be challenged. Knowing them, especially Dr. Richard Land of the SBC's Ethics & Religious Liberty Commission, I trust and expect this process will continue. Art Toalston, editor of Baptist Press, the SBC news service, was an early backer of this project.

My own rabbi, Steven Engel, of the Congregation of Liberal Judaism, is a gifted and sympathetic clergyman who was kind enough to read my chapter on the Jews and offer his insightful views. Rabbi Sholom Dubov of Congregation Ahavas Yisrael (Chabad) in Maitland, the "rabbi around the corner," not only read the Jews chapter but also helped me put on *t'fillin* (phylacteries) while I was writing the book. Rabbi Daniel Wolpe of Temple Ohalei Rivka in Orlando offered the unique perspective of a *Simpsons* fan who, like Krusty, comes from a family of distinguished rabbis.

In California, I would like to thank Antonia Coffman at *The Simpsons* and attorney Susan Grode for their assistance in this project, making things possible when they could have just as easily made them impossible. Writers and producers Mike Scully, Al Jean, Mike Reiss, Steve Tompkins, Jeff Martin, and Ian Maxtone-Graham were extremely forthcoming about their craft, as was the actor and writer Harry Shearer. And thanks especially to Matt Groening (whom I still hope to meet one day) for graciously providing the image of Bart for the cover of this book and for green-lighting this line of inquiry and examination.

David Dobson, my wise and light-handed editor at Westminster John Knox Press, bolstered my shaky confidence as a first-time author from our first telephone conversation.

Finally, I would like to thank the Reverend Robert Short, who blazed this particular trail of religion and popular culture more than three decades ago with *The Gospel according to Peanuts*. He was most generous with his time and encouragement.

Other Titles of Interest

THE GOSPEL ACCORDING TO PEANUTS
by Robert L. Short
With a new foreword by Martin E. Marty

With more than 10 million copies sold, Robert Short's classic continues to provide a modern-day guide to faith, fully illustrated with the beloved comic strips of Charles Schultz.
ISBN 0-664-22222-6

WATCHING WHAT WE WATCH:
PRIME-TIME TELEVISION THROUGH THE LENS OF FAITH
by Walter T. Davis Jr., Teresa Blythe, Gary Dreibelbis, Mark Scalese, S.J., Elizabeth Winans, and Donald L. Ashburn

Much like the process of reading a book, *Watching What We Watch* teaches how to "read" a movie or television show and to do so in light of one's faith, values, and beliefs.
ISBN 0-664-50193-1

To order these books, visit our Web site at www.wjkbooks.com or call 1-800-227-2872.